Praise for *Crucible*

M000006595

"When you read *Crucible Leadership*, Warwick Fairfax's account of the ups and downs of his life and the lives of many famous leaders, you won't be able to help but reflect on your own life and leadership. With themes such as faith, character, purpose, and vision, this book has lessons that will serve every leader well. Roll your sleeves up and start reading—it's going to be an adventure!"

> **—Ken Blanchard**, coauthor of the *New York Times* bestseller
> *The One Minute Manager®* and *Servant Leadership in Action*

"Warwick Fairfax weaves together history and his own fascinating life experience to offer a series of vital leadership insights. Whether you are responsible for a company, a foundation, an arts organization, or a government agency, you will find nuggets of leadership gold in this book. If you aspire to lead a group of people and to do so with integrity, self-awareness, and a big, worthy mission, start reading *Crucible Leadership* today."

> **—Nancy Koehn**, James E. Robison chair of Business
> Administration, Harvard Business School and author of *Forged
> in Crisis: The Power of Courageous Leadership in Turbulent Times*

"Clear and compelling lessons about leading and living well, drawn from lived, sometimes painful personal experience. *Crucible Leadership* is filled with thoughtful reflection on what it takes to move beyond failures and setbacks to achieve new levels of success and satisfaction in business and life."

> **—Joseph L. Badaracco**, John Shad professor of Business Ethics,
> Harvard Business School and author of *Step Back: How to Bring
> the Art of Reflection Into Your Busy Life* and *Leading Quietly*

"It's rare to get an inside look at what it takes to bounce back from a big and very public failure, but Warwick Fairfax lived it and now shares it with all of us. The result: a riveting, honest, and in the end, hopeful account of how to grow your leadership and build a meaningful life while doing so."

> **—Sydney Finkelstein**, Steven Roth professor of
> Management, Tuck School at Dartmouth College, author
> of *Superbosses*, and host of the podcast, *The Sydcast*

"Having grown up in Australia, the Fairfax family was iconic, so I knew of Warwick Fairfax—and his brutal public fall—long before I came to actually know him as a friend. A humble leader with a servant's heart, Warwick has penned a deeply profound book that will help anyone who's ever been knocked down by life and yearns to make sense of their struggle and chart a more meaningful path forward. His hard-won wisdom, shared with utmost honesty, will help you come to see that those experiences you thought were ruining your path were really just revealing it."

—**Margie Warrell**, CEO, Global Courage Leadership, columnist at *Forbes.com,* and author of *You've Got This: The Life-Changing Power of Trusting Yourself*

"One of my favourite questions when interviewing people for a job is 'Tell us about a mistake you've made and what you learned from it.' The people who say they've never made a mistake don't get hired. This is what *Crucible Leadership* is all about. Warwick Fairfax gives a searingly honest account of the mistakes he has made in his life and the lessons he has learned from those experiences about resilience, the importance of listening, keeping focused on your vision, and living by your fundamental values. This is heartening and inspiring to anyone who has ever made a mistake as a leader—and that means all of us!"

—**Dame Helen Ghosh**, master of Balliol College, Oxford

"*Crucible Leadership* is equal parts memoir and master class about overcoming life's challenges to live and lead with purpose and significance. Few of us have known the kind of trials Warwick has experienced, but all of us can benefit from his inspiring, insightful exploration of moving beyond them. He has figured out exactly who he is (and who he isn't) and how he can most effectively pursue his life's vision—and he can help you do the same."

—**John Ramstead**, CEO, Beyond Influence, host of *Eternal Leadership* podcast, and author of *On Purpose With Purpose: Live Your Best Life* and *Discover Your Core Values*

"Warwick Fairfax's early journey was a hard path to travel. But in the process of picking up the pieces and moving on, Warwick learned valuable lessons about identity, vision, and most of all, *faith*. He shares those hard-won insights in this book to help us all gain a better understanding of how to handle the difficult times."

—**Jim Daly**, president, Focus on the Family

"We love success stories ('Wow! Look at them!'). We love failure stories ('Serves them right!'). But the story that rarely gets the press is the most important story of all: how to find your way from failure to meaning and from meaning to authenticity as a leader. In *Crucible Leadership*, Warwick takes us by the hand and shows us the way."

—**Sheila Heen**, senior lecturer on law, Harvard Law School and co-author of *Difficult Conversations* and *Thanks for the Feedback*

"If you've ever failed and wondered if you would regain your footing, this book will encourage and equip you—not to try to be someone else but to be fully and authentically who you are created to be. *Crucible Leadership* will inspire you to embrace the truth that each of us can lead somewhere. Drawing from his own public and costly failure at a young age, Warwick Fairfax unfolds a path of hope for those who determine to get back up. He illustrates the principles of crucible leadership through vulnerable disclosures about his own life, woven with parables and examples from leaders who have shaped history. You will find yourself drawn in by the stories, questions, quotations, and authentic counsel from one who has lived through what he counsels other leaders-in-development to consider."

—**Paige Comstock Cunningham, PhD, JD**, former president, Taylor University

"The perspective Warwick offers in *Crucible Leadership* highlights the opportunity hidden within the setbacks and tragedies we all endure. I know from my own experience as a paraplegic plane crash survivor that life is won and lost above the shoulders, that emotional recovery is in many ways the toughest hurdle to clear when you've been through a crucible. Warwick has lived it, learned from it, and shares those lessons with admirable authenticity. This book is a gift."

—**Ryan Campbell**, youngest pilot to fly solo around the world and author of *Born to Fly: The Inspiring Story of an Australian Teenager's Record-Breaking Flight Around the World*

"Warwick Fairfax knows what it's like to live a life and pursue a destiny that wasn't his. He had many unkind names attached to him by critics after his failed takeover of the family media dynasty he stood to inherit— but he hasn't let any of those false identities stick. He has persevered to create a new reality aligned with who he was created and called to be. *Crucible Leadership* is a bold declaration that our best life is one in which we offer the best of our true selves in service to others."

—**Esther Fleece Allen**, author of *No More Faking Fine* and *Your New Name*

"*Crucible Leadership* is a deeply personal and engaging reflection on leadership. Warwick Fairfax understands what it is like to go through a terrible trial in business, to fail, and yet to be sustained by his faith in God and tutored by the experiences of history's greatest leaders. He is refreshingly honest about his own part in these events and uses his experience to show readers a better way as they pass through the crucible of test and trial, and even failure."

—**Peter Jensen**, retired Anglican archbishop of Sydney

"Warwick Fairfax has written a truly extraordinary book arising from the rebuilding of his own life after the crucible of catastrophic business failure. In Australia in 1990, John Fairfax Ltd., a five-generation, multi-billion-dollar family media business was lost, as he puts it, 'on my watch.' Warwick shares intimately of his own life leading up to and including these very public events and their aftermath. Alongside this truly poignant autobiographical thread are masterful summaries of key moments in the lives of many notable leaders, combined with insight from the Bible and Christian experience. Now a qualified and experienced executive coach, Warwick equips us to better understand and respond to the crucible moments of our own lives, and develop leadership-enhancing life-skills. Relevant, insightful, refreshing, and practical; time spent in this book will make you a better person and a better leader."

—**Dr. Stuart Johnson**, author of a PhD dissertation
in history that examined John Fairfax and the mid-
nineteenth century *Sydney Morning Herald*

"When all seems hopelessly lost . . . when your world crumbles . . . when an innocent mistake or a sinister injustice strikes . . . can good come from the ashes of devastation and disappointment? Warwick Fairfax answers with a resounding 'yes!' in *Crucible Leadership*. Your greatest heartache can actually open the door to the life you've always wanted! Having walked with Warwick for twenty years, I've personally benefited from the leadership lessons he espouses in this book—they have helped me become the leader I was designed to be. Apply them and discover that God can indeed work all things in your life for good."

—**Greg St. Cyr, DMin**, lead pastor, Bay Area
Community Church, Annapolis, Maryland

CRUCIBLE
LEADERSHIP

CRUCIBLE LEADERSHIP

Embrace Your Trials to Lead a Life of Significance

WARWICK FAIRFAX

MOUNT
TABOR
MEDIA
AN IMPRINT OF
MORGAN JAMES

NEW YORK

LONDON • NASHVILLE • MELBOURNE • VANCOUVER

Crucible Leadership

Embrace Your Trials to Lead a Life of Significance

Published in New York, New York, by Mount Tabor Media, an imprint of Morgan James Publishing. Morgan James is a trademark of Morgan James, LLC. www.MorganJamesPublishing.com

Morgan James BOGO™

A **FREE** ebook edition is available for you or a friend with the purchase of this print book.

_____

CLEARLY SIGN YOUR NAME ABOVE

Instructions to claim your free ebook edition:
1. Visit MorganJamesBOGO.com
2. Sign your name CLEARLY in the space above
3. Complete the form and submit a photo of this entire page
4. You or your friend can download the ebook to your preferred device

ISBN 9781631954764 paperback
ISBN 9781631954771 eBook
Library of Congress Control Number: 2020952383

Cover Design by:
MTWdesign.net and
SIGNAL.csk Brand Partners

Interior Design by:
PerfecType, Nashville, TN

MOUNT TABOR MEDIA

VERITUM REVELATUM - "TRUTH REVEALED"
A BRANDED IMPRINT OF MORGAN JAMES

To Gale,
the love of my life,
who has always supported, encouraged, and believed in me.
And to Will, Gracie, and Robbie,
who have given me such joy
and helped me see that my story was not yet finished.

CONTENTS

PART 4 | **LEAD AND LIVE WITH IMPACT**

ACKNOWLEDGMENTS

Firstly, I want to thank my family. I am blessed to have an amazing, loving wife, Gale, to whom I have been married for over thirty years. Through the trials and the aftermath of the takeover, and the years where I tried to find my way back, she has always been supportive, loved me for who I am, and believed in me. I am grateful to have three wonderful children: Will, Gracie, and Robbie, who are now young adults. I am blessed to have them as my children. They are all unique in their own way, and it is a pleasure to see who they are becoming.

I am also grateful for my immediate family: for my father, Sir Warwick Fairfax, and my mother, Lady Mary Fairfax. My father had a nobility of spirit that went beyond his title, a sense of fairness and open-mindedness. My mother had a joy for life and a smile and a laugh that could light up a room, along with passion and an ability to persevere through life's challenges. I am grateful for my younger sister and brother, Anna and Charles, who brought more life into our family. I also want to thank my older sister, Annalise. She was instrumental in my coming to faith in Christ. Her example of faith and desire to lead a normal life amidst the privileged upbringing in which we were raised were models for me as I was growing up.

For my book, I want to start by thanking the whole team at Morgan James Publishing, including Chris McCluskey of Mount Tabor Media and David Hancock, the CEO and founder of Morgan James. I love the book-publishing model at Morgan James. They empower authors, listen to their voice, and enable them to have their messages heard.

I have many to thank on the Crucible Leadership team. Over four years ago, I came to Cheryl Farr, the visionary founder and CEO of Signal.csk Brand Partners. I had a manuscript, and I knew I needed a brand. Out of our discussions grew the brand of Crucible Leadership and the brand philosophy embedded in the book of helping leaders at all levels lead lives of significance. Cheryl has become a good friend and trusted adviser. Her brand insight and, even more so, her strategic insight have been of incalculable value. The team Cheryl has assembled at Signal is amazing. Day-to-day implementation is led by Alexandra Mollón. Alex keeps everything moving; nothing gets dropped with her attention to detail and her passion for the brand and insights into how to achieve what we are trying to achieve are critical. Jeremy Grant, the creative director at Signal, has a keen insight into how to graphically and visually bring the brand and the concepts of Crucible Leadership to life. The website and all the visuals of Crucible Leadership are superb because of his creative vision and leadership. The whole team at Signal, including Cristina Ferreri, Meghan Engdahl, and Tony Vardaro, is terrific. At the start of my journey with Signal, Haley Sevalstad was a key component of the team. Many of the original words and brand insights came from the groundwork laid by Haley.

Gary Schneeberger, president of ROAR, is a huge part of the Crucible Leadership team and has also become a good friend and valued counselor, helping me set and execute my vision. Originally brought on to help us out with public relations, Gary's skill set, which includes many years in journalism, is such that he covers multiple bases. Perhaps most significantly, he is my co-host on my podcast *Beyond The Crucible*. Gary has a creative mind and a great radio voice and leads our efforts to find superb guests. He has also helped with looking at the book and ensuring that as the Crucible Leadership brand has grown, the book is in step with that growth.

Steve Reiter and his team at Right Turn Media first suggested that a podcast could really work for our brand and our message. Steve has helped us create high-quality, professional podcasts.

Our newest team member, Keri Childers of Keri Childers Consulting, is also passionate about the brand and what we are trying to achieve with Crucible Leadership. Keri has extensive experience in helping authors connect with their audience by finding venues where their messages can be heard and has enthusiastically—and with excellence—worked to expand the Crucible Leadership footprint.

I have been so blessed by the editors who have helped me refine and hone the message behind Crucible Leadership. Most recently, Arlyn Lawrence of Inspira Literary Solutions helped me get this book into a manageable size while ensuring the key message is still heard. Cortney Donelson of vocem, LLC has helped me get over the last few yards with proofreading, formatting, and expert assistance organizing references.

But this book has been a long journey, years in the making. Back when I was dialoguing with those in book publishing circles in Australia, there were a couple of people who were so helpful. Maggie Hamilton is an author and former senior book-publishing executive. Maggie connected me with two wonderful editors who provided some initial editing of my manuscript: Susin Chow, who gave me invaluable structural editing advice, and Clara Finlay, who gave me great copyediting input. I also want to thank Fiona Inglis of Curtis Brown, an Australian literary agency. I am grateful for Fiona's advice.

I want to conclude with a key moment where the idea for a book about learning from your crucibles and getting beyond them was born. In 2008, Greg St. Cyr, the lead pastor of my church, Bay Area Community Church, asked me to give a short sermon illustration during a message he gave on David, who was a righteous man falsely persecuted by King Saul. While I don't see myself that way, as I brought a lot of my challenges on myself, that talk I gave was a catalyst for this book being written. It was also a catalyst for my own life of significance. For weeks and months after I spoke, people came up to me and told me how much my story had helped them. I am very thankful to Greg for the opportunity to share my heart that day and, more than that, his friendship and encouragement.

INTRODUCTION

While still in my twenties, I was seen as largely responsible for the loss of a family dynasty. From the time I was born, I was on a path to holding a leadership position in the Fairfax family media company founded in 1841 in Australia and to have its largest shareholding. By the time I came on the scene, the business had been in my family for five generations. Named after its founder, my great-great-grandfather, John Fairfax Ltd. (later Fairfax Media), it was one of the largest diversified media companies in the country.

At its height, John Fairfax Ltd. included newspapers, television stations, radio stations, magazines, and newsprint mills. With the *Sydney Morning Herald,* the *Age* in Melbourne, and the *Australian Financial Review,* we held the Australian equivalent of *The New York Times, The Washington Post,* and *The Wall Street Journal* in the United States.

In 1987, at age twenty-six, I launched an AUS$2.25 billion (the equivalent of more than US$1.5 billion) takeover bid of the company for reasons I will fully explain later. Within three years, the company went bankrupt. For the first time since its inception, John Fairfax Ltd. was no longer in my family's control. The media called it "The Fall of Fairfax"— and it was global news. A five-generation family media dynasty was gone. And it ended on my watch.

Needless to say, the takeover and its aftermath were very painful for me. In my efforts to save the company, it seemed like I had helped to destroy it. The media didn't help with these thoughts of failure, either. In fact, they made them worse. Through pointed articles and satirical cartoons, they found an easy target for painting a less-than-flattering portrait of who I was and what I had been trying to do.

Yet through it all, I started to learn a lot about myself—who I was and also who I was not. The trials I went through led me on a journey of introspection that has given me clarity about what my unique design, purpose, and passions really are.

A key turning point in my search for purpose came in 2008 when the lead pastor of my church in Maryland asked me to give a seven-minute talk as part of that Sunday's message. In essence, he asked me to share my story. So, I did. I shared from my heart.

In those seven minutes, I was forthright about what had happened at the family media company, the takeover, the bankruptcy, what I'd gone through, the pain it caused me (self-inflicted or otherwise), my faith, the journey back to a fulfilling life, and what I had learned through it all. Most of those sitting in the church that day knew nothing of my takeover story, still less of Fairfax Media. Australia was a long way away.

I used to think, *Who could possibly relate to my story? How many other people have lost a 150-year-old family empire?* But, amazingly, what I said seemed to resonate. What I found was that people related to the sense of devastating failure and profound loss. My story was helpful to them. This led me to think: *If my story can help other people, perhaps other leaders, then maybe there is a purpose to the pain. Maybe they can learn from my mistakes and the lessons I've learned, as they recover from their own failures and seek their own lives of significance.*

Over time, I developed a point of view on how we can each leverage our setbacks and failures as turning points toward living with uncompromised authenticity and leading lives of significance. I call it "Crucible Leadership." The concept is built upon the four key lessons I have learned from my experiences, and I'm sharing them with you in this book in hopes they will be helpful as you discover your own life of significance. They are:

Lesson One: **Failure can be of great value. It can be the most refining time of your life.** Difficult experiences can change you. In a sense, they can make or break you. Choose the path that makes you a better, more whole, and more resilient version of yourself. Failures and setbacks—your crucible moments—can feel like insurmountable obstacles, causing you to feel stuck or lost. But they can also offer an introspective inflection point that moves you toward more effective leadership and a life of significance.

Lesson Two: **The quest for leadership is first an inner quest for discovering who you are.** You can't fight your design. We all come out of the box a certain way, with certain innate gifts. Those gifts can be nurtured and influenced over time, but we all have our own unique wiring we just can't override. A life that is tied to your innate gifting, overlaid with your passions, values, and beliefs, is like rocket fuel.

Lesson Three: **You cannot inherit a vision.** I tried and failed. The only vision that can succeed is one that is uniquely true to you and who you are. Vision occurs when deep-seated beliefs and passions are combined with your unique wiring. Crafting a vision for yourself that fully aligns with who you are sets the foundation for you to live and lead with uncompromised authenticity. A vision that is not tied to who you are, what you believe in, and what you are passionate about will tend to go nowhere, however noble it is.

Lesson Four: **A vision unfulfilled is a vision lost.** Hard work, perseverance, and honest assessment are what turn vision into reality for leaders. When you have a vision that you are passionate about, that you were designed to do, that vision will have a far greater chance of becoming reality. There will still be obstacles, but because you are clear about who you are and what your life of significance is, you will be much more likely to persevere.

How This Book Can Help

Crucible Leadership is for anyone seeking significance, authenticity, and effectiveness in their leadership—and throughout their life. Each of us can be a leader irrespective of our positions, be it as a leader of a large organization or a leader of a local community group. This book is for you if your journey in life has been full of highs and lows, successes and failures, and promising opportunities and devastating setbacks. It is for you if your path hasn't always been straight. It is for you if you desire to lead a life of significance.

As you seek to improve in all areas of life, the advice you'll likely hear is to focus on the wins, focus on what works, and learn from those who teach from a position of unwavering success. But it's not success in the traditional sense that you want—you want success that comes from a place of leading and living with authenticity and significance. You are ready to embrace the painful moments of your life journey and move forward in a way that is authentic to you. If this sounds like you, you've picked up the right book. I wrote this for you. In it, I use my story-driven philosophical approach and iterative process to teach what it means to become a crucible leader and chart a course to leading a life of significance and uncompromised authenticity.

This book is not a "how-to manual," but rather a personal journey, pointing toward how you can authentically lead a life of significance. Its four sections align with the four core building blocks of a life of significance, rooted in those lessons I outlined above. Within the sections, I have structured each chapter to highlight a key leadership principle and why it is an anchor for Crucible Leadership. I then follow with illustrative stories as demonstrable proof of each principle in action. The stories either illustrate the principle exemplified or the consequences of its lacking. The principles embedded within the stories transcend generation and situation—and are highly relevant to the situations each one of us faces today.

The key to leadership growth is the continuous journey of applying timeless principles to our leadership and our lives. With that in mind, there are stories and illustrations of three kinds, or "strands," woven into this book. One strand includes my personal story, as well as the stories of key members of my family who were involved in the family business. For example, my great-great-grandfather, John Fairfax, who founded the family business, and my father, Sir Warwick Fairfax, significantly influenced my philosophy of leadership. I greatly admired them both, and they taught me invaluable lessons on leadership and life.

Another strand features historical leaders. I have always loved history. History is one of the ways my father and I bonded. As I was growing up, he often told me inspiring stories of heroes accomplishing great deeds against the odds. We can learn a lot from great historical leaders—through how they faced adversity and the timeless lessons that overcoming adversity teaches us.

The final strand shares lessons from inspirational and biblical figures. Faith is foundational to who I am and what I believe about life and leadership. This book is not a polemic on any particular faith, though I am clear on the role that my faith has played in my life. Just as with historical figures, we can learn much from the lives of biblical and inspirational figures, such as David, Esther, and Gandhi.

Through the tapestry of stories provided by these three strands, I demonstrate in what I hope is an honest, self-reflective way for you can make sense of your own talents and trials to lead with uncompromised authenticity in all areas of life.

I conclude each chapter with reflective questions that will help you unpack the core principles and translate the lessons into your own personal application on your journey to leading a life of significance. A willingness to be vulnerable is crucial to becoming a crucible leader—and to leading and living with complete authenticity. I positively challenge you to open yourself up to developing a practice of purposeful vulnerability as you read this book and to reflect on each part. Doing so will help you get the most out of this process so you can achieve the results you seek.

It is my hope that *Crucible Leadership* will inspire us all to be better leaders: that we will stop trying to be who we are not and instead start being who we were designed to be. My hope is that we will be people of character and that the crucible experiences we have gone through—and will go through—will make us stronger, more effective, and more fulfilled in our leadership roles and our lives in general.

I want to see us create huge visions, which inspire people and nations to be better than they ever thought possible . . . and for these visions to become reality. And because life is not easy, and we do get knocked down, I hope we will pick ourselves up and persevere, even if it means starting all over again. My vision is that *Crucible Leadership* will help us all move toward lives of significance so that together, we will make the world a better place. This is my heart's desire.

Part One

EMBRACE YOUR CRUCIBLE

Without exception, any study into the life of people who lead and live with impact will reveal this truth: their lives have been marked by challenging experiences, which have refined and shaped them. These "crucible moments" provide opportunities to reflect, re-assess, and redefine our identity, purpose, and vision in life and leadership.

Sometimes the crucible moment was the result of personal failure. Perhaps it was due to forces beyond our control. And perhaps it was a combination of the two. Regardless, these moments bring us to crucial crossroads in our lives and provide invaluable opportunities to take stock of ourselves. They lead each of us to deal with this foundational question that will determine the quality of our leadership and the trajectory of our lives:

Will the flames of a crucible experience consume us or will they be a refining fire from which we emerge purified, solidified, and forged with purpose?

Crucibles make or break a leader; we are never the same after going through such an experience. What is a crucible? According to the *Oxford English Dictionary*, a crucible is a container in which metals or other substances are melted or subjected to extremely high temperatures. But the secondary meaning is what this book is all about: "a severe trial in which different elements interact to produce something new."

It's a situation that produces a strong test of character. A painful life experience of failure or loss. A time when we are put through the fires of a life-altering trial and forever changed. Through a crucible, we may become a better person and grow, or we may be destroyed. The choice is ours.

This is the essence of any crucible. We have to ask ourselves: *Am I going to let this situation destroy me, or am I going to learn from it? Will I become bitter at the injustice of it all, or will the accusations and unfair circumstances make me a better person?*

In this first section, we will explore what it means to embrace the crucible moments of our lives and leverage them to be our best selves. Understanding how we've been refined will help us understand who we truly are, so we can move forward from crucible moments and lead lives of impact and significance.

Chapter 1

MY CRUCIBLE

So much of the cultural narrative about leadership is how success breeds success. The problem is that, for most of us, our paths haven't always been on a straight progression.

When I was born in Australia in 1960, I was heralded as the heir apparent who would one day lead the family media business. I would be the fifth generation in the business founded in Sydney by my great-great-grandfather, John Fairfax, when he bought the *Sydney Morning Herald* in 1841. While I was growing up, John Fairfax Ltd. was a large, diversified media company that included newspapers, television stations, radio stations, magazines, and newsprint mills.

I was a child from the third marriage of my father, Sir Warwick Fairfax, to my mother, Lady Mary Fairfax. When we were living in England for about a year in the late 1960s, my parents adopted my younger sister and brother, Anna and Charles. I also have half and stepsiblings from my parents' previous marriages, so when people ask me how many brothers and sisters I have, the answer is complex! From my father's first marriage, there was a daughter and a son, Caroline and James. From his second marriage, there was a daughter, Annalise, and a stepson, Alan Anderson. My mother also had a son, Garth, from her first marriage.

The family dynasty was founded in the Victorian era and managed to retain many of that time period's values into modern times. The custom was that only male children would go into the family business, and of those, typically only the older sons. My father asked his oldest son, my half-brother James, to join the business in the 1950s and gave James some of his shares to lessen the impact of estate taxes. But by agreement, the bulk of James's shares would come to me one day. (I was the next son after James, who was more than twenty-five years older than me.) Adding to the pressure for me to join the company was the fact that James never married and did not have children. My father's cousin, Sir Vincent Fairfax, also had a significant shareholding. His son, John B. Fairfax, would also join the company.

For my father, whose family line had more shares than other family members, keeping our line going was very important. Thus, I was seen by my father—indeed by both of my parents—as destined one day to become the managing director or chairman. Since I stood to inherit my father's shares and the bulk of my brother James's shares, I would also be the leading shareholder among the family.

I well understood my parents' and family's expectations, both spoken and unspoken. I did everything I could to make them proud, to be worthy of the mantle, and to live up to their expectations. I worked hard at school. Like my grandfather, father, older brother, and other relatives, I went to Oxford University. After graduating, I worked on Wall Street at Chase Manhattan Bank then went to Harvard Business School, graduating with a Master of Business Administration (MBA).

My father died in January 1987 when I was twenty-six, while I was in my second year at Harvard Business School. After his death, rumors were flying that our family company might be taken over. Management was making decisions I thought were questionable. I had concerns over whether the company was being run in line with the ideals of the founder.

How would I respond?

High Stakes, High Expectations

My family, especially my parents, looked to me to carry on the traditions of the family and the family name. They expected me to go into the family business, help it continue to exist, and pass it on intact—and hopefully greater—to the next generation.

What made it tougher, and the expectations higher, was that this was no ordinary company making, say, widgets. John Fairfax Ltd. was a media company that played a vital part in the nation. Some people go into public service to improve their nation, or others go into the military to defend their country. My family saw its role in the newspaper business in a similar vein: to speak truth to power and uphold those who were trying to make Australia a better place. This was more than a business. It was a sacred cause.

Another aspect that raised the stakes for me was the tradition in our family of preserving the ideals of the company's founder, John Fairfax. It was not only important that the company be successful and do its job well; the *way* it did its job mattered to me. In my vision, a newspaper company should not be a place of cynical journalism that sees all politicians and businesspeople as corrupt, just waiting to be found out. Some might be corrupt, certainly—but not all. My vision was of a newspaper company that treated people fairly. If wrongdoing were to be found, we would expose it. If someone was doing a good job, we would write about that, too. Reporting was not to be an exercise in bringing people down for fun or political gain or slanting the story to make it more interesting. The company's newspapers would bring down figures in society when warranted, lift up others when deserved, and generally seek to preserve and advance the good of society in Australia.

The vision I had was also of a company where people loved to come to work, where they were treated as human beings with aspirations, gifts, and goals. They would be respected, developed, and encouraged. Our role as the family behind the company was in part to see that employees were treated fairly. The company would, in a sense, be a family.

These were high stakes and high expectations indeed.

Even as young as I was at the time, I had a sense that both aspects of this vision had been lost, or at least watered down, over the years. It seemed that newspapers were more sensationalistic, less concerned with the truth than slanting news to make an ideological point. It seemed the business was not as well run as it used to be. I had begun to see an evolving image of a company where people did not always like coming to work.

I was also keenly aware that my father had stood in the gap to try to stem the tide of what were arguably poor management decisions. One such poor management decision, at least from my parents' and my perspectives, was a series of capital-raising proposals. In the mid-1980s, management proposed a couple of schemes that sought to bring in capital while preserving family control. Initially, the company proposed to issue participating irredeemable preference shares (PIPS). These would be non-voting shares.

While the rest of the family, management, and the other directors were in favor of the company issuing PIPS, my parents were adamantly against it. They feared a corporate raider would snap up the PIPS and somehow force these non-voting shares to become voting shares and thereby gain control of the company. As it happened, the Sydney Stock Exchange (now part of the Australian Stock Exchange) ended up setting requirements on PIPS that would allow these shares to become voting shares under certain conditions. This was enough for the family, management, and board to abandon plans for issuing PIPS. In essence, the Sydney Stock Exchange confirmed my parents' fears that PIPS could become voting shares, which raised the possibility of the family losing control of the company.

Another poor management decision was John's Fairfax Ltd.'s response to Rupert Murdoch's efforts to seize control of one of our chief competitors.

In late 1986, Murdoch, owner of News Ltd., launched a takeover bid for the *Herald and Weekly Times*, one of the largest newspaper companies in Australia, controlling major papers in Melbourne, Brisbane, and Adelaide, and television stations in Melbourne and Adelaide. This would put the family business in a difficult, competitive position. John Fairfax Ltd. initially made a bid for the *Herald and Weekly Times'* Brisbane newspaper, then ended up making a takeover bid for the whole of the *Herald and Weekly Times*. But the bid was too late, and Murdoch's News Ltd. gained control of both.

In part a consequence of John Fairfax Ltd.'s legal action to try to stop News Ltd.'s takeover of the *Herald and Weekly Times*, our company gained control of the *Herald and Weekly Times'* Melbourne television station, enabling John Fairfax Ltd. to add this station to its Seven Network stations in Sydney and Brisbane. However, complicating the purchase of the Melbourne television station was the proposed cross-media ownership legislation. Previously, a company could not own more than two television stations in Australia. After the purchase of the Melbourne television station, John Fairfax Ltd. would own three stations. The new proposed legislation would allow a company to have any number of television stations up to a certain percentage of the national audience. However, the proposed legislation also said that a company could not own a television station and a newspaper in the same market. Since John Fairfax Ltd. also owned a major profitable newspaper in Melbourne, there would be a problem. The net result was that the company was forced to sell the recently acquired Melbourne television station, and it did so by selling all three of its television stations. This drew criticism in the press at the time; a media company selling television stations, arguably core assets, was deemed unwise. In short, it seemed our company got the short end of the stick.

Fateful Decisions

Then, in February 1987, John Fairfax Ltd.'s stock price rose. Presumably, the market felt, with the upheaval from the *Herald and Weekly Times* takeover drama and the recent death of my father, the company might be in play. At the time, I felt the market must believe that even though the Fairfax family had close to 50 percent of the public shares in the company, 48.6 percent was not close enough. Corporate raiders were lurking. Given my thinking at the time that I must preserve family control of the company, I felt it important that the family have over 50 percent of the shares, not just 48.6 percent. So on behalf of my father's shareholding, I bought 1.5 percent of the shares, taking the combined Fairfax family shares in the company to 50.1 percent. But while this effort did raise the family shareholding, it also hurt relations with other major family shareholders.

All these events—my perception that the company was being mismanaged, the botched dealing with the *Herald and Weekly Times* takeover, the purchase and subsequent forced sale of the Melbourne television station, and the "risky" capital-raising schemes—formed in my mind the need to do something. *Who knew what other poor decisions management was going to make? Could I afford to wait and find out?*

At the time, I believed the answer was no. So in late August 1987, at the age of twenty-six, I launched an AUS$2.25 billion takeover bid (the equivalent of USD$1.5 billion at the time). It was a high price to pay for the shares of the company, though given the nature of the market at the time, some commentators said the price was too low.

As it turned out, 1987 was one of the toughest years of my life and the turning point. It was the key crucible moment. My life would never be the same. Before 1987, I was on a path to one day having the largest shareholding in the company and being chairman and possibly chief executive. After 1987, that all changed.

In hindsight, once I launched the takeover, success was going to be elusive, if not impossible. One of the key assumptions I made was that the rest of the family would not sell after I moved to consolidate family control. I felt I needed to be in charge of what, in a sense, would be a privatized company in order to change management and ensure the business was run along the ideals of the founder. However, this meant that for the other major family shareholdings to stay in, they would have to remain shareholders in a private company without any ready ability to get out and with a twenty-six-year-old (me) in charge. What rational person would want to do this? Who would agree to be in a minority position in an essentially privatized company?

After the other two family shareholdings realized the position they were in, they decided to sell. I was told the terms of the takeover bid were such that I had to accept all offers at the price offered, including from these other major family shareholdings. I did not want them to sell, but they did. This added a huge amount to the debt load.

The other major event that hurt the company was the October 1987 stock market crash. We had planned to finance part of the takeover through selling some assets, which became even more necessary after the other major family shareholdings decided to sell. The stock market crash depressed the prices we were able to obtain for these assets.

By the end of 1987, the takeover had succeeded in the sense that I was in control of the company and was able to change management. I brought in a new chief executive, Peter King, who, in his first year, increased operating profits by 80 percent. This seemed to justify my belief that the company had not been managed as well as it could have been. However, by late 1987, the debt load was crushing. For a while, we limped along, fueled in part by the considerable increase in operating profits. We tried numerous refinancing options, even issuing bonds (so-called junk bonds) through Drexel Burnham Lambert. In the 1980s, when a company had a lot of debt and needed creative financing, Drexel was the one to turn to. However, by late 1990, Australia had gone into a recession. Traditionally, newspaper revenues were cyclical with advertising revenues, and in particular, classified advertising revenues (made up of text ads for jobs, cars, houses, and so on) being extremely cyclical. When the economy went down so did newspaper revenues.

The recession was having a marked effect on the company's profitability. With the amount of debt we had, there was no margin for error. As a result, we were forced to file for receivership. I was no longer in control of the company. My shares were now held by the banks. I had lost the family's control of the family business.

Picking up the Pieces

In early 1991, I left Australia to live in the United States, away from the notoriety and the limelight. I felt I could not lead a normal life in Australia. I had always liked America, so if I had to leave Australia, that seemed the logical place to go. I had met my wife, Gale, who is American, while she was visiting friends in Australia in 1988. She ended up living in Australia during the time I was involved in the family business, and we married during those years. My wife is very close to her family, so she was happy to be nearer to them when we decided to move to the U.S.

The ten years or so after the company went into bankruptcy were very hard for me. They were years of introspection. *How could I have assumed the rest of the major family shareholdings would not sell? Could I have done anything differently to stop the company from going into receivership after the takeover was complete? Could I have convinced the other members of my family that management needed to be changed without feeling like I had to do a takeover? What would life have been like for me if I had not done the takeover? I would have been wealthier, perhaps, but would I have been happier?* These are questions that have no easy answers. Moving on was difficult. I was haunted by the thought that God had a plan for my life, and I had blown it.

Will a Crucible Break You—or Make You?

So much of the cultural narrative about leadership is how success breeds success. The problem is that, for most of us, our paths haven't always been on a straight progression. We are unique individuals, forged by our own life experiences, our family's past and present, our God-given talents, and of course, the crucibles we've faced. My own story is but one example of this reality.

The truth is that life is rarely a journey of ascending success. Many, if not most, of us have faced significant crucible moments. These trials create a crossroads where we can wallow in our setbacks, or we can turn toward a life of significance.

Some of history's greatest leaders have been shaped by crucible experiences. Franklin Roosevelt was struck by polio in the 1920s. Winston Churchill found himself in a political wilderness in the 1930s and then had to face the might of Nazi Germany in the Second World War. Without those crucible experiences, Roosevelt and Churchill would not have had the impact on the world they had. They were tested and were not found wanting.

> Crucibles provide the forge at which great leaders are hammered out, the anvil on which the sword of leadership is refined.

Nobody wants to face a crucible experience, but they are tough to avoid. Some of us face trials that are more public than others. But whether we are well known or not, life is such that crucible moments *will* strike us. Crucibles provide the forge at which great leaders are hammered out, the anvil on which the sword of leadership is refined

For me, life could not be much better than it is today. I have a wonderful wife, two sons, and a daughter. We live in scenic Annapolis, Maryland. I am a writer, leadership adviser, and executive coach. I host a podcast that allows me to use my gift of reflection and innate curiosity to explore the ways in which the guests I interview have moved beyond their crucibles. I am an elder at my church and have been on the board of my children's school. I love my work, which I truly feel called to, and I have been involved with organizations whose missions I care deeply about.

Today I feel blessed. I am following a vision that is *my* vision, not anyone else's. I am living in light of who I was designed to be. I am using my skills and abilities in areas I feel passionate about. And I am using my failures and pain to help others. Life could not be much better. I am now living my life for a purpose that honors God and which has brought much fulfillment and fruitfulness to me and to others.

To Sum It Up

Think about your crucible moments. You may not have lost a multi-billion-dollar family business, but all of us face crucible experiences in our lives. We either have faced or will face trials. Whether those crucible moments are our fault or not, whether they are public or not, they are painful, they are real, and they can be debilitating.

How do we move on from such crucible moments, such periods of trial by fire? Part of it is a decision: *Will I let this experience destroy me, or will I try to move on? Will I learn from this experience? Will I learn more about who I am and who I am not? Will I use this experience as an opportunity to lead a life of significance and of serving others?*

At the end of the day, moving beyond a crucible experience is a decision. What will you take away from it? What lessons will you learn about yourself to help you move forward?

This next chapter sets the stage for moving beyond failure and living a life of significance. In order to serve others in a vision that is part of a higher purpose, you have to start from within. Building a life of significance starts from the ground floor. It starts with who you are.

Reflection Questions

1. What blessings have been hidden in your crucible moments?
2. What has your crucible experience taught you about yourself?
3. How could your crucible experience be used to help others?

Chapter 2

LEADERSHIP FORGED IN THE FIRE

I learned the hard way that you can't solve everything. Even when your analysis of the problem is right (and it won't always be), often you won't have the power or ability to fix the problem right away—or possibly ever.

What have I learned from my own crucible moment in 1987? Several things. One is that there are no do-overs. You cannot go back and try several different hypothetical tracks to see which one works out the best. If I had not attempted the takeover and instead, slowly over the years, tried to ensure the company was better managed and restored to the ideals of my great-great-grandfather, would life have been better? Maybe. Maybe not. This scenario and how it would have panned out are unknowable.

The takeover didn't work, and I needed to quit beating myself up. Yes, I made some business decisions that perhaps were not the best. I made mistakes—some that were on a big scale. But I had to move on and live my life. This may sound obvious, but trust me . . . it's easier said than done. Without my faith and my family, I don't know how I would have moved forward.

Lessons Learned

I've recognized that my biggest mistake, even bigger than the takeover, was in trying to be who others wanted me to be. My parents saw me as the savior of the family company. I bought into this dream and sought to prepare myself to fulfill it. But here's the major problem: it was not my dream. It was my parents' dream. The role this dream forced me to take on did not fit with my personality or innate gifts.

At heart, I am an adviser, not an upfront, take-charge leader. Being in charge of a huge company, having to make dozens of momentous decisions each day, did not fit with how I was designed. But when I was growing up, I never took the time to ask myself what I wanted to do. What did I feel God calling me to do, in light of the gifts and abilities He had given me? I always assumed my calling had to be John Fairfax Ltd. I never allowed myself to be open to other opportunities.

The hardships and failures of the 1987 takeover and the pain of those ten years after the company went into receivership have also given me a measure of understanding and compassion for people who have suffered misfortunes. I attended Oxford University and Harvard Business School, which some may think is quite an accomplishment. But after some of the mistakes and decisions I have made, I hardly feel arrogant about my education; frankly, I feel a bit embarrassed.

Now, if I meet somebody who says they have lost all their wealth or destroyed their marriage due to alcohol or drug abuse, I don't sit in judgment. We all make mistakes. Some are more public than others. Some have bigger consequences than others. And some mistakes are life-altering.

My crucible has also made me more tolerant and forgiving of others' mistakes. It is one thing to have compassion for someone who has been through difficult circumstances. It is another to be tolerant of people who don't perform up to your expectations. I have to say this one is still a work in progress.

One hard lesson of the takeover has been recognizing my own impatience. I have learned to temper my passion for doing what needs to be done with patience. Change rarely happens overnight. In my role as a board member of my church or previously as a board member of my kids' school, I have had to learn that patience and perseverance are required. Sometimes, others will not consider a particular initiative to be as important or urgent as you do. You may be right. They may be right. Regardless, patience is a must.

> We all make mistakes. Some are more public than others. Some have bigger consequences than others. And some mistakes are life-altering.

I learned the hard way that you can't solve everything. When I see a problem, especially when it is one of injustice or things being run in a way that hurts an organization's ability to accomplish its mission, I want to fix it right away. But I have learned that even when your analysis of the problem is right (and it won't always be), often, you won't have the power or ability to fix it immediately—or possibly ever. The realization that God is in control has helped me see that I can't solve all the problems of the world. Solve the ones you can, and don't obsess about the problems you can't solve.

Paradoxically, another key lesson I gained from the takeover is to speak up. Even for the most reticent among us, there is a time and place to express opinions and a helpful manner in which to express them. This lesson of speaking up has been hard-won. During the months leading up to the takeover bid, I was asked to sit in on several board meetings of John

Fairfax Ltd. There I saw some of the board's deliberations at the time, including the discussions around selling the company's newly acquired Melbourne television station and the other Seven Network stations we owned. What struck me was the absence of tough questions. *Where were the questions asking how we got into the mess of being forced to sell at least one television station, if not more? Where were the questions asking whether a media company should be selling television stations?*

You might ask what I said at these meetings. I may have asked some questions. I don't believe I said a lot. In fairness, I was not a director of the company at the time and was attending those meetings at the board's invitation. I was also only twenty-six and not one to fire away in an environment like that. However, some of the directors of the company had been there a long time and had considerable business experience, yet they were largely silent, too.

I have never forgotten this. When good people say nothing, bad things happen. It is the job of the directors of a company to speak up. They have a duty to the shareholders, to the employees, and to the community. Speaking up may not make you popular with management or your fellow directors, but it is your job.

Now, as a board member or director, there are times when I ask tough questions that may make things uncomfortable for some people. As a director, that is my job. I do not want it said of me that I did not speak up when I knew things needed to be said. This is probably one of the biggest lessons I have learned from the takeover experience. But again, not every issue that comes up before a board requires you to pound your fist on the table and say, "What are you thinking?" Discretion, wisdom, and judgment are required in knowing what to say, when to say it, and how to say it.

Another outcome of the takeover is that my faith was forever affected. I will discuss this in more detail later on, but for now, suffice it to say that when the takeover failed and I lost a great amount of money, position, and prestige, I had to ask myself, *Where do you put your security, Warwick? In what or in whom do you trust?* Putting your trust in money, position, or power can be dangerous.

There's a passage in the Bible that says, "Come now, you who say, 'Today or tomorrow we will go to such and such a city, and spend a year there and engage in business and make a profit.' Yet you do not know what your life will be like tomorrow. You are just a vapor that appears for a little while and then vanishes away." (James 4:13–14, NASB) The wisdom in this spoke to me and changed my perspective.

Life is a vapor. Money, power, prestige, and reputation are fleeting. We can spend our whole lives seeking these things, trying to hold on to them. But they can all be gone in an instant. Like a vapor, they can vanish. Certainly, money and power will vanish for all of us one day as we pass from this life. But God never changes. His love never changes. It is not dependent on our wealth, status, accomplishments (or failures), or anything we do. It is given by *grace*.

Once the takeover failed, that truth became very real to me.

A Legacy of Overcoming—John Fairfax

My process of coming to these self-revelations (and learning from them) was enhanced by considering the achievements—and challenges—of my great-great-grandfather, John Fairfax, founder of John Fairfax Ltd. His impact in shaping who I am today cannot be overstated. He went through many of his own crucible experiences, from which I have learned much.

John Fairfax was born in the county of Warwickshire (hence my first name, also my father's) in England in 1804. He did not grow up with wealth; his father was in the building and furnishing trade (though there had been a time when the Fairfaxes of Warwickshire were prominent). John's great-grandfather, also named John Fairfax, was the mayor of the town of Warwick and a wealthy man. However, his son, John's great-uncle, squandered the family's estates.

The Warwickshire Fairfaxes also had a distant connection to the Yorkshire Fairfaxes, a far more prominent family. Lord Thomas Fairfax was the commander of the Parliamentary forces during the English Civil War that began in the 1640s. Oliver Cromwell, who was under his command, later executed King Charles I, which horrified Lord Fairfax, who wanted greater democracy but did not want the monarch to be executed.

Eventually, Lord Fairfax's descendants moved to America, and at one point, a good part of Northern Virginia was land controlled by Lord Fairfax. Fairfax County in Northern Virginia is named after him. (This means that while people in the U.S. may not be able to spell or pronounce my first name, Warwick—the second *w* is silent—at least those in the Washington, D.C. area have heard of my last name.)

But back to John and the less-famous Warwickshire Fairfaxes. Since his family was not wealthy, John was removed from school by his parents and apprenticed to a local bookseller and printer at twelve. At twenty, he moved to London and worked for a newspaper called the *Morning Chronicle*. A few years later, he moved back to Warwickshire and settled in the town of Leamington. At the time, Leamington had a spa (natural springs), which made it a fashionable resort for those seeking to improve their health. John worked with a number of newspapers in Leamington before founding the *Leamington Chronicle* in Leamington Spa in 1835.

In 1836, an event occurred that would alter the course of John Fairfax's life. His newspaper published an article condemning the conduct of a local lawyer. The lawyer sued, but the court ruled in favor of the *Leamington Chronicle*. The lawyer again sued, knowing John Fairfax had limited resources, and the court again ruled in favor of the newspaper. Since, at the time, defendants had to pay their own legal costs, irrespective of the verdict, the heavy legal expenses forced my great-great-grandfather into bankruptcy.

John's bankruptcy left him devastated. All he had worked for and dreamed of seemed to be over. However, he had many friends in Leamington and was very active in his local church. His involvement helped build the church from a congregation of no more than six to one of the most influential houses of worship in Warwickshire. Townspeople held meetings to support John and raised money to help the *Leamington Chronicle* continue. At one such meeting, a resolution was passed saying the townspeople admired the *Chronicle's* "fearless independence" and its "careful abstinence from . . . all libelous matter, slander, and vituperation."

However, John would not accept their charity and instead decided to seek a new life in a distant country—in a wider, freer atmosphere where he could build another newspaper. So in 1838, John, his wife Sarah, and their three children departed for Australia. At the time, the voyage from England was a forbidding one. A month into the four-month voyage, Sarah gave birth. The new baby, Richard, was not a strong child, and this added to the stress of the journey. (Richard died a few months after their arrival in Sydney.) At last, they caught sight of land, but it was a barren spot on the west coast of Australia. John's heart sank as he thought of bringing his family to this seemingly hostile place, and he had little money to provide for them.

As he was looking out at this new land, Sarah sensed his despondence and came up from below deck to find him. As recorded in a 1941 biography by John Fitzgerald Fairfax, my father's cousin, Sarah apparently said the following to her husband. It is one of the most moving passages I have ever come across from a spouse supporting the one they love:

> *I knew, John, that despair was in your heart as you looked across those cold, grey waves at that horrid, unfriendly coast, and I know that you were worrying about me and ours and your ability to fend for us . . . Do not worry about me and the children. I will be brave and helpful, and whatever God may send or take away, my love for you is the strongest thing I have in life and it will have no death. I do not worry about you; I know what you can do, and it is much. I know your strength of purpose, your sound, vigorous brain and your sense of honor. You are well armed, John, for any fray, and you will win and I will win, not only success, but content and great happiness.*

In 1841, three years after stepping onto Australia's shore, John and journalist Charles Kemp together bought the *Sydney Morning Herald*, which over time grew into a large company. Sarah's prophecy and John's dream came true. Out of misfortune came a blessing that John would never have known without the court case and subsequent bankruptcy of the *Leamington Chronicle*. Twelve years later, Kemp retired, leaving the Fairfax family in control of what would one day become John Fairfax Ltd. John tirelessly devoted his energy to building up the *Sydney Morning Herald* and subsequent additional publications.

When John Fairfax died in 1877, he left his son James Reading Fairfax to head the family business. James Reading Fairfax's son, James Oswald Fairfax, had one child—my father, Warwick Fairfax.

Doing His Duty—My Father

My father was the greatest man I have known. He was not perfect; like all of us, he had his flaws. But there was a nobility of spirit about him. At over six feet tall, he had the bearing and features you would expect of a nobleman. Some said the people closest to him almost worshipped the ground he walked on. I certainly did.

My father was born in Sydney in 1901 on the shores of Sydney Harbor in the suburb of Double Bay, in the same house, Fairwater, that I later grew up in. He just missed being born in the Victorian era, as Queen Victoria had died earlier that year, but the Victorian way of thinking continued until the First World War. This was a generation of Australians, at least among the well-to-do, who still thought of England as the mother country, and "going home" meant going back to England.

My father used to take this tradition a bit far in that he would cheer for England in the Ashes cricket test matches between England and Australia. This used to drive me crazy. The cricket test series against England is one of the most important sporting events in Australia. At stake is a symbolic urn, which supposedly contains the ashes of a bail (an item of cricket equipment)—hence the term "the Ashes." I couldn't understand how my father could cheer for England when our family had been in Australia since the 1830s. To me, this was carrying respect for your heritage a bit far. I sometimes wondered whether he cheered for England just to annoy me.

He grew up amid wealth, as had his father, and was the fourth generation of the Fairfax family to go into the family business. He was the only child of Sir James Oswald and Lady Mabel Fairfax and was definitely the heir to the company. James and his brother Geoffrey ran the business alongside their father, Sir James Reading Fairfax. Geoffrey and his wife lived next door to my grandparents and had no children. As a result, my father almost had two sets of parents and was rather spoiled as a boy.

At heart, my father was a reflective philosopher rather than a businessman. John Fairfax, his great-grandfather and founder of the family business, had been a deep thinker, but he had also been a great businessman. Somehow the business genes were not passed on in great measure to my father. I have often thought he would have made a great philosophy professor at a university. He had a curious mind and loved learning for its own sake. Much to my mother's chagrin, he preferred to spend his evenings reading rather than socializing. But despite his diffident (some would say "shy") nature, he enjoyed discussing theology, politics, and history with other interesting people. He enjoyed these discussions even when he disagreed with their views.

My father, as I did, saw it as his duty to preserve the family business for future generations. I am sure that, like me, he never seriously thought of doing anything other than going into the business. He was involved in John Fairfax Ltd. from the 1920s, when he came back from Oxford, until his death in the 1980s. For much of that time, from 1930 to 1976, he was either the managing director or the chairman of the company. He was still a director of the company when he died.

My Father's Crucible

My father went through a number of challenges and crucible moments in his life. He ascended to the leading position of the family company in 1930 when he was twenty-nine, a couple of years after my grandfather, Sir James Oswald Fairfax, died suddenly of a heart attack. This was an unexpected ascension for my father, as his father was only sixty-five when he died. My father became managing director of the company and later became chairman when it went public in 1956. He held the leading position for more than forty-five years.

While ascending to the top leadership position at such a young age was quite a test, other tough challenges followed. Like many family businesses, over the years there were frictions and disagreements within John Fairfax Ltd. The seeds of bitterness and perhaps rivalry were sown many years earlier.

The years of 1961 and 1976 were two of the most challenging years in my father's life. In early 1961, after a difficult divorce from his second wife and subsequent marriage to my mother, there was a lawsuit by my mother's first husband against my father over the breakup of my mother's prior marriage. Some members of the family who were involved with the company felt my father needed to resign his position. While they said this was to be only temporary until the legal actions were settled, he took it very personally. As it happened, within a few months, the legal actions were settled and my father again assumed the chairmanship. But he felt betrayed by the other family members.

So, when in 1976 these same family members who had pressured him to temporarily resign in 1961 now successfully pressured him to resign permanently as chairman, it was especially hard to take. At the age of seventy-four, my father was in great health and had lots of energy. He had plans to update the *Sydney Morning Herald* and continue to modernize the company, and he was shocked when some family members told him they felt it was time for new leadership. To my father, it seemed they had tried unsuccessfully to get rid of him fifteen years earlier, and now, they had finally succeeded. Given the decision had come from within the family, it was very difficult for him to get over.

Being forced to resign was a crucible experience for my father. It was a test of his character. How would he handle this crisis? Would he let bitterness overwhelm him? In the end, he decided to step down and say nothing about the fact that he had been pressured to resign. He did so partly to ensure that my future with the company would not be endangered by a public fight with other family members.

He also felt that the best thing for the company would be for him to resign gracefully. I was fifteen, and that period of time is one of the most memorable for me as I think of my father and the great man he was. Over the next year or so, he forgave the other family members, as best as he could, who had removed him from the position he loved. He told me God commands us to forgive, and so that is what he did. It was the right thing to do, both for the family and for the family business. I have never forgotten what my father did during those days—and his attitude in doing it. It is to me one of the greatest examples of integrity I have ever seen.

What I Learned from My Father and Great-Great-Grandfather

What did I learn from my father's crucible experience of 1976 and its aftermath? For one, I learned it is important to do the right thing, no matter what. My father felt that a public fight would be wrong and not in the company's best interests or mine, so he did not oppose the actions of these other family members. Despite feeling marginalized in the last eleven years of his life, he stayed an active board member and tried to positively contribute. He was not one to pack his bags and go away feeling sorry for himself. He had a job to do, and he would do it.

My great-great-grandfather taught me a great deal as well; although, I never met him. He was a man of vision, and he had the strength of will and the perseverance to make it happen. After ten years of dreaming of and working toward owning his own newspaper, this dream seemed to be dashed in 1836. Many in this situation would have become bitter and given up. As a small-business owner committed to running a business on sound moral principles, how can you compete against the unscrupulous tactics of some? Not only did he not give up, he had the presence of mind to see that real opportunity lay in Australia, in a new land, where things were not so set as in England. This sense of vision, of what is possible, is also shown in his work with his church in Leamington and later in Sydney. The things John Fairfax became involved in tended to grow and expand.

John dealt with his crucible experience of being bankrupted by an unscrupulous lawyer by not letting go of his vision of founding the newspaper of his dreams. He would persevere until he succeeded. He was supported by his wife, a woman of character and courage. (I also have a wife who has always supported me and believed in me, even when I doubted my own abilities and was not particularly hopeful. Even in those times when I could not always see my capabilities or the good within me, my wife could. That is an incalculable gift. The value of a strong partner in life cannot be overestimated.)

John Fairfax was a newspaperman through and through, but there was more to him than newspapers. He was a loving husband and devoted father. He was active in the community. But his greatest outside interest was his church. He was a member of the Pitt Street Congregational Church, where he was a deacon. The church still stands in downtown Sydney today. John was passionate about his faith in Christ. He spoke of being "busy for both worlds," which I will discuss in more detail later.

John had, and still has, a powerful effect on my life. John Fitzgerald Fairfax's biography of him, published in 1941 on the one-hundredth anniversary of the Fairfax family's ownership of the *Sydney Morning Herald*, is a loving, warm tribute to a great man. I read this book growing up and have read it many times since. There is so much about my great-great-grandfather that I want to emulate.

When he arrived in Sydney in 1838, John Fairfax hardly had anything to his name. He was not a man of inherited wealth who was content to live off the success of previous generations. He worked tirelessly and earned the respect of those around him. He was admired by those in society in Sydney, those at the *Sydney Morning Herald*, those at his church, and most of all, his family. John was a man of great faith and integrity. He was probably a nineteenth-century liberal, which has different connotations than the word does today. He believed in treating everyone fairly, and this was reflected in his editorial values for his newspapers. His biographer captures John's vision for the newspaper he wanted to build in Australia:

> *It would be a free, hard-fighting, vigorous newspaper, unchoked and untrammeled by the limiting throngs of a country town. His paper would be molded on the lines of all those things he held most dear; it would be without fear to express opinion, it would be without the reproach of self-interest, sworn to no master and free from the narrow channels of sectarianism.*

In fact, the *Sydney Morning Herald*, even before John Fairfax and Charles Kemp bought it, had mottoes that fit right into John's editorial philosophy: "In moderation placing all my glory, while Tories call me Whig—and Whigs a Tory." In other words, the *Herald* was not to be a party newspaper as some nineteenth-century newspapers were. (Whigs and Tories refer to the two major political parties in England in the nineteenth century, which became the Liberal Party and the Conservative Party.)

John Fairfax did not put on airs or try to be who others wanted him to be. He knew who he was and where he was going. He loved newspapers and had a dream of founding a great one. John Fairfax was secure and did not need to pretend. His faith was the root that grounded him, and a huge part of who he was. He overcame adversity, persevered, and found gain in his pain. It's a legacy he passed down to me, and one I want to impart to others.

Overcoming Disability—Franklin Delano Roosevelt

So many great leaders of history have been forged in the fire of a crucible. Franklin Delano Roosevelt is one of those leaders. Roosevelt is regarded by historians as one of the greatest American presidents. He helped bring America out of the worst Depression the country had faced and served as the nation's leader throughout most of the Second World War. Clearly, Roosevelt faced many crises. But the crucible experience that changed his life occurred when he contracted polio in August of 1921.

The image we have of Roosevelt in his early years is of a fun-loving, aristocratic, privileged young man, who came from what is perhaps the most patrician background of any president. Between his mother's family, the Delanos, and his father's, the Roosevelts, he had no fewer than twelve Mayflower ancestors. He became a Democratic state senator in New York in 1910, then assistant secretary of the Navy in 1913 under the Wilson administration, and in 1920, he was the Democratic nominee for vice president on the ticket with presidential nominee James Cox. But then, in 1921 at age thirty-nine, Roosevelt contracted polio—a greatly feared and stigmatized disease in those days, as a vaccine had yet to be developed.

On the way up to his family vacation home on Campobello Island in New Brunswick, Canada, Roosevelt visited a Boy Scouts camp. A photograph taken there is the last one that shows him walking freely, unaided by braces. Later on, at Campobello, Roosevelt swam in the cold waters and hiked two miles home. That August evening, Roosevelt retired early, feeling tired and chilled. By the next day, one leg was paralyzed. The following day, both legs were paralyzed.

At the time, most would have said Roosevelt's political life was over. His mother urged him to retire to the family estate in New York as an invalid. Fortunately for Roosevelt, his wife, Eleanor, knew that if he gave up on his active lifestyle and his interest in politics, his soul would die. During the next seven years, he sought to get back on his feet. Though he would never walk again without the aid of braces, Roosevelt never gave up hope. Right up to the time of his death in 1945, he refused to believe that he would not recover. He was determined not to let polio hold him back. While recovering at Hyde Park, each day he would walk down the driveway with his braces on and aided by his crutches, saying, "I must get down the driveway today—all the way down the driveway." This was some considerable distance, about a quarter of a mile.

Roosevelt knew that to have any future in politics, he could not appear as an invalid, believing that to use crutches would be political poison. So he developed the appearance of walking. With his heavy braces on, he would lean on the arm of one of his sons and use a cane with the other arm. Despite the difficulty of walking this way, he would laugh and smile at crowds, appearing to casually take his time walking to his car or from his seat to the podium to speak. In 1928, he was asked to speak at the Democratic National Convention in Houston to nominate Alfred Smith as the party's nominee for president. With 15,000 people in the audience watching, Roosevelt walked on his son Elliott's arm from his seat to the podium.

Later that year, he became governor of New York, and in 1932, in the midst of the Great Depression, he became president. In his inaugural address on March 4, 1933, Roosevelt uttered these now-famous words: "This great Nation will endure as it has endured, will revive and will prosper. So, first of all, let me assert my firm belief that the only thing we have to fear is fear itself—nameless, unreasoning, unjustified terror, which paralyzes needed efforts to convert retreat into advance." One wonders, would a physically healthy Franklin Roosevelt have become the Democratic nominee for president in 1932 and won the presidency? A good-looking privileged man of noble birth, a fun-loving man with an eye for the ladies—was that the type of man America, in the throes of suffering and poverty, would vote for? Was that the man who could identify with your pain and your fear? I am doubtful.

Even though the full extent of Roosevelt's disability may not have been known at the time, it was clear to all that he had come back from adversity. He had not let fear cause him to remain an invalid. Conquering his fear and physical challenges, he appeared for all the world as an energetic man on the move who would take action to solve the nation's problems.

In some sense, polio made him the man he was. To picture Roosevelt without polio or Roosevelt before polio is to picture a very different man. The same is true for any of us. Who we are now is not who we would have been without our crucible experience. Crucibles make or break a leader. Clearly, polio could have broken Roosevelt. He could have listened to his mother and retired to the private life of an invalid at the family estate at Hyde Park. He got much different advice from his wife, Eleanor, who urged him not to give up and kept his name up in political circles while he was recovering.

Fortunately for us and for history, Roosevelt listened to his wife and not his mother.

Reflection Questions

1. Are there any figures in your own family history whose stories have influenced you? Who are they, and how have they inspired you?
2. What famous people, either past or present, have you admired for their legacy of overcoming? What about them strikes you as a quality you'd like to emulate in your own life and leadership?
3. If you had to identify just three important lessons you learned from your own crucible experience(s), what would they be?

Chapter 3

KNOWING (AND BEING) YOURSELF

Being authentic is one of the biggest gifts you can give to yourself and to other people. Simply put, you cannot lead if you are not yourself.

The Ancient Greeks had a saying, "Know thyself." That's great advice—but easier said than done. To really know yourself, you have to know what you are good at and what you are not good at, what you can and can't do, and even what scares you. In essence, how can you be authentic if you don't know who you really are?

This might sound obvious. However, we live in a fast-paced world, where technology is always changing and crises in the world and the workplace are constant. Our days are spent just trying to keep up with the challenges at work and somehow to keep work and family balanced. To many, this can feel like a losing battle. Who has time to contemplate the direction their work is going, how their family is doing, and especially, *who they really are?* Who has time to figure that out—and does it really matter anyway?

I've spoken a lot up to this point about how my father and great-great-grandfather have influenced me. My mother, Lady Mary Fairfax, also had a significant impact on shaping who I am today. She was a complex figure. I am a combination of both of my parents. So to understand who I truly am, my authentic self if you will, it is important to know who my mother was. She was truly unique.

A Picture of Determination and Perseverance—My Mother

My mother, Mary Wein, was born in Poland in the 1920s to Jewish parents. They left for Australia when my mother was three, before the Second World War when Nazi Germany took control of Poland. The Nazis killed three million Polish Jews, more than 90 percent of their pre-war population.

I have often thought about how fortunate my mother and her family were to have immigrated to Australia when they did. My mother's parents were Zionists; that is, they were Jews who believed in the creation of a Jewish homeland in Israel. As I have been told, many Zionists were not particularly religious, and this was true of my mother's parents. For the first few years of my mother's life in Australia, they lived in Broken Hill in outback New South Wales. After that, the family moved to the eastern suburbs of Sydney. My mother's first marriage ended in divorce, and she married my father in 1959.

Mary Fairfax was many things, but she was definitely an original. She was a determined, driven, and uninhibited person. If she wanted to accomplish something, she would generally achieve it. Her determination and perseverance were off the charts. She was incredibly outgoing, always the life of the party. After studying chemistry at the University of Sydney, she started seven fashion shops in Sydney; at one point, she told me, she was the highest self-employed female wage earner in New South Wales.

Her concept was to offer the styles of expensive fashions that "factory girls" (as she put it) could afford. The shops were very successful, and they enabled her to buy a nice house on the water in Elizabeth Bay in Sydney.

When I think about my mother, I particularly remember the amazing parties she would host at Fairwater in the 1960s and 1970s. She could put on fabulous dinners for three hundred or more as if it were nothing, often with wandering minstrels in the garden playing Italian music. Many of the guests would be in *Who's Who,* and she would look up their entries and seat those with common interests next to each other. The picture of my mother I have back then was of a woman of incredible vibrancy, glowing like an incandescent flame. The laughter and the gaiety stand out in my memory.

My mother and I had a complex relationship, mostly because she had definite ideas about how things should be and what people should do—including and especially me. She was very strong-willed, as was my father, for that matter. I have inherited this trait from both parents, I suppose. I, too, can be stubborn. There were times when I was growing up that my mother would push me to do something or meet someone, and I would push back. She would push harder, and inevitably I would feel forced to push back harder myself. I am sure my mother found this frustrating. But I was both my mother's son and my father's son. So I suppose I came by my stubbornness honestly!

Despite the challenges in our relationship over the years, I dearly loved my mother. She had her flaws, like all of us. But she was an amazing woman. She was highly intelligent and had a prodigious knowledge and appreciation of art and poetry, among other things.

At one point, she was on a list of the ten best-dressed women in the world. She was formidable, but she could be kind and generous and would help people she met. She believed strongly in philanthropy and giving back. She is probably best known for establishing Opera Foundation Australia, which gives scholarships to young Australian singers to be trained in some of the best opera houses in the world, such as Bayreuth in

Germany, La Scala in Milan, and the Metropolitan Opera in New York. So grateful was the Australian Opera for what my mother had done for young Australian opera singers that, on her birthday, they would often send an opera singer to sing for her.

My mother was a creative thinker; she would call herself "the ultimate lateral thinker." I have probably inherited some of her creative thinking, though while I appreciate art, my knowledge and passion for it is not at the same level as hers.

I have benefited from my mother in numerous ways, some due to genetics and some because of her example. From my father, I get my reflective, philosophical side. Like my father, I was quite shy and diffident growing up, though that is not as obvious now—my kids tease me that after church I am usually the last one there, talking to someone. From my mother, I have inherited determination and perseverance. That never-say-die attitude that was a part of her is certainly a part of me. My mother was a very passionate woman who loved life intensely and who could get very excited about things, including people she met. Beneath my often calm and reserved exterior, I, too, am a passionate person with strong convictions about things.

To Thine Own Self Be True

Shakespeare wrote this line—"to thine own self be true"—over 400 years ago, and the fact that it's still often quoted today serves to show us that authenticity is not just a modern-day value. Know who you are and how you got to be that way—then be who you are! This is timeless advice.

But to be authentic, you have to know what you are trying to be authentic *to*. For example, you might sense that you're being taken off-course by praise or criticism, but unless you know who you are, how would you know for sure?

An analogy might be useful. Let's say your company is thinking of buying another company. Your company would closely investigate the other one, analyzing what market it is in, how the economy is affecting it, how it is doing against the competition, and importantly, researching its strengths and weaknesses.

Maybe the company has talented people, but they are spread too thin with too many products in different markets. Maybe they have great products, but the market need for their products is shrinking. Coming up with a balance sheet of the target company's strengths and weaknesses is critical in making the decision whether to acquire it. Shouldn't you know your own strengths and weaknesses as well as or better than some company your firm is thinking of acquiring?

There are several ways to find out your strengths and weaknesses. For example, psychological and behavioral assessments can be helpful. There are a number of well-known tools, such as Myers-Briggs (which uses the theory of psychological types described by Carl Jung) and DISC (which looks at people's behavioral differences). Another popular survey for figuring out your strengths is Strengths Finder, originally put out by the Gallup Organization. (This assessment is easy to obtain; you just have to buy the *Strengths Finder* book and you then have access to it.)

Another popular method widely used in organizations for finding out your strengths and weaknesses is the 360 Assessment or 360-Degree Feedback. This involves asking those around you what they think you are good at and what areas you could improve in. A 360 gets input from your boss, your peers, and those who report directly to you—in other words, those above, alongside, and below you (hence the name). One 360 Assessment I like is the Leadership Practices Inventory (LPI) from the work by James Kouzes and Barry Posner in their book, *The Leadership Challenge*.

While assessments can be helpful, just asking simple questions can get you a long way. Ask those around you, including your boss, your peers, and those who work for you, to tell you the areas you are good at and the areas in which you could improve. While some may be reluctant to tell you, if they genuinely feel you want to know the truth and that you will not rip off their heads if they give you an honest answer, you can get useful information.

If all those around you say the same things about your strengths and weaknesses, they may be right. It is amazing how often leaders dismiss the results of a 360 and say everyone else is wrong and that they are right about who they are. This kind of reasoning makes little sense. (But then, humans have a great capacity for self-delusion.)

As John Fairfax Ltd. grew to be a large, diversified media conglomerate, the company and those leading it were very influential. In Sydney in particular, the Fairfax family was respected not just because of its wealth, but also because of its status in the community. The Fairfaxes were "old money," high up in both the economic and social spectrum of society. Because I grew up in this environment, which sometimes could feel artificial, I have always valued authenticity.

From what I know of John Fairfax, the company founder and my great-great-grandfather, he, too, valued authenticity. He knew what mattered to him, and he never wavered from it. My father was authentic, too. He did what he wanted, when he wanted, and with whom he wanted. Currying favor with others to benefit himself—or the family business— was not something that would have occurred to him. That said, growing up under the cloud of my family's wealth and status exposed me to people who wanted to use us to move up the social or economic ladder. It meant wondering whether people wanted to be my friend for me or because of who I was—"a Fairfax."

For most of my growing-up years, we lived in the eastern suburbs of Sydney in the large house on the water, Fairwater, which my grandfather had bought around 1900. My parents held a lot of parties. We hosted prime ministers, politicians, ambassadors, business leaders, visiting dignitaries, and Hollywood stars.

I attended a private boys' school called Cranbrook. The school's motto was *Esse quam videri*—literally, "to be rather than to seem to be." I have often thought that for many in the upper reaches of society, such as those who frequented my parents' parties, the motto should have been, "to seem to be rather than to be." Even as a child, I could discern that much of the posturing was all about being the person you thought others wanted or expected you to be. Put on the air of self-assurance, whether or not you feel confident. Pretend to be wildly successful, even if things are not going so well in your business. Make sure you pay rapt attention to people you find immensely boring. Laugh loudly even when the joke is not remotely funny.

Being brought up in this kind of environment has made me intensely allergic to inauthenticity and the putting on of airs. Not surprisingly, I have a fairly low tolerance for inauthentic people and much prefer to be around men and women who are real. Also, not surprisingly, this has meant that my friends and those I spend time with now are not from the same social or economic stratum I grew up in. It is tough to find the authentic amid the rich and powerful.

My world now is so different from the one in which I grew up. It is sometimes difficult for me to believe that my former life really happened, or that it happened to me and not some other person. My life is full and enjoyable. I have a wonderful wife, Gale—an American whom I met for the first time at Sydney airport in 1988. Some mutual American friends were in Sydney and told me they were going to the airport to pick up a friend. Since they weren't used to driving on the left side of the road, I offered to drive them. Sometimes, good things happen when you do a good deed. That is how I met Gale, who I say blew into my life. She spells her name like the wind.

Gale and I have three children—two sons and a daughter. We have lived in Annapolis, Maryland for almost thirty years. I feel very blessed to have a wonderful family, good friends, and to have been involved with organizations and work that I believe in and where I feel I am honoring my true, authentic self. This is more rewarding than any power or status that money or social standing can provide.

Why is Authenticity so Hard?

Being authentic is one of the scariest and most difficult things you can be. It flies in the face of our culture and conventional thinking. You could even say it flies in the face of conventional business thinking. Marketing teaches us to identify the needs of the target market and then design the product and the communication about it to meet the needs of the consumer. Give the consumers what they want and tell them why that product meets their needs. This may work in marketing products but not in leading people. People want to know who their leaders really are.

Being authentic is one of the biggest gifts you can give to yourself and to other people. Simply put, you cannot lead if you are not yourself. People do not want to follow inauthentic leaders. However, being authentic, being truly you, takes courage.

It is one thing to be rejected while you are wearing a mask. In that case, people are not really rejecting you; they are rejecting your mask. Putting on a mask is safe. You can craft a mask that appeals to the broadest possible group of people. Do people want you to be outgoing? Then you can be outgoing. Do they want you to be witty and intelligent? Then you can be witty and intelligent. Whatever role is called for, you can play. All it requires is a bit of training, perhaps the right degrees, and observations of people who have the characteristics you desire, and you can be whoever you want to be. But when you are so concerned about being who your target audience wants you to be (or who you think they want you to be), you forget who you really are.

Consider politics. Candidates poll test what the hottest issues are for a given election cycle. Then they appear to know what they are talking about on those issues. This strategy sends the message that real solutions are not as important as appearing to be knowledgeable, credible, and understanding. So whether it is health care, energy, the economy, foreign affairs, or the great social issues, candidates try to appear knowledgeable and compassionate. Above all, they want to appear to be more knowledgeable and compassionate than their rivals. But many, if not most, avoid authenticity.

As Jack Nicholson famously says in the movie *A Few Good Men*, "You can't handle the truth!" Can you imagine a candidate telling the public what he or she thought the important issues were, even if they were not even among the top ten issues their pollsters said people were concerned about? It is the ultimate taboo: telling the public not what you think they want to hear but what you believe they need to hear—and being yourself as you do so. Maybe your pollsters are telling you that the public wants you to be compassionate and empathetic, but you are more of a tough, no-nonsense, tell-it-like-it-is kind of person. The pollsters will tell you that if you have to deliver painful medicine, i.e., the truth, say it in a way the public wants you to say it. Don't be yourself when delivering the bad news.

The point here is not that cold and gruff wins or that being compassionate and understanding is bad. Nor that it is wrong to try to be compassionate. It is that you have to be yourself and do what you believe. That is the hallmark of authenticity. Simply put, it is being who you are, rather than who you are not.

You might be thinking, *Okay, I buy the fact that you need to advocate for what you really believe in and be yourself, not some other person. So what's next?* The problem is that being yourself and advocating for what you believe in is more difficult than you might think. Who do you know who stands up for what they believe in, no matter what anyone thinks, and who are truly themselves without a thought of putting on airs or a

> Be yourself and do what you believe. That is the hallmark of authenticity.

mask? Think of your friends, your co-workers, and your family. Think of people in the public eye—politicians, entertainers, or people in the media. Think of people in history. How many people can you think of? It is difficult for most of us to come up with more than a handful.

Authenticity in leadership is rare. The higher you go in the economic and social spectrum, the harder it is to find authentic leaders. It is easy to criticize leaders for being phony. That is certainly my tendency, and though I may be more sensitive to this than some others because of my background, I believe this is a common experience.

The challenge is that as a person rises in leadership, the temptation emerges to put on airs and be who others want them to be or to be the "right" kind of person to fit in or get ahead. It is like a virus that creeps up and infects a person. How many times do we read about people who have been changed by success or a rise to prominence? They ditch their old friends from the neighborhood. Those people simply wouldn't fit in, they tell themselves—they wouldn't feel comfortable in these circles. They acquire the trappings of power and success: the large house, the nice cars, and of course, the right friends—people who are comfortable with the house, the cars, and their new status. Not only do they have these "designer friends," but they may also have "designer wives." While there may also be "designer husbands," it seems to be all too common for a man to "make it" and then ditch his wife for the younger model who he believes can better showcase the fine clothes and jewelry he can now afford.

It is easy to look down on all of this and condemn those who rise to economic and social power, seeing how their souls corroded and how they seem to sell out to the lifestyles and values of the rich and famous. However, try being in this situation and withstanding the pressure to conform. I know how tough it is.

Authenticity in the Spotlight

Growing up as the heir apparent to a 150-year-old family media empire, I lived in the proverbial goldfish bowl where I felt my every move was scrutinized, and I couldn't afford to fail. I had to work hard at my studies, do well at university and business school, and prepare myself to, one day, lead the family business. This is not an environment that makes for authenticity. I was reticent about letting anyone know what I really thought or felt or see who I really was. I didn't so much pretend to be someone else as much as I did not let people see who I really was.

Once the takeover was completed toward the end of 1987, I was in control of a large, diversified media company. For the next three years, until the company went into receivership, the spotlight was on me. Leading up to the takeover and during the years I was in control of John Fairfax Ltd., while I received my share of criticism, I also received plenty of supportive comments—some of them sincere, and some from people perhaps seeking to ingratiate themselves with me. Sincere or not, it was tough for this attention not to have an effect.

Some of these people told me I was bright and hard working, that I was in the mold of John Fairfax himself, a man of great faith. Some said they had been praying for years that God would raise up a man of faith in the media in Australia. I was an answer to prayer, they said. My name was in the headlines. My face was in the media.

All this can take a toll on a person's sense of self. Who was I? Was I going to believe the news reports? Was I the hotheaded kid who could have had it all but just couldn't wait, launching the unwise takeover that led to the company going bankrupt and the passing of family control? Or was I the young knight who was coming in to save the company and restore the ideals of its founder? You do tend to lose your sense of self between the media onslaught on the one hand and, on the other, the "support" of "friends" who seem to think you are the second coming. Perhaps both are wrong.

So when you are in the public eye and feel that you are at the top of your socioeconomic sphere, how do you stay authentic and be who you really are? In general, lessons are better caught than taught. Typically in this book, I share the lessons I've learned on leadership and life through stories and parables. However, authenticity is so important in general—and so important to me—that a few words about *how* to be authentic might be helpful, and that is the topic of the next chapter.

Reflection Questions

1. Why is authenticity such a key component to leadership?
2. Why do you think authenticity is so rare in our culture?
3. Whom do you admire for their authenticity? What is it about them that makes them authentic?

Chapter 4

ANCHORED IN AUTHENTICITY

Authenticity is the foundation of good leadership.
In our fast-paced, pre-packaged, often artificial
world, people crave the real, the authentic.

Telling someone generically "how to be authentic" can seem challenging. Based on personality, life circumstances, and any combination of other variables, different people will express authenticity in a wide number of ways. This is especially true in the wake of crucible moments. They have a way of bringing our vulnerabilities out into the open, sometimes privately and sometimes for the whole world to see.

Trying to avoid failure and trying to hide our failures are two ways we frequently circumvent the development of authenticity in our lives. Such behaviors impede our freedom and commitment to be real about who we truly are. Our failures do not define us; rather, they shape us. The sooner we embrace and apply this concept, the sooner we can enjoy the fruit of the self-awareness and confidence it can bring as we move beyond our crucibles to pursue lives of significance.

In the next chapters, we will explore ways to discover our own unique design—the "flavor" of who each of us is as individual. Your family, your beliefs and values, your life circumstances, and a variety of other factors will all contribute to who you are and what is important to you.

I've discovered, though, that regardless of the things that make us unique, there are some critical core principles that inform how to live our lives with authenticity. I believe we all can benefit from these guiding principles to help us live with purpose and without the masks that hide our true selves from the world.

Have an Anchor

The first key to authenticity is being solidly grounded in something immovable. For me, this was—and remains—my faith. Being rooted in something outside yourself, particularly when difficulties arise, is like being a boat tied to an anchor that is tossed on stormy seas. Without an anchor in your life, you can be buffeted off course by the wind and waves. You don't know which end is up.

Case in point: the higher you rise up the economic and social ladders, the stronger the wind and waves become, and consequently, the greater the need for a strong anchor. The lack of such an anchor has led to many people losing all sense of self. You can see it in professional athletes, entertainment stars, and politicians. How many begin to believe the adulation they receive then implode with extramarital affairs, drugs, or both? The extramarital affairs and the drugs are just a symptom. The real problem is that they don't know who they really are anymore. They are lost. They are confused. They need something to distract them and dull the pain, the sense of loss, and the feelings of hopelessness. "Successful" people can be some of the most lonely, distraught people out there.

My faith is the most important thing in my life. It is the anchor that rescued me from the darkness that threatened to envelop me after the takeover failed. After John Fairfax Ltd. went into receivership in late 1990, the following several years were tough. Without the anchor of my faith, I shudder to think what would have happened to me. Even with faith, my sense of self-worth sank.

However, I knew that no matter what mistakes I may have made, God would always love me and support me. For me, having key Bible passages memorized allows me to call them to mind whenever I feel lost, confused or afraid. My faith helps keep me grounded on what, for me, I know to be true. It helps me weather life's most devastating storms. It helps me stay true to my guiding values and beliefs.

Here are a couple of Scriptures of particular significance to me:

Trust in the Lord with all your heart and lean not on your own understanding; in all your ways submit to him, and he will make your paths straight.

—Proverbs 3:5–6

But whatever were gains to me I now consider loss for the sake of Christ. What is more, I consider everything a loss compared to the surpassing greatness of knowing Christ Jesus my Lord, for whose sake I have lost all things.

—Philippians 3:7–8

These Scriptures and others like them have helped keep me anchored, have helped me keep my sense of self, and at times have kept me from the depths of despair, or at least brought me back if I sometimes descended there.

Without my anchor of faith in those years after the takeover failed, I may well have drowned. *Who am I? What is my purpose in life? What am I going to do with my life now?* These were all frightening questions I had not faced before but had to face at that time. My faith taught me that I was a beloved child of God, that He still loved me despite the mistakes I had made, and that He had a plan for my life. That, for me, remains the starting point for determining who I am.

Find True Friends

Another key to authenticity is having good, real friends—friends who tell you the truth, not just what you want to hear. They tell you the truth in love. They are unlike the people who love telling you the "truth" to pull you down out of jealousy or revenge. Truly loyal friends who have your best interests at heart and will tell you the real truth in love are worth their weight in gold.

When you work with people with similar values in organizations you care about, invariably you make good friends. At different times in different places—Oxford, New York, Sydney, and Annapolis—God has provided me with good friends. Some of the closest are the elders I have worked with at my church and those on the school board on which I served. God has also provided me with the ultimate friend I could have on this earth, my wife Gale, who always speaks truth to me. She has been a great counselor, confidante, and ally.

Many times, especially while wrestling through crucibles, we may want to seek out companions who feed our ego, make us feel good, grant us access to people or experiences we desire, help us accomplish material objectives, or who are simply convenient for a good time. These kinds of "friends" will not contribute to our leading lives of significance. I would rather have a few close, authentic friends than a large number of superficial ones.

Over the years, as hopefully, I have gained a bit of wisdom, I have found it valuable when I am struggling with something to ask my close friends for their opinions. Even friends are not always willing to speak the truth to you all the time, but the really insightful ones will often respond by asking me a series of questions to help me think through the issues myself.

It's true that often the best way to get a point across and speak the truth is to ask a penetrating question. It could be as simple, "What do you think is the right thing to do?" Typically, when asked the right questions, we know what we should be doing. We know which choice is true to who we are and what we value. We just need a trusted friend to help us think things through. These kinds of friends are crucial sounding boards and accountability partners who help us remain true to our authentic selves.

Find the Right Environment

A third factor in cultivating authenticity is making sure your environment reinforces who you are, rather than who you are not. Society and the workplace have created immense pressure to conform—to be who the organization needs you to be—rather than your authentic self. For example, if your values are honesty and integrity, and you are working for a company that is so focused on the stock price, and management is willing to do almost anything to prop it up, it could be a problem. They may not be doing anything illegal or grossly unethical, but they may ask you to "shape" the story you give your customers in a certain way. *After all,* they urge, *don't you want to put the company's best foot forward?*

Illegal or grossly unethical behavior is easier to spot and withstand, but the subtle shades of grey are harder. Over the course of your career, the dewy-eyed, idealistic young man or woman you started out as can gradually become bitter, cynical, and hardened. It is like the boiling lobster. If you slowly turn up the temperature of the pot, the lobster does not realize it is cooking to death. You do not want to be like the lobster and slowly die to your values, your ethics, and your true self—the real, authentic you.

With this in mind, it can be helpful to consider a few important things when you evaluate your environment—in this case, your work environment. First, know who you are. *What are your strengths and weaknesses? What are your values?* Then consider the organization you are working for (or are considering working for). *Do its personality and values match yours? Does the organization's environment work for your strengths and weaknesses?* For instance, if success requires rapid decision-making and you are a slower, more thoughtful decision-maker, it could be a problem.

How about where you live? If you love the outdoors and getting away to the mountains, and you're holed up in an apartment in a big city, maybe that is not a good match. The job may pay well and you may like the organization, but does the location fit who you are? Does the location help you be who you truly are?

I have often wondered how much my father enjoyed being the managing director and chairman of the company, which he was at various points during his tenure with John Fairfax Ltd. He did seem to enjoy the journalistic and political side, with the *Herald* reporting and commenting on the major issues of the day. But being responsible for continuing the Fairfax family legacy and dynasty, as well as overseeing the company—I wonder how fulfilling that actually was for him and whether or not he was his best, authentic self in that role.

I remember seeing some photographs of him from the 1940s or 1950s. One showed my father at the office, looking rather dour. Another showed him wearing country clothes and a straw hat while at Harrington Park, our farm outside Sydney. The difference was that in the photograph at Harrington Park, my father seemed relaxed and had a broad grin on his face. He loved the country and his Poll Hereford cattle.

I have also often wondered whether, rather than being a corporate executive, my father would have preferred to be a professor at a university, where he could write and debate philosophical, theological, and political issues. These activities and environment clearly captured his imagination and passion more than the business side of newspapers.

This point about the environment we work in, both the organization itself and its location is that it's important. Due to the natural human desire to conform, we risk becoming people who fit into the location or mission of the organization but are unrecognizable as our true selves.

Conformity as a form of inauthenticity is a trap that is difficult to break out of once we've started down that path. There are few things worse than living a life that is a lie. That's what you're doing when you are not being who you are but rather who others want or expect you to be.

Do What You're Great At

One final thought I try to live by is this: Don't merely do what you are *good* at but what you are *great* at. A friend mentioned this idea to me; I believe it is a quote from Dick Halverson, a former chaplain of the U.S. Senate. It may sound presumptuous, but I believe that we are all great at something.

Unfortunately, we all too often, find ourselves in situations where we are not drawing on our core strengths, and in some cases, may actually be operating in our area of weakness. When I was in leadership at John Fairfax Ltd., I think at some deep level, I realized I did not have the disposition or the desire to head up a large media company. I am, by nature, somewhat shy and retiring. For my personality and gifts, being in the limelight of what was then one of Australia's biggest takeovers in a company that held some of the most renowned media assets in the country was not a good fit. I was no Rupert Murdoch or Kerry Packer, to name two of the leading media figures in Australia at that time. The company needed more of a take-charge, self-confident action man, someone who was at ease with himself and at ease with other people, especially while leading a charge. That was not me. That was certainly not me in 1987 at age twenty-six.

In my current season of life, I am utilizing and capitalizing on my core strengths. I love writing and being a reflective adviser. I love hosting a podcast and asking guests questions about their trials and triumphs. I also love working with organizations whose missions I care deeply about. The crucible experience of the takeover and its aftermath has been a great gift. The takeover made what I am *not* good at very clear; but it—and subsequent experience—has made what I *am* good at evident, too.

I am naturally very contemplative. A friend of mine calls himself a recreational visionary, meaning he dreams of what could be all of the time and everywhere. I am similar in that I love reflecting. It is easier for me to consider and reflect on something than to make a decision and act. While there are downsides to this characteristic, being reflective actually helps my writing, enables me to give thoughtful input on the nonprofit boards I have been a part of, and helps my executive coaching.

This is by design. I could have put myself in a lot of other situations where I am not gifted. Why put yourself in situations that involve doing things you are not good at? Why not put yourself in situations where you can do things you are great at?

Authenticity in Action—David

History provides many useful examples of great leaders and allows us to see their authenticity (or lack of it) in action. One of the greatest examples of authenticity, I believe, is the biblical figure King David, who started out as anything *but* kingly. He was the youngest in his family, mocked and marginalized by his brothers, and relegated to menial jobs like sheep herding and delivering food to his brothers on the front lines of battle while they did the "important" jobs. I'm sure David felt like a failure sometimes.

As a boy, David conquered Goliath with just his slingshot and enabled the soldiers of Israel to prevail over the Philistines. A mere lad, he showed more courage in taking on the giant Goliath than anyone else in the army. Throughout his life, David was a man of courage who did not shrink from tough decisions. He became King Saul's leading commander, and whenever he was sent out to battle for the Israelites, his courage would win the day.

David made serious mistakes, as well, such as his affair with Bathsheba and his subsequent orchestration of the death of her husband, Uriah. But when confronted by the prophet Nathan over his sin, David confessed and was contrite. The Psalms are filled with his expressions of authenticity to God: anger, fear, hopelessness, and uncertainty—he hid nothing about who he really was and what he truly felt from his Creator

Other biblical accounts provide similar examples of David's authenticity. There is one incident when David was bringing the Ark of the Covenant, one of Israel's national treasures and the symbol of God's presence with the nation, back to Jerusalem. The ark was an ornate gilded chest containing stone tablets on which the Ten Commandments were inscribed. As the ark was being brought into the city, David stripped off his outer clothing and danced in the street in his linen underclothes, celebrating with unabashed abandon. His wife, Michal, the daughter of King Saul, despised him for this "unkingly" display. To her sarcastic comments, David replied that if that was what it took to celebrate before his God, he would become even *more* undignified!

David was clearly an authentic leader. He was a courageous and bold commander and a person of deep faith. He was flawed, but when confronted with mistakes, even gravely serious ones, he owned up to them. He certainly did not put on airs or try to be someone he was not. These are qualities that would serve us all well as we cultivate authenticity in our own lives and leadership.

Authenticity in Leadership—Abraham Lincoln

Abraham Lincoln is another classic example of authentic leadership. He experienced significant failures in his life but went on to harness those failures into a political career that changed the course of U.S history and the lives of millions of people.

Lincoln was the sixteenth president of the United States, from 1861 to 1865, during the American Civil War. He is routinely listed as one of, if not *the*, greatest presidents in American history. In a 2017 C-SPAN survey among top U.S. presidential scholars, Lincoln was rated the best president, ahead of George Washington and Franklin D. Roosevelt. Lincoln is not only acclaimed in the United States; he is thought of by people from many different cultures as one of the great leaders in history.

Born in 1809, Lincoln grew up in humble circumstances in Kentucky, experiencing several notable failures before winning the White House—was defeated in a bid for the state legislature, had failed in business, and twice lost campaigns for the U.S. Senate from Illinois.

Considered to be somewhat "backward," as he lived at the time in the then-wilds of Illinois, Lincoln garnered little respect from the U.S. East Coast establishment. But in his bid to earn a place in national politics, he did not apologize for his humble beginnings or his values. He was true to who he was and what he believed.

As the nation was on the brink of civil war, about to be torn asunder over the issues of slavery and states' rights, Lincoln ascended to the presidency at a crucial time in U.S history. He believed passionately in the preservation of the Union and came to believe that slavery was morally wrong and needed to be abolished.

> I believe authenticity is not only a key to effective leadership; it is a key to leading a fulfilling life. It is one of my most cherished values. I don't want to be anyone else; I just want to be me.

His beliefs were not poll-tested to fit the mood of the country. At various times, the North grew tired of war, and not everyone was willing to continue fighting just over the issue of slavery. But Lincoln would not back down from his beliefs in the preservation of the Union and the abolition of slavery.

Lincoln was a man who knew himself, and he was far more intelligent and wise than he appeared on first impression. His opinion of himself was not bound up in what others thought, and he remained steadfast in his beliefs, no matter what. A man who did not seek excessive praise, he was known to seek input and was almost impossible to offend. The history books tell us that Lincoln's authenticity and self-awareness enabled him to draw together a talented group of men in his cabinet, and ultimately, win the respect and admiration of the nation.

I believe authenticity is not only a key to effective leadership; it is a key to leading a fulfilling life. It is one of my most cherished values. I don't want to be anyone else; I just want to be me. From my faith perspective, I want to be who God created me to be. Nothing more. Nothing less.

Authenticity is also the foundation of good leadership. In our fast-paced, pre-packaged, often artificial world, people crave the real, the authentic. That's why being authentic is an essential starting point for people to want to listen to you . . . and ultimately, for wanting to follow you.

Reflection Questions

1. What are your strengths, weaknesses, and personal values?
2. In what situations or scenarios might you be putting on a mask rather than being your authentic self? Why do you think that is?
3. How can your authentic self inspire and help others?

Part Two

DISCOVER YOUR PURPOSE

Leadership, especially in times of crisis, must be paired with conviction and character if it is to be successful. That's why to lead others well, you must understand yourself: your passions and talents, your strengths and weaknesses, and what you hold most dear.

Just before he died, my father was working on a book called *Purpose*. In its conclusion, he noted a number of things that summarize both his theology and his character. He wrote, "But I prefer an incomprehensible God to a meaningless world" and the following:

How can I say what I should aim at?
To live beyond my understanding.
To act beyond my love.
To serve beyond my life.

Faith in something larger than yourself is the bedrock on which the ability to weather storms is built. And putting into practice the principles you believe in—aligning your inner self with your outward behavior—is critical to living a life of purpose and significance.

Chapter 5

THE GOVERNING POWER OF FAITH

Ground zero in this journey of living with purpose is to recognize and live from an immovable anchor that steadies your life when the harsh winds come. For me, that anchor— the course-corrector and course-steadier—is faith.

Part of the human condition is that life is rarely a smooth journey: crucibles are common, if not unavoidable. All of us—or at least everyone I know—have faced trials that have knocked (or threatened to knock) us off balance. The important question is, *What will we do when we are faced with these trials?* When a proverbial hurricane hits us, or our organization, how will we get back to center? How will we keep our business on track? How will we remain on course, personally, to be the leaders we want to be? Without an anchor, a solid and immovable object to hold us steady in the storm, the answer is clear: we won't. The question is not whether you and your organization will get blown off course, but when.

The road back begins with learning the lessons of your crucible and knowing and understanding yourself—self-awareness. What are your deepest values? What, in essence, makes you tick? Understanding your innate design—how you have been wired and then developed in light of that wiring—is critical to being able to craft a vision for your life that is truly yours and to living a life of significance that benefits others. Ground zero in this journey of living with purpose is to recognize and live from an immovable anchor that steadies your life when the harsh winds come. For me, that anchor—the course-corrector and course-steadier—is faith.

> The question is not whether you and your organization will get blown off course, but when.

Faith is much maligned in some quarters of society today. People of faith, almost irrespective of their religious tradition, are considered by many to be narrow-minded bigots who seek to foist their beliefs on others. They are also often dismissed as anti-intellectual. There are certainly some people of faith who fit this mold. But, just as certainly, not all, or even most. Just as one example: I think of C.S. Lewis, the Oxford academic, theologian, and writer who was one of the foremost Christian thinkers of our time. He wrote such classics as *Mere Christianity* (one of the best primers on the Christian faith) and the beloved children's series *The Chronicles of Narnia*. He was certainly no narrow-minded, anti-intellectual figure. In other faith traditions, you could also point to the current Dalai Lama, who is the fourteenth in a succession of Dalai Lamas that goes back to the late 1300s. The Dalai Lama is a key figure in Tibetan Buddhism and is respected around the world.

I am passionate about my faith, but I try never to impose it on others. By nature, I'm a listener; I seek to understand other people's perspectives. It's possible for people of different faiths to respect each other and have a constructive dialogue. My brother Garth is a follower of Orthodox Judaism. Both he and I are passionate about our respective faiths. Yet while we follow different religious traditions (though there is certainly some commonality between Judaism and Christianity), we respect each other's beliefs and have good discussions. It is from this foundation that faith is best brought into leadership contexts where it can serve as a stabilizing force for you—and your organization.

Why Faith?

You may accept that you and your organization need an anchor to withstand the storms of life that will come your way. But, you might ask, why should this anchor be faith?

The crux of the issue is that to be solid and immovable, the anchor we are looking for must be based on something absolute, not something relative. For example, you might decide to base your anchor on a set of values or principles you believe most people in society or your organization would agree with. In reality, much of the time, such an approach might work out only in the short term. If you survey a group of people, for instance, you may well find that honesty and integrity are their key values. Perhaps some would say fairness or even humility. Based on these principles, you could work up your own set of values or a mission statement for your organization. But the problem is that public opinion on acceptable values can change over time. What is the use of having an anchor that can shift? Over a long enough period, the drift in your anchor—and the changes in your trajectory—will be apparent if you choose to look carefully.

Imagine you could go to Germany in the 1930s, while the Nazi party was in power, and survey people about what they valued. Perhaps people would say they valued racial purity, rooting out weakness, and unswerving obedience to leaders. As another example, we might go to the pre–Civil War South of the United States. What principles would we find there that people might consider their anchor? We might hear values supporting the rule of white people and the importance of property rights, where they would consider slaves as property. I think we can all agree we might find certain values that were once cornerstones of public opinion, which ultimately proved to be reprehensible values on which to base a nation's ideals.

In the United Kingdom, from after the Reformation of the sixteenth century up until the Catholic Emancipation Act of 1829, Catholics could not vote or become members of Parliament. Imagine what values might have been prevalent then. Being Protestant, and having allegiance to king and country and not to Rome, would be up there. To many in British society at the time, such "bedrock principles" might have seemed an obvious choice. To us now, they seem nonsensical and abhorrent.

The point of these examples is that basing your anchor, your set of immovable principles, on what society believes at any given time may make sense to you now, but in the light of history, it may make no sense at all. The "principles" may, in fact, not be *principled* at all in hindsight.

So what *does* provide an anchor whose principles do not shift but remain true for all time? For that you have to delve into something eternal, something timeless. For myself, I seek to anchor my principles of leadership not based on man's thoughts but God's thoughts. I find the Bible has much to say on leadership and contains numerous examples of great leaders who exhibit some touchstone qualities of leadership. It provides teachings that do not shift with time and culture. It provides an anchor that ensures the central tenets of my leadership and life remain the same yesterday, today, and tomorrow.

Coming to Faith

My great-great-grandfather, John Fairfax, was a man of great faith. He was active in his church and had a strength and fervor to his faith. His son, James Reading Fairfax, also had a strong faith.

There is a haunting letter James Reading Fairfax wrote to his adult sons, which seems to reinforce the idea that there was a shift in the nature of faith in succeeding generations. In essence, it pleads with them to swear allegiance to Christ and accept Him as their Lord and Savior. The fact my great grandfather felt he had to write this letter to his sons speaks volumes.

He wrote, "Now that my sons are men of mature years, does it not seem reasonable to suppose that they have given serious thought as to whether they accept the faith in God their fathers professed, and acknowledge Jesus Christ as their Savior . . . ?" He continued, "Do not my dear sons, wait till years go on . . ."

James pointed out in his letter that the time must come when we all must receive or reject Christ's offer of salvation, and he pleaded with his sons to tell God that they were His sons and would serve Him. He finished his plea with this quote, from Acts 16:31: "Believe in the Lord Jesus Christ and thou will be saved and thy house." (KJV) Given how faith in my family seemed to become more traditional after James Reading Fairfax's lifetime, I am not sure the letter had the impact he desired.

I grew up in the Anglican Church in Sydney. While I believed in God, faith was not a very active part of my day-to-day existence growing up. I went to church somewhat infrequently, at Christmas and Easter and a few other times a year. I had a father who was very interested in theology and philosophy and a mother who believed there was a Creator. My mother had studied chemistry at university and would tell me how perfect the table of elements was—to her, there was no way this world was an accident.

My sister, Annalise, came to faith in Christ, along with a few of her friends, while at Ascham, a private girls' school in Sydney, and she has always been an example of faith to me. Annalise has led confirmation classes at the local Anglican church we attended, St. Mark's Darling Point in Sydney, and has even preached several sermons over the years. She has always been caring, supportive, and understanding of me. She would give me different versions of the Bible on birthdays and other such occasions and certainly made me open to the Gospel.

The turning point in my faith journey occurred when I was at Balliol College, Oxford. This was a challenging time for me. I was eighteen when I started at Balliol, at the other end of the world from my family and where I had grown up. While I had done well at school in Sydney, Oxford—and Balliol College in particular—had exceptionally bright students. The competition was stiff and the pressure was high. I studied philosophy, politics, and economics (PPE), as my father had done. To me, the other students doing PPE were geniuses—and I was clearly not.

One uniqueness about Oxford is that it uses the tutorial method of teaching. Every week, you meet with your professor and one other student and take turns reading out loud the essay you had written. When it was the other student's turn to read out their essay, it was always written in the most beautiful prose with no extraneous language, touching on every point that could possibly be made on the subject. The professor would then ask me if I had anything I wanted to add. I would sit there somewhat stunned, wondering what there could possibly be to add.

Compared to my fellow students, I felt a complete dunce. It was a humbling and somewhat frightening experience. Particularly during that first year, I felt out of my depth and overwhelmed. At the end of the first year, students "sit prelims" (preliminary exams), which are either pass or fail. If you fail, you go home. During this arduous time, I often took long walks in the University Parks that go along the river Cherwell. Even though I had not yet come to a personal faith in Christ, I remember praying to God. I asked Him to please not let me fail. I did not want to disappoint my father or let my family down. I was keenly aware that I was seen as someone who worked hard, was bright, and would hopefully carry on the traditions of the family media company, as laid down by John Fairfax. I felt I had to be almost superhuman to fill those shoes: to have the integrity and character of John Fairfax yet the business acumen to lead the large, diversified media company.

I worked hard and passed prelims. PPE is a three-year degree. Once you pass prelims, there are no more exams until the end of your third year. I studied hard and gradually became a little less intimidated; by the time I graduated, I actually did pretty well. But this experience did keep me praying. I remember continuing to take long walks, saying to God, "Please let me survive another term."

During my final year at Oxford, a friend invited me to visit a local Anglican church, St. Aldate's. It was different from most other churches I had attended. It was a student church with many Oxford students. The messages were penetrating and relevant, and some of the liturgy was sung instead of merely spoken. They sang contemporary Christian choruses, and the congregation seemed to hang on every word of the liturgy.

The same friend subsequently invited me to an Oxford and Cambridge retreat at an Anglican retreat center in Devon, Lee Abbey. The week I was there, in late March 1982, changed my life. The weather was perfect, unseasonably warm and sunny. Each morning, we would gather together, hear testimonies, hear thoughts about Christ, sing Christian choruses, and pray together. I had never experienced anything like that. In the afternoons, we would go on long walks in the Devon countryside. It seemed to me that these students had such peace and joy in their lives. With the pressures on me and the pressures to come, I knew I needed that peace and joy.

One day, I asked a woman who was part of the St. Aldate's team for a modern version of the Bible. I guess that was a dead giveaway that I was seeking to deepen my faith. She took me aside and asked me about my faith. I spoke a bit about my life, my background, and the pressures on me. She asked if I had fully committed my life to Christ. I said that I had not but that I knew I needed to. I knew I would not be able to withstand the pressures on me without Christ in my life. There and then, I invited Him into my life. Those next few weeks back in Oxford, attending St. Aldate's and a new believers' Bible study, were amazing. I was so full of joy. I had found the answer. It was all about God and trusting in Him. I had found my anchor.

Busy for Both Worlds—John Fairfax

Several books have touched on the life of my great-great-grandfather, and a recent portrait of John Fairfax's faith has come to light in the writings of Stuart Johnson. Reading about his life in J.F. Fairfax's biography, as well as having Johnson's in-depth portrait of his faith, have given me a greater perspective on what it means to be a person of faith. He was a devoted husband and father, active in his church, and a much-loved head of the newspaper company. In terms of a businessman of faith, to me he is the gold standard.

John Fairfax had a characteristic phrase I mentioned earlier: to be "busy for both worlds." His life mission was to "work on, in the world and the church." In essence, he believed a person should apply himself or herself diligently both at work and in the church. He believed people of faith should be role models. In an 1856 address to the YMCA in Sydney, he said:

> *Christian young men should be the most active, the most industrious, and then they will also be the most successful . . . [W]e sometimes hear . . . 'That is a good young man, but somehow he doesn't get on. He believes in God's providence, but doesn't seem to like work; is early at church, but late in business; is "fervent in spirit" but not "diligent in business".' What an enigma . . . and how he injures others, and how he belies the Christian profession he makes! If all young men were like him, what a miserable colony this would become.*

John believed in working hard at work and being faithful at church. He was a man who lived his faith. He grew the *Sydney Morning Herald* into the largest and most successful newspaper in the colony, often working long hours. He was also active in good works. But the lifeblood that fueled his work in the newspaper world and the community was his faith. There is a great quote from John, recorded when he was working for a London newspaper in the late 1820s:

I do humbly hope that there is one spark of divine grace and love even in my poor and cold and hard heart, and it is my earnest prayer that that spark may be fanned into a pure flame of unquenchable love to the great and ever blessed Redeemer. This is what I want. I have been taught to lisp the praise of my Maker while an infant, told repeatedly that nothing but religion could possibly make me happy . . . that if I ever lived and died without Christ I should be miserable to all eternity . . . humbly I would beseech Thee to grant, O God, that this desire and thirst after the eternal good which Thou hast to bestow may continue as long as life remains.

John worked as hard for his church as he did for the newspaper, serving as a deacon and continuing to teach a Sunday school class until he was fifty. With his family, he attended services or classes four times on Sundays (at 9:30 a.m., 11:00 a.m., 2:30 p.m., and an evening service at 7:30 p.m.). He was also active in leading and funding the Congregational Home Mission Society, which sought to plant Congregational churches in New South Wales and beyond. Summing up his life, on the Sunday after his death in 1877, the pastor of the Pitt Street Congregational church chose as his text 2 Samuel 3:38: "Know ye not that there is a prince and a great man fallen this day in Israel?" (AKJV)

Faith of My Father

My father's faith—perhaps evidence of the change in the family's religious practice after James Reading Fairfax—was more traditional than evangelical. He was an intellectual who read widely on philosophy and religion and was curious about other religions. Among other books, he read the Bhagavad Gita, a sacred Hindu text. He met theologians of different denominations, including Anglican ministers and Catholic priests. One minister with whom he had regular discussions was Bruce Wilson, who became the Anglican bishop for Bathurst, a regional city west of Sydney.

Early in his career, Bruce Wilson was the curate (basically the assistant minister) of the church we belonged to. He was an Anglican who held to the evangelical perspective. As I recall, he would try to get my father to think about the personal side of the Christian faith. *Who was Jesus? What did He look like?* This was a stretch for my father, who felt more comfortable talking about the philosophical rather than the personal side of faith.

In 1976, when pressured to resign as chairman of John Fairfax Ltd. by some of his family members, he was devastated. The newspaper company was his life, and at the age of seventy-four, he was still very fit and mentally active. However in the end, he resigned, not revealing publicly that he had been pressured to resign or what he felt about being forced to do so.

My father's faith in God governed how he acted, and he forgave the other family members who had put him in that position. For all of his philosophical musings, he certainly lived his faith. It may not have been the personal faith in Christ as Lord and Savior that I adhere to, but it was a real faith nonetheless. Indeed, how my father handled himself in that devastating moment, and in general, had a profound impact on me, becoming a key building block for my own spiritual journey and ultimately for my faith in Christ—and my understanding of what good leadership is founded on.

I do wrestle a bit with my father's ecumenical approach to trying to find a synthesis among a variety of religious and philosophical traditions. But interestingly, soon after I had made a commitment to Christ at Lee Abbey in Devon, I phoned him. I wanted him to know. I was so excited. In hindsight, my father's reaction was interesting and quite revealing. He did not seem to think I had become some misguided, overly emotional evangelical or a "holy roller." Quite the reverse. He observed that my faith in Christ was in line with that of John Fairfax. He was clearly pleased and proud. There was no admonition.

A few years later, in 1985, he wrote me a letter upon my acceptance into Harvard Business School. After leaving Oxford and working at

Chase Manhattan Bank, I was not able to see my father much, and he died two years later in January 1987. In his letter, he observed that since leaving Oxford and starting at the bank, I had "matured as a man and as a Christian." He said that his "faith had been strengthened too." The next line is one I will cherish forever. He wrote: "So the two people we are now can grow even closer than before."

Today, my faith in God and in Christ as described in the Bible is my anchor for life and leadership. It gives me a measuring stick to gauge how I am doing as a leader, how I am doing as a father, how I am doing as a husband, and how I am doing as a human being. The more I keep my life focused on my faith, the more centered my life is and the better I am able to deal with its storms.

Reflection Questions

1. Why is it important to have an anchor rooted in something more unchanging and eternal than public opinion?
2. What is the anchor that guides your life and leadership? How does it help you live and lead with purpose and significance?
3. Think of a time where you felt a crucible knocked you off course. How did your anchor help you get back on course?

Chapter 6

FAITH THAT GUIDES LEADERSHIP

These principles do not shift with public opinion or
the whims of society. They are eternal and changeless.
They are true yesterday, today, and tomorrow.

When we are trying to bounce back from our most trying crucible experiences, the anchor of faith can provide us with truths and values that are key principles of leadership. These include humility, integrity, servant leadership, and self-sacrifice, as well as the greatest commandments, those of loving God and loving others. I want to spend some time here unpacking these values and their impact on our leadership. These principles do not shift with public opinion or the whims of society. They are eternal and changeless. They are true yesterday, today, and tomorrow. They are true irrespective of culture or background.

Humility

Who wants to be around someone who clearly thinks he or she is better than others and knows everything—and that he or she is *entitled* to be followed? By contrast, it is refreshing to be around people who admit they don't have all the answers and that they, too, screw up regularly. That kind of leadership, offered in authenticity and humility, gives us the freedom to offer our own ideas, knowing that if we take a risk and fall short, others will cut us some slack.

Arrogance divides while humility unites.

In more exact terms, humility means that we see ourselves rightly, as created beings who are answerable to our Creator for our attitudes and actions. We are here to do His will, not our own. Since we are created beings, we should not primarily serve ourselves but should serve God, who made us.

My faith perspective teaches that we are sinners by nature, that we all fall short of God's perfection, and that, as a loving father, He has a plan to rectify that situation. We get to enter into relationship with Him because of Christ's death on the cross, which atones for our sins and makes us clean in His sight. From that perspective, what is there to be arrogant about? All we have and are is because of His grace and goodness.

There are many passages in the Bible that talk about humility. Some of my favorites are:

> *Do nothing out of selfish ambition or vain conceit. Rather, in humility value others above yourselves.*
>
> —Philippians 2:3

> *Who is wise and understanding among you? Let them show it by their good life, by deeds done in the humility that comes from wisdom.*
>
> —James 3:13

These are the ones I look on with favor: those who are humble and contrite in spirit, and who tremble at my word.

—Isaiah 66:2

The Bible says that humble people think of others as better than themselves. It says that if we are wise, we will have humility. It says that God is against the proud (the "arrogant," if you will) but gives some slack to the humble. God admires those who feel bad and are remorseful when they mess up. Doesn't it just make sense to be humble? When we are humble, others will be more forgiving when we make mistakes, and we all do.

According to Numbers 12:3, "Moses was a very humble man, more humble than anyone else on the face of the earth." Moses lived at a time when the Jewish people were being held captive in Egypt, which was ruled by Pharaoh. Moses was actually raised by Pharaoh's daughter after a clever scheme by his mother spared his life in the face of Pharaoh's edict that all Jewish boys born at the time should be killed. Moses could have lived a life of luxury in Pharaoh's household, but he chose to defend his people—a choice for which he had to flee for his life.

Moses was clearly not looking for greatness. In fact, when God confronted Moses at the burning bush and told him to return to Egypt and deliver his people out of captivity, Moses responded, "Who am I, that I should go to Pharaoh and bring the Israelites out of Egypt?" (Exodus 3:11) Moses was also not looking to be the key spokesperson of the Israelites. So God allowed Aaron, Moses's brother, to be the spokesperson. Moses humbly tried to serve God his whole life and obey Him. He led his people out of Egypt—millions of them!—and after wandering forty years in the desert, he would lead them to the brink of entering their Promised Land.

Moses's leadership had an incredible impact on the Jewish nation and its history. It is interesting to note that what Moses is remembered for most is not primarily his great leadership abilities but rather his humility.

Integrity

To me, integrity means doing the right thing no matter what. Interestingly, that is not quite the dictionary definition. Integrity comes from a root word meaning "whole" or "undivided." According to the *Oxford English Dictionary*, integrity means having strong moral principles. There is also the sense of consistency, honesty, and responsibility.

You can rely on people who have integrity. When they tell you something, you know this is what they truly believe. They are not duplicitous or deceptive. In essence, what you see is what you get. They are men and women of their word. They mean what they say, and they do what they say they will.

Who wants to work with someone who tells you they have your back, that when you offer your perspective in the meeting they will support you; and then says nothing in the meeting, leaving you hung out to dry? Or say you are assembling a big customer order with an important deadline. For you to fulfill that order, critical components have to be delivered to you on time from your supplier. If the supplier says they can deliver those components to you on time, how important is that to you? The cost of the supplier not having integrity, and not delivering those components, could be huge. It could cost your company a significant amount financially and in lost reputation.

In the real world, of course, unforeseen problems do happen. But a supplier who has integrity will not overpromise, and if something unexpected does happen, they will give you a heads-up as soon as possible and give you the straight story, not some made-up convenient excuse.

Here are a few passages that demonstrate God's concern for integrity:

Whoever walks in integrity walks securely, but whoever takes crooked paths will be found out.

—Proverbs 10:9

The integrity of the upright guides them, but the unfaithful are destroyed by their duplicity.

—Proverbs 11:3

"Teacher," they said, "we know that you are a man of integrity and that you teach the way of God in accordance with the truth. You aren't swayed by others, because you pay no attention to who they are."

—Matthew 22:16

A person of integrity can sleep well at night. He or she doesn't have to worry about being found out because there is nothing hidden or damaging to be discovered. It is a lot easier to keep your story straight if it is the truth than to remember a web of lies you have told people. Sooner or later, your lies will catch up with you.

Joseph is a great biblical example of a person of integrity. Joseph was the younger son of Jacob. He was his father's favorite, and he was a bit too proud of this. His older brothers, who were jealous, sold him to slave traders, and they took him to Egypt where he was eventually sold to Potiphar, one of Pharaoh's officers.

Because of Joseph's character and integrity, Potiphar made Joseph overseer of his household and everything he owned. Potiphar's wife tried to seduce Joseph, but he rebuffed her. This angered Potiphar's wife, who accused Joseph of trying to force himself upon her. So Joseph was thrown in prison.

There is much more to be told of Joseph's life and I hope you will look up his story in the Bible if you are not familiar with it. (See Genesis 37–50.) But for our purposes, I will stop here to point out that despite the personal risk to himself, Joseph was not angling to get ahead. He was just trying to do what was right. Some men might have gone along with the desires of Potiphar's wife, supposing she might help them. But Joseph was a man of *integrity*. He did what was right, irrespective of the consequences.

Ultimately, God delivered Joseph from prison and raised him up to the highest level of leadership in Egypt, second only to Pharaoh himself. That's a big promotion from having been in prison for attempted rape. But it's a poignant example of how God honors integrity. When we choose to do what is right—even at a cost to ourselves—it will eventually come back around, and God will remember and honor us in the long run.

Servant Leadership

Servant leadership has for years been considered one of the most important touchstones of leadership. Many leaders are no longer asking how their people, or their organization, can serve them. Instead they are asking how they as leaders can serve their people and their organization.

Some leaders are even asking how their companies and organizations can meet the needs of their community and society and have a positive influence on the environment or culture. The concept of an organization having societal responsibilities is now commonplace. In fact, it has become almost rare for corporations not to promote how they give back and contribute to society.

But where does this concept of servant leadership come from? I would argue it comes from the Bible; in particular, it comes from the model of Jesus and how He lived His life. Jesus came to serve, not to be served. When large crowds gathered to hear Him, He would often withdraw to pray and meditate in quiet or to be with His disciples. He did not come, as some had hoped, to lead a revolution to overthrow the Romans. He came to lead a movement of the heart, to turn people's hearts back to God, to help people live what they said they believed. Jesus' whole life was one of service.

One of the greatest speeches ever given, one that changed the world, was Jesus' Sermon on the Mount. (See Matthew 5–7.) Jesus did not tell us to be brave, bold, courageous, unafraid, and resolute, or to be the leader who laughs in the face of death. Rather He told us to be meek, poor in spirit (that is, to realize our need for God), hunger and thirst for righteousness, merciful, pure of heart, and peacemakers. We are to love our enemies, give to the needy, pray, and seek treasures in heaven rather than on earth. We are not to judge others. In effect, Jesus, in the Sermon on the Mount, described the path for the servant leader. He described who the servant leader is and what he or she does.

Many, if not all, of the great figures of the Bible are described as servants. Moses was said to be the servant of the Lord, as was Joshua. David spoke of being Saul's servant, when Saul was king, and of being God's servant when he, David, was king. The prophets Elijah and Isaiah both spoke of being God's servants. Jesus' disciples were referred to as servants. Paul is described as a servant of Christ Jesus and the Gospel.

There are some great passages in the Bible on service and being a servant:

The greatest among you will be your servant.
                                                                   —Matthew 23:11

Anyone who wants to be first must be the very last, and the servant of all.
                                                                   —Mark 9:35

Be shepherds of God's flock that is under your care, watching over them—not because you must, but because you are willing, as God wants you to be; not pursuing dishonest gain, but eager to serve.
                                                                   —1 Peter 5:2

This last passage in particular provides some great thoughts on leadership. It instructs leaders to care for those under their authority, not to be focused on getting rich because of their position, but to be eager and willing to serve. How we need to hear this in our day and age when it seems the reverse is so often true! We have leaders who are paid well even when their organizations are performing poorly. How much are today's leaders—business, politics, sports, entertainment—focused on eagerly serving those under their care, rather than eagerly serving themselves?

I believe the most descriptive illustration of service is when Jesus, on the last night of His life on earth before He was crucified, took off His outer clothing, wrapped a towel around His waist, and washed His disciples' feet, then dried them with that same towel. Jesus told His disciples that they were to follow His example in caring for others: "Now that I, your Lord and Teacher, have washed your feet, you also should wash one another's feet. I have set you an example that you should do as I have done for you." (John 13:14–15)

At Taylor University in Indiana, the towel image is used as part of the graduation ceremony. All three of my children graduated from Taylor, a great university with a strong academic reputation and an amazing Christ-centered community. After being there for a few years, it is hard to leave, so caring, supportive, and fun is the community. Taylor's mission statement is to "develop servant leaders marked with a passion to minister Christ's redemptive love and truth to a world in need." During the graduation ceremony, Taylor gives all its graduates a towel along with their diploma. This symbolizes that Taylor graduates are primarily meant to be servants as they seek to live out Christ's mission for their lives. It is a very moving moment and a poignant picture of what it means to be a servant leader.

What better illustration could there be for us as leaders for how to serve those entrusted to our care? We are to serve them in humility, proverbially on our knees, figuratively naked in our humility and authenticity. This image of the leader as a servant, washing the feet of those under his or her care, is not one we often see in leaders today, despite many leadership thinkers advocating the importance of leaders serving others. The power of a leader serving his or her people in such a manner is so strong that it can move mountains. Who would not want to follow a leader like this?

Self-Sacrifice

Self-sacrifice goes hand-in-hand with servant leadership and is not a popular leadership principle. Some may buy that humility and integrity, even servant leadership, are all part of what constitutes a great leader. *But self-sacrifice?* That connotes images of self-flagellation or being the willing martyr. Self-sacrifice also suggests death, as in the death of the "hero." Going under the bus for a cause sounds a bit melodramatic.

But being willing to go under the bus for a cause or principle is part of what true self-sacrifice is about. The *Oxford English Dictionary* defines self-sacrifice as being willing to give up your own interests in order to help others or advance a cause. Self-sacrifice may mean being willing to give up your life, or it may mean being willing to give up your position, your reputation, or even your career. There are few higher forms of leadership than a willingness to sacrifice everything for the good of those in the organization or for the good of the country.

> There are few higher forms of leadership than a willingness to sacrifice everything for the good of those in the organization or for the good of the country.

The key is motivation. Is your desire to promote your own heroism and ego to reserve your place in history? Or is it to do your duty, to sacrifice yourself for a higher cause or ideal, whether or not anyone ever knows or cares about your sacrifice?

When we think of self-sacrifice, we cannot help but think of the brave men and women who have given their lives in defense of their country, especially when that cause is to preserve the freedom of that country or other countries. In Australia, we might think of soldiers receiving the Victoria Cross, and in the U.S., of soldiers who have received the Congressional Medal of Honor. Soldiers receive these medals, in many cases, by sacrificing their lives to save their comrades in arms. They were not thinking of being heroes. They were thinking of saving the lives of their fellow soldiers. That is true self-sacrifice. The theme of the Congressional Medal of Honor Society sums it up well: "Ordinary people doing the extraordinary."

History is full of great examples of self-sacrifice. William Wilberforce is one. He was a British politician in the late 1700s and early 1800s who could have had a brilliant career in politics and may well have become the prime minister of Britain one day. Wilberforce was outgoing, popular, and had an engaging personality, which was a great asset in politics and at the influential parties to which he was invited.

Wilberforce was good friends with William Pitt, a prime minister known as William Pitt the Younger to distinguish him from his father, who had also been prime minister. It could have been possible for Pitt to pass the mantle of leader of his party and future prime minister on to his friend. However, Wilberforce's focus was the abolition of the slave trade in the British Empire. This cause was not popular with everyone in his party or others in power. By clinging to the cause of the abolition of slavery as the major thrust of his life, Wilberforce gave up the possibility of being prime minister. In effect, he sacrificed his own political self-interest for a higher cause. That is self-sacrifice. Wilberforce's life was not about his ego or desire for glory; it was about doing what was right for his country and for humanity. This also brings to mind images of those who have fallen in battle, laying down their lives for their fellow soldiers: "Greater love has no one than this: to lay down one's life for one's friends." (John 15:13)

The story of Esther, found in the Bible, is another great example of self-sacrifice. Esther was a Jew who became the wife of the great Persian king, Xerxes. She lived at a time when the Jewish people had been conquered and taken to Babylon as captives. (Babylon became the capital of the Persian Empire.)

Esther's cousin Mordecai uncovered a plot whereby one of Xerxes's officials, Haman, had schemed to have all the Jewish people killed. Mordecai sent a message to Esther, pleading for her to help save her people. Esther was initially reluctant, reminding him that for anyone to go before the king without being summoned could well mean death. Mordecai's response—that it was her duty to try to save her people—is still a poignant exhortation to anyone who finds themselves in this kind of precarious position, wavering between self-preservation and self-sacrifice: "And who knows but that you have come to your royal position for such a time as this?" (Esther 4:14)

Esther went to King Xerxes and implored him to spare her people, and Xerxes granted her request, sparing the Jews from certain slaughter. Esther risked her life to save her people.

The Great Commandments

The Great Commandments are another cornerstone of leadership, tying how we relate to *God* to how we relate to *others*. They help us focus vertically on God and horizontally on our relationships with other people—and they are tremendously instructive in guiding us as we chart a course back from our crucible experiences toward a life of significance.

In the Great Commandments, the Bible provides the clearest answer to the question of where we should find the immovable anchor for our leadership. The answer is that our anchor needs to be in God. Looking to God, who He is and what He stands for, will help us understand how to relate to other people.

The Greatest Commandment, given in Matthew 22, is in response to an expert in Jewish law who asked Jesus: *Which was the greatest commandment in the law?* This was Jesus' response:

> *Love the Lord your God with all your heart and with all your soul and with all your mind. This is the first and greatest commandment. And the second is like it: Love your neighbor as yourself. All the Law and the Prophets hang on these two commandments.* (Matthew 22:37–40)

The Ten Commandments, found in Exodus 20 and Deuteronomy 5, can also be tied to the two concepts found in Matthew 22, loving God and loving others. The first four commandments of the Ten Commandments refer to loving God: loving God alone, not worshiping idols, not misusing the name of the Lord, and keeping the Sabbath day holy. The last six commandments refer to loving others: honoring your father and mother, not murdering, not committing adultery, not stealing, not giving false testimony, and not coveting your neighbor's wife or his property.

The concept of loving one another is also referred to by Jesus in John 13: "A new command I give you: Love one another. As I have loved you, so you must love one another." (John 13:34) Jesus stated this principle in positive terms. But it is also found in negative form in many of the great world religions and ways of thought, including Judaism, Hinduism, Buddhism, Islam, and Confucianism:

> *What is hateful to you, do not do to your fellowman. This is the entire Law; all the rest is commentary.*
>
> —Judaism

> *No one of you is a believer until he desires for his brother that which he desires for himself.*
>
> —Islam

> *Do not do to others what you would not like yourself. Then there will be no resentment against you, either in the family or in the state.*
>
> —Confucianism

So, what has all this to do with leadership? Everything. All these passages point to the centrality in the world's great religions and philosophical traditions of loving others. Loving others is a key commandment of ethics, morality, and religion. But how do we love others? In particular, how do we love others who hate us and persecute us? This is not easy. The answer is to look to God and understand how He loves us: "This is love: not that we loved God, but that he loved us and sent his Son as an atoning sacrifice for our sins." (1 John 4:10)

When we look to God and understand how He loves us, it better enables us to love others. To lead well, we need to love those who work for us. We need to love those who supply goods for our company. We need to love those who provide money for our company to run. We need to love those who buy our company's products. If we love all these people, honor who they are, and respect them, all things being equal, things will go well for us.

Look at it from the point of view of your clients or customers. We hear some companies say they want to *value* their customers. Isn't that the same as saying that we should *love* our customers? If we treat our suppliers well, perhaps during times of shortages they will be more likely to give us the critical parts we need for the products we make. If we treat our shareholders and lenders well, keeping them informed and making sure they are truly heard, during difficult times they may be more patient with our company than with others. If we truly cherish our employees—as some companies say they do—that will help us attract and keep the best and the brightest.

More companies are becoming concerned with being socially responsible, caring for the environment and the welfare of their workers in diverse, often poorer countries. They view their performance as more than financial, sometimes using the phrase the "triple bottom line," which looks at the social, environmental, and financial contexts. Being socially and environmentally responsible elevates such companies' stature in the community and often makes them more desirable places to work. More people in society today are seeing that loving others just makes good business sense.

As a caveat, loving others does not mean being a doormat and giving others whatever they ask for or taking from them whatever they want to give you without any questions. Of course you want to charge a fair price for the quality of product or service you are providing. Of course you expect quality parts from your suppliers. In a family, loving your kids does not mean saying yes to all of their demands. But loving others, respecting them, listening to them, and helping them does make sense. Those you love are more likely to love you back. They are more likely to respect you, listen to you, and want to help you. Don't you want others to treat your company that way?

Principles for Yesterday, Today, and Tomorrow

To be clear, when discussing the importance of faith to leadership, particularly crucible leadership, I am not saying we ask the question, "Does the leader believe in Jesus?" or "Does the organization believe in Jesus?" The question is whether the leader is living in accordance with some of the timeless principles that are so well documented in timeless religious texts, such as the Bible. Is the leader *humble*? Are they a person of *integrity*? Are they a *servant leader*? Are they someone who will *sacrifice* themselves for the greater good? Do they believe in some greater good, some higher calling? Do they love others in the organization and beyond? Whether or not a leader is overtly a person of faith, these qualities are a critical foundation for being a good leader.

Reflection Questions

1. Think of someone who has a great deal of integrity or is very humble. What behaviors lead you to that conclusion?
2. When you think of self-sacrifice and putting it into practice in your leadership, what thoughts come to mind?
3. Think of a time someone you worked for, or served with, exhibited servant leadership to you. How did it make you feel and perform?

Chapter 7

LIVING WHAT YOU BELIEVE

Character, then, is the key link between your faith and
how your faith manifests itself in your leadership. If you
have a high degree of integrity and humility, it would seem
almost impossible for you not to be of good character.

We've discussed the importance of having an anchor in your life that
governs your leadership, such as faith. Faith that provides a touchstone to keep us authentic, particularly as we seek to regain a foothold in
the aftermath of a devastating crucible experience.

But *how* does faith work itself out in our life, and from a business
perspective, how does it affect how we lead? It does so through character.
Character is the outworking of faith in our lives. (To be clear, here again
I am using faith in the general sense, meaning a transcendent way of
thought that governs your life.) Faith that is not linked to how you live is
very hollow.

When I was in my teens, and my father asked me if I wanted to go to Balliol College, of course, I wanted to please him and pursue the intellectual challenge an Oxford education would give me. Later on, I worked at Chase Manhattan Bank and then went to Harvard Business School to get my MBA to get the financial and business knowledge and experience to make a contribution to the family business. None of it was about what I wanted or where my passions or abilities lay. It was all about not letting down my family, especially my father.

> Faith that is not linked to how you live is very hollow.

Ironically, my father never gave me any big speeches about how it was my duty to follow him into the family business. It was just assumed. But if I had not gone into the newspaper company, it would have devastated him. As I've said, I loved my father very much, and there was no way I would even have considered something I knew would disappoint him.

I have always been idealistic, and despite a few knocks and some experiences that you would think would sap my idealism, I still am. I remember as a boy thinking, *God, help me not to become world-weary.* I realized the world could sap you of idealism and hope, of belief in what was possible and belief in what people could become. I never wanted to become cynical and world-weary as I grew older. This was one of my greatest hopes: that my idealism—my sense of hope, belief, and optimism—would not fade. Somehow (I would have to say through God's grace), it is still there.

How Character Helps Us Lead Well

In the Bible, James makes the point that faith and deeds have to be working in tandem: "But someone will say, 'You have faith; I have deeds.' Show me your faith without deeds, and I will show you my faith by my deeds . . .

You see that his (Abraham's) faith and his actions were working together, and his faith was made complete by what he did." (James 2:18 and 22)

Faith without deeds in a sense is not really faith at all. If you say your faith teaches you to be humble, patient, and caring, yet you never show any sign of these qualities, others might question whether you really believe what you say you believe. This does not mean you will always exhibit, in every situation, all of the key characteristics of your faith; but on the whole, over the course of your life, you will be seen to have those characteristics.

Character, then, is the key link between your faith and how your faith manifests itself in your leadership. The *Oxford English Dictionary* defines character as "the mental and moral qualities distinctive to an individual." Character, as we are using it here, could be defined more specifically as "*good* character."

So, what are the attributes that make a person of good character? A man or woman of good character is honest. They are reliable. They are respectful. They are fair. They are trustworthy. They accept responsibility for their actions. They do what is right, whether that is popular or unpopular. But above all, they have two of the qualities discussed in the previous chapter: integrity and humility. If you have a high degree of integrity and humility, it would seem almost impossible for you not to be of good character.

Humility and Integrity: Foundations of Character

Why are these two foundational components of character so important? If you have integrity and humility, you will tend to know yourself well and will not think of yourself more highly than you ought. If you have integrity and humility, you will have enough self-confidence to surround yourself with capable people. You will not feel threatened by their strengths.

Psychologist Daniel Goleman found that self-awareness is one of the cornerstone qualities of leaders who exhibit high emotional intelligence. People with integrity and humility tend to be thoughtful, not prone to making rash decisions. They know their own weaknesses, which tends to promote thoughtfulness.

Leaders who are humble and have integrity will want to do things the right way. The goal is too important, the mission too great not to do things right. Almost by definition, leaders who are humble and have integrity will be moral. If you realize your own failings and want to do things right, it is hard to live a life patterned on immorality. And it is far more likely you will be able to move beyond your crucible experience to live a life of significance.

In 1962, General Douglas MacArthur spoke to the Corps of Cadets at the United States Military Academy at West Point in New York. MacArthur played a prominent role in the Pacific in the Second World War. He later became supreme commander for the Allied Powers in Japan and was significantly responsible for Japan becoming a modern democratic state. He also became commander-in-chief of United Nations forces during the Korean War. (Funnily enough, my father met MacArthur during the Second World War when the general was in Australia. Years later, my father told me that his first thought was that MacArthur was one of the greatest men he had ever met. His second thought was that MacArthur was one of the most opinionated men he had ever met.)

Here are MacArthur's words to the cadets: "*Duty. Honor. Country.* Those three hallowed words reverently dictate what you ought to be, what you can be, what you will be. They are your rallying points: to build courage when courage seems to fail; to regain faith when there seems to be little cause for faith; to create hope when hope becomes forlorn."

These words also remind me of the great British hero Lord Horatio Nelson, who led the British fleet at the Battle of Trafalgar in 1805 during the Napoleonic wars. He is probably my favorite British military hero, as he was for John Fairfax and my father. His exploits, in fact, were introduced to me in rousing detail by my father when I was a boy. As the British fleet prepared to do battle at the Battle of Trafalgar, Nelson sent this signal to the fleet: "England expects that every man will do his duty."

"Duty" is not a common virtue in our contemporary society, but it was in generations past when "duty" and "character" were important virtues. My great-great-grandfather, John Fairfax, was an example of this. As I've noted, when John was in charge of the *Leamington Chronicle* in 1836, a local lawyer sued the paper for libel and succeeded in bankrupting him, even though the charge was found to be without merit. There is one other page in the story of the court case that led to the bankruptcy of the *Leamington Chronicle* and John's subsequent move to Australia.

Years later, in 1852, John and Sarah returned to England and visited Leamington. While John's main purpose for going back was to visit friends and family and buy printing machinery for the *Sydney Morning Herald*, there was another reason: he wanted to repay his debts. They had been wiped clean in bankruptcy all those years ago. But that was not John Fairfax's code. He had a black notebook he had long kept, listing the names of those to whom he had owed money before those debts had been absolved when he went bankrupt.

When he returned to England, he wrote to all those he owed money and paid them back with interest. He even paid the expenses of the lawyer who had unfairly sued him. John was not one to hang onto the legal definition of bankruptcy. Legally, he did not have to do anything. But he felt a moral obligation to repay his creditors, even the man who had sued him.

To repay your regular creditors is one thing, but to repay the man who sued you twice and lost both times is remarkable. But such was his integrity that he was willing to err on the side of doing the right thing, even when many would have said there was no debt to repay. He had a higher standard of what he thought was right. Afterward, he received letters from some of his former creditors expressing surprise, gratitude, and admiration.

John Fairfax's character also showed itself in the effect it had on other people. On arriving in Australia with virtually nothing, he worked first as a printer for a local journal before obtaining the position of librarian of the Australian Subscription Library (now the State Library of New South Wales) in Sydney. In the library, he talked with several prominent figures of the day. He also met Charles Kemp, a political and law reporter for the *Sydney Morning Herald*. They became friends, and finding that they shared a vision for the paper, in 1841, they bought the *Sydney Morning Herald* together.

John's faith, and the way he lived it, won him the deep devotion of his employees. But probably the greatest testament to his faith and the way he lived it was the affirmation from his family. On his fiftieth birthday, John's children gave him a large, ornate silver centerpiece. In the accompanying letter, they wrote: "Your children [wish] to express their gratitude for the generosity of their parent—their respect for him, and the deep respect they entertain for his character [and] for the unchanging parental love that has ever watched over them." They hoped this silver centerpiece would serve as an expression of their "affection and esteem" and love and a remembrance of the years of happiness that they had spent together.

John was clearly moved, as anyone would be by such a gift and letter. He wrote in reply: "Your gift is elegant and costly, and your letter is precious. The former surprised me; the latter affected me to tears."

The center of John's life was his faith, which worked itself out in all areas of John's character and had a profound effect on his life and other people. He felt that a person of faith should be the hardest working, the most industrious, and the most active. It was important to him that people of faith live what they believe, not just in words but also in deeds in every area of their lives. Convictions are lived one moment at a time. Indeed, often the strength of your beliefs is determined by how you handle the little things. John would have little or no work done on the Sabbath and had an embargo on advertisements lodged on Sunday, except in the case of death announcements or funerals.

Lessons in Character—My Father

Like all of us, my father had his flaws, and he made his share of mistakes. But he was a great man, and I count myself privileged to have had him for a father. He achieved some significant things during his life. He was knighted by the Queen of England, becoming the third generation of his family (following his grandfather Sir James Reading Fairfax and father Sir James Oswald Fairfax) to be knighted in their own right (in other words, not by heredity) for services to the community and to their country.

During his almost fifty years of service to the family business, he saw it expand from a stable of a few newspapers, dominated by the *Sydney Morning Herald*, to a large diversified media conglomerate owning large metropolitan daily newspapers, television stations, radio stations, magazines, and newsprint mills.

However, it was his character, his humility, and his integrity that meant the most to me. During the 1930s, he and his first wife, Betty, were friends with Sir Robert Menzies and his wife. They spent time together at Palm Beach, north of Sydney. At the outbreak of the Second World War in 1939, Menzies was a conservative prime minister of Australia (the leader of the United Australia Party). However, over the first couple of years of the war, my father came to believe that Menzies was not the right man for the job. My father and the *Sydney Morning Herald* had issues with the policies of the Menzies government and questions as to whether Menzies had the right temperament for a wartime leader. These views had been expressed in the *Sydney Morning Herald* and in letters from my father to Menzies.

In July 1941, my father wrote these words in a letter to Menzies: "The *Herald* [the *Sydney Morning Herald*] has never in all its history been a party paper, and is watchful and critical of all Governments." Later that year, Menzies's government lost power, and John Curtin of the Labor Party became prime minister. My father and the *Sydney Morning Herald* welcomed Curtin and the Labor Party to power. My mother told me that for the rest of his life, Menzies blamed my father and the *Sydney Morning Herald* for his election loss and never forgave him for it. This was despite the fact that in 1949, Menzies again became prime minister and remained so until 1966, the longest-serving prime minister in Australia's history.

Perhaps Menzies felt that my father, being generally conservative in his views, should have ensured that the *Sydney Morning Herald* supported him. The point of this story is that when he came to believe that Menzies was not the right man to lead Australia during a time of war, my father did not let their friendship get in the way of doing what he believed was right for the country. These are just a few stories that help to explain why I loved and admired my father so much. They also help to explain why I wanted to lay a similar foundation of character, one of humility and integrity, in my own life—no matter what.

Ironically, my father never gave me any big speeches about how it was my duty to follow him into the family business. It was just assumed. But if I had not gone into the newspaper company, it would have devastated him. As I've said, I loved my father very much, and there was no way I would even have considered something I knew would disappoint him—again: duty, honor, country (or family/company).

Foundations of Character

When I was growing up, plenty of the boys at my school had wealthy parents, but no one seemed to be in the same league as my family. I say that not because *I* felt they were not in my league but because *they* did not. Cranbrook wasn't an inexpensive school. But while other boys' fathers might have been bankers, lawyers, and doctors, mine was the chairman of a large media company. Even in a good private school, I felt a bit out of place.

A few of the boys would say to me from time to time, "Warwick, you think you're better than us because of all that money and the cars your dad has." My father had some wonderful old cars, including a 1928 Bentley and a mid-1960s Aston Martin DB6 (almost the same car that James Bond drove in the movie *Goldfinger*). Those taunts only fueled my desire that the wealth I grew up with would not define me. I would strive for humility and modesty.

While my father loved nice cars and was quite happy being driven to work every day in a Rolls Royce, I was not going to drive a fancy car. I had no desire to live up to the stereotype of the spoiled rich kid. When I was in control of the family business, I would drive to work in my red Toyota Camry and park alongside the Jaguars and the Mercedes in the executive parking lot. This actually may not have been very "humble," but in some perverse way, it gave me a kick to drive into the executive parking lot in my unassuming little car. Over the years, I have driven Toyota Camrys and Honda Accords, those kinds of cars. I actually did break down a number of years ago and buy a Volvo, and later, an Audi. I don't think I could buy a Rolls Royce.

Like me, my father grew up in a life of privilege. He could appear aloof, although that was more often due to his shyness, the fact that he was more at home with books than with people. He was not one to show his emotions and express his love in words. So instead, he and I communicated by talking about history. So fascinated was I with history that I did not always appreciate that other boys did not grow up talking about its intricacies with their fathers.

One afternoon, when I was six, I had a school friend over to play. I had several Greek toy soldiers, and I had set them up in a Macedonian phalanx, a formation the Greek soldiers used against their enemies and which was used by Philip of Macedon and his son Alexander the Great. Each soldier held his shield on the outside of the formation to create an impenetrable wall. My friend asked me what I was doing, and I told him that I had formed the soldiers into a Macedonian phalanx. He asked, "What is that?"

I was startled. I said, "You mean you don't know what a Macedonian phalanx is?" Come to think of it, I did not show a whole lot of humility there—but I was only six!

Despite the Rolls Royce and the driver, my father exemplified humble character in several ways. He was humble in the sense that he did not look down on people, no matter what their station in society, and he respected the right of everyone to hold different views than he did, certainly differing political or theological views. He never treated people differently because they may not have been his "equal" in society's eyes. However, he did not seem uncomfortable in the position of privilege he grew up in, unlike me. He did like being a knight and therefore being called "Sir Warwick." When we visited America when I was seventeen, people did not always understand the difference between a knight and a lord and would sometimes call him "Lord Fairfax," which would have been a promotion. My father did not always bother to correct them—but this was more out of amusement than pride.

In our home, we had several staff working for us. They were very loyal to my father and respected him tremendously, and he returned that respect. If a staff member disagreed with him, that was all right. I remember traveling into outback New South Wales one time with my father and his driver from the office. (I was too young at the time to drive and to spell my father from the task, so he'd brought his driver.)

We were going through Bourke when my father and his driver got into an argument about which direction was the right way to go. My father's driver was a no-nonsense kind of bloke who had been a truck driver in the Second World War. He was not going to take any grief from anyone. So here they were, my father and his driver, heatedly arguing about which was the right way to go. It never occurred to my father that his driver should not be arguing with him. My father may have thought the driver's opinion was wrong, but he felt he was entitled to it and was entitled to defend his opinion vigorously. In my father's eyes, people were people, and every person was entitled to his or her opinion.

This openness extended itself to politics. One of my father's friends was Bob Hawke, who subsequently became prime minister of Australia, but when I was growing up, he was the leader of the trade unions in Australia. He was highly intelligent, a Rhodes Scholar at Oxford, but was also pretty left wing at the time. My father was a conservative by political persuasion but open to different ideas. He enjoyed conversation with a very bright man, whether or not he agreed with his politics.

This openness to the ideas of others meant he was humble enough to realize that, despite his considerable learning, there was always more to learn. He loved learning about politics and history from politicians and others, and he also loved learning about theology and other faiths.

This is some of the background of why I believe character is so foundational to great leadership. In part, it is because of how character was modeled by my father and John Fairfax. But I have also drawn inspiration from great figures of history who exemplify character—in particular humility and integrity—and we will examine some of these in the next chapter.

Reflection Questions

1. Define character in your own words. As you look at your definition, who's the first person who comes to mind? Why?
2. What, in your experience, are the foundations of character?
3. Why is character so important to the day-to-day expression of faith?

Chapter 8

GROWING IN CHARACTER

Being aware of our shortcomings, as well as our strengths, is a great help to establishing good character. If you know the areas where you are likely to fall down, it makes it a lot easier.

So, how do we put all of this together to understand and refine the state of our own character? One way is to look to the example of other leaders. We can assess them and say, "I want to be like them." Studying history and the lives of those who lived it helps us to identify qualities and actions we want to emulate—or avoid.

Whom are the leaders whose character you most admire? They may be great leaders in history or leaders you have known or worked for. Leaders can come in all forms. They can be our parents, or our brothers and sisters. In my case, I've learned much about character from the example of my great-great-grandfather and my father. Like them, family is very important to me. I aspire to be a person my children can admire and respect. The attainment of that goal in large part depends on me.

Models of Character

One of the people from whom I learned a lot about character wasn't a historical giant or a relative. His name was Mr. Petrosian, and he was my high school history teacher in Australia.

Mr. Petrosian had some significant physical challenges. He could not walk properly and had to shuffle his legs to move. His hands were turned inward, so he had to write on the blackboard with his hands reversed. But despite these challenges, he was one of the most upbeat, positive people I have known.

He loved history—American history in particular. He would play us tapes of the campaign songs of those running for the presidency in bygone days, which to our ears sounded more like folk songs. He would ask us questions to which the answer was always "South Carolina." Which state was the first to secede in the Civil War? South Carolina. Which state was at the center of the Nullification Crisis? South Carolina (which in the 1830s attempted to nullify a federal tariff).

Another running joke was his banter with me about the newspaper business, knowing full well I had grown up in it. In front of me, he would tell the other boys, "You know, I love the *Herald*. I especially like the flavor of the ink when you wrap fish and chips in it." He would call the *Herald* "the fish wrapper."

What I admired about Mr. Petrosian was his attitude about life. He did not feel sorry for himself because of his physical challenges—his crucible experiences. He had tremendous energy, laughed a lot, and was filled with such joy. He inspired me with a love for American history that has persisted to this day.

Thanks to his teaching, when my dad asked me after I got into Oxford where in the world I would like to go for a trip, I said America. My dad would have taken me anywhere I wanted to go. But I had been inspired by Mr. Petrosian and his love of American history, and I wanted to tour America. We ended up driving from San Francisco, down through the southern states, and up to New York. Later, of course, I married an American girl and now live in America. So you could say that Mr. Petrosian had a big effect on me. The power of teachers!

Besides family, friends, and teachers, I've found examples of character worth emulating in literature, religion, and—thanks to my father's influence—history. Gandhi, for me, is one of these figures.

In many ways, Mohandas Gandhi, who became known as the *Mahatma,* which means "the Great Soul," was great not so much because of what he did but because of who he was. We remember him as the leader who helped India gain its freedom through his ideals of nonviolence and social justice. He influenced civil rights leaders, such as Dr. Martin Luther King Jr. in the United States and Nelson Mandela in his struggle against *apartheid* in South Africa. Yet, Gandhi held no elected office and represented no government. His influence came from the quality of his character.

We also remember Gandhi today from his famous quotes, many of which are so profound, some humorous in their truth. Here are just a few:

"If we could change ourselves, the tendencies in the world would also change."

"What do I think of Western civilization? I think it would be a very good idea."

"I like your Christ. I do not like your Christians. Your Christians are so unlike your Christ."

The quote about how changing ourselves can change the world is so true: the essence of this is living the way you think others should live, being the person you want others to be. A large part of this comes down to your character. Indira Gandhi, herself a prime minister of India, and the daughter of Jawaharlal Nehru, India's first prime minister, said of Mahatma Gandhi: "More than his words, his life was his message."

Gandhi was born in 1869 in Porbandar, India to Hindu parents who were somewhat well-to-do. His father was the prime minister of the local state. A turning point in Gandhi's life came during his years living in South Africa, where he went to practice law and where he faced discrimination against Indians. Like Nelson Mandela, he spent many years in prison for his protests. In 1922, he led Indians in the Non-Cooperation Movement, boycotting British goods; in 1930, he led a protest of the British-imposed salt tax with a 240-mile march called the Dandi Salt March, and in 1942, he called for the British to quit India. Even though he never held an elected office, eventually the British government had no choice but to negotiate, and in the end, he helped India gain self-rule. *Time* magazine named Gandhi one of the key people of the twentieth century. He was nominated several times for the Nobel Peace Prize; though, somewhat inexplicably, he never won it.

Gandhi the man was not your usual "saint." He was a skinny, bent figure who wore a white loincloth and spectacles. He was a devoted vegetarian who avoided all spices as a discipline to his senses and took a nap each day with mud on his stomach and forehead. Every afternoon, he spent up to a couple of hours spinning wool on a small handwheel to demonstrate to Indians the importance of not relying on foreign goods. He railed against Western industrialism, technology, and material pleasures. Gandhi's religious beliefs were influenced by Hinduism, Buddhism, readings from the Koran, and Jesus' Sermon on the Mount.

What was the secret of Gandhi's influence on India and on leaders such as King and Mandela? I believe it was his character and authenticity. Here was a man who grew up privileged in India and studied law in England. He worked as a lawyer in South Africa. Yet this man adopted a life of poverty and preached non-violence, not only advocating simplicity and the value of village life but truly living it. He did not just preach the value of economic independence from foreign products; he practiced it by spinning cloth each day. In 1930, when he led the Dandi

Salt March, he started out with seventy-eight followers, but by the end of the march, so many had joined in that 60,000 people ended up filling the jails because of their civil disobedience! He also preached a philosophy of religious tolerance and was greatly saddened when, because of religious differences, part of India was partitioned to become the predominantly Muslim nation of Pakistan in 1947.

Clearly, Gandhi led a simple, humble life. He did not seek political office and was never the leader of his country. Yet on his death in 1948, Jawaharlal Nehru said in a radio address to the Indian people that the "father of the nation" had died. He had truly lived a life of significance—and unswerving character.

An "Indispensable Man" of Character—George Washington

One of the greatest examples of a leader of character, a leader with humility and integrity, was George Washington. King George III of England and Napoleon Bonaparte of France both sang Washington's praises. In fact, George III said the general who orchestrated the defeat of his British armies was "the greatest man in the world." And Napoleon, after he had been imprisoned on the island of Elba, said, "They wanted me to be another Washington."

What led these two men to make such statements? As with Gandhi, Washington's greatness came from his character. There have been strong leaders in history who came to power professing noble principles but in the end, betrayed the principles on which their revolutions were founded—think of Caesar, Cromwell, Lenin, Mao, Castro, and, of course, Napoleon himself. What separates these leaders from Washington is that they never gave up power voluntarily. Washington did.

George Washington was born in 1732, the son of a leading Virginia planter in what were then the British colonies in America. When Washington was eleven, his father died—a definite crucible moment. While

Washington's two older half-brothers had been educated in England, the death of his father made that impossible for George. So, by age fifteen, his formal schooling was over—another crucible.

But Washington refused to let those setbacks limit him. At the age of twenty-one, he obtained a commission in the Virginia militia. After serving during the French and Indian War (a conflict between the French and the British over colonies in America and Canada), Washington was given command of Virginia's entire military force in 1755. In June 1775, with the outbreak of war against Britain, the Continental Congress of the American colonies appointed Washington to take command of the Continental Army (the army, such as it was, of the American colonies fighting the British).

The war between the American colonies and Britain would last years. Finally, in September 1783, at the Treaty of Paris, Britain recognized the independence of the United States. But earlier that year, in March, in what came to be known as the Newburgh Conspiracy, some of the army's officers believed the Continental Army should challenge the authority of the Continental Congress. Historians have speculated that those behind the Newburgh Conspiracy might even have wanted the army to conduct a coup.

Certain officers had criticized the Continental Congress's conduct of the war, blaming Congress for the army often being without pay or proper clothing. This made some feel that republics were weak, and disaster would fall on America unless Washington was made a dictator in a military takeover. In response, Washington gave a speech to these officers, declaring that any attempted coup by the army would be a repudiation of the principles they had been fighting for and an assault on his own integrity.

On December 23, 1783, after word was received that the peace treaty had been signed in Paris, Washington said farewell to the soldiers of the Continental Army and to the Confederation Congress meeting in Annapolis, saying, "Having now finished the work assigned me, I retire from the great Theatre of Action . . . I here offer my Commission, and take my leave of all the enjoyments of public life." No wonder George III described him as "the greatest man in the world." What leader leaves public life at the height of power? Not only that, but he refused to accept a salary while he was commander in chief, reflecting his thought that the purity of his motives must match the purity of the cause he served.

While Washington assumed he was going to retire permanently to private life, he was later asked to chair the Constitutional Convention (a meeting of delegates of the American Colonies to draft the U.S. Constitution) and in 1789, was elected as the first president of the United States. He was elected unanimously by the electors of the individual states, the first and only president to be so ratified by the Electoral College. There was no campaign for the presidency in 1789. Washington was chosen for who he was, not for what he thought. The nation trusted Washington. He was thought of as the indispensable man.

Where did George Washington's greatness come from? He was not a particularly well-educated man. Nor was he the most successful military commander. He lost more battles than he won and was often up against superior generals on the British side. Washington's greatness was not in his education or his military genius. It was in his character. He was the one man the American colonies could rally around to lead their army. He was the one man the new nation could rally around to be their first president and to set a model for future presidents to follow. It could be said that in times of trial and temptation (such as the Newburgh Conspiracy), character is most tested. It was Washington's honesty, integrity, and humility that compelled the nation to love and respect him so.

(An interesting side note to this story, for me, is the Fairfax family connection with George Washington. It turns out there was a Lord Thomas Fairfax who moved to Virginia while George Washington was a teenager. Lord Fairfax owned much of the land that is now Northern Virginia, and Fairfax County is named after him. When Washington was sixteen, Lord Fairfax gave him his first job, surveying some of his lands. As I have been told, Lord Fairfax was impressed with Washington's ability and bought him a commission in the army, which I assume was the Virginia militia mentioned earlier. So, apparently it was a Fairfax who gave George Washington his first job and his start in the army!)

Obtaining Character

Since character is so important to leadership and significance, it's important to know how to obtain it, particularly in the wake of a crucible experience, especially a crushing one. This is no easy feat, and it is tempting to say that either you have it or you don't. However, it's not that simple. Let's explore how we can develop or refine our character.

Like leadership, character must be grounded in something immovable, such as faith. The most reliable anchor for character is, I believe, a religious tradition, something that has stood the test of time and is grounded in unchanging values. Related, for me the two important elements of character to tie to that anchor are integrity and humility.

That does not mean that these are the two most important qualities for everyone. Some people may want to be above all else compassionate and giving. I value being compassionate and giving, but if you asked me which two elements of character I would want to be known for, I would reply, "Above all else, I want to be known as a man of integrity and humility." Even the order says something. My gut reaction is to put integrity first, humility second.

If I want to know what humility looks like or perhaps refresh my memory, I might reference a Bible passage, such as: "Do nothing out of selfish ambition or vain conceit. Rather, in humility value others above yourselves." (Philippians 2:3) This passage informs me that if I claim to be humble, I will not focus on my own agenda for glory and gain, but instead, I will look to the interests of others and helping them achieve their dreams. I might also look to personal examples in the Bible, such as Moses, who was never looking to be a hero. In fact, Moses initially tried to escape God's call to lead the Israelites out of captivity! Or I might look at Jesus, who, instead of coming to Earth as a conquering and powerful king, came as a carpenter's son, born in a manger in a stable.

The Bible clearly demonstrates what humility is, both by defining it and by giving us examples of people of humility. I can use the same process for integrity, referencing passages such as this one about Jesus: "'Teacher,' they said, 'we know you are a man of integrity and that you teach the way of God in accordance with the truth. You aren't swayed by others, because you pay no attention to who they are.'" (Matthew 22:16)

A person of integrity teaches what they believe. They are not swayed by the audience to which they are speaking. They say what they believe and they live what they say. We can think of David, who served as the commander of Saul's army—even though Saul became jealous of David and tried to kill him. In one incident, when Saul was murderously pursuing him, David hid in a cave. Not knowing that David was there, Saul came into the cave to relieve himself. David could have killed Saul at that moment, but he did not. What an incredible example of integrity! How many of us would faithfully serve a boss who not only persecuted us—but tried to murder us? Or when given the chance to get even with the boss, how many of us wouldn't take it? David conducted himself and led the troops under his leadership with remarkable integrity and character.

Becoming Self-Aware

This brings up another element critical to having character: being aware of our shortcomings, as well as our strengths. If you know the areas where you are likely to fall down, it makes it a lot easier to compensate.

If you have experienced a crucible moment and have spent time learning the lessons of your setback, you may be able to honestly ask yourself, "Why should I be arrogant? After all the times I messed up, what is there to be arrogant about?" This is a healthy perspective.

One of the great benefits of going through the trials of a crucible experience is that you tend to become aware of your own failings. One of the things I learned about myself during the takeover bid is that I am, as I noted earlier, pretty stubborn and can be impatient. There were some who advised me at the time that I should pull back, that circumstances had changed. (The October 1987 stock market crash had had an effect on our asset sale program, thus adversely affecting the financial state of the company.) I was also given advice that, once the takeover was launched, legally I could not back out. But would I have backed out, even if I thought I could?

I was resolute. I believed at the time the takeover was necessary, and I was not going to back down. I was going to press ahead. Being resolute may be an admirable quality in most circumstances. Unfortunately, many virtues have their opposites, qualities that are not so beneficial. The reverse side of resoluteness is stubbornness.

I can also be impatient, which my wife and children know only too well. At times, I just want to get something done, get it finished. In this, I think I am somewhat typical of many fathers. If we are going to go on a family trip, I want to leave on time and get to the destination on time with a minimum of stops. Sound familiar? Invariably, we leave late, have more and longer stops than I would like, and get to our destination later than I would like. This all makes for an impatient me.

Lack of self-awareness in matters of character can destroy marriages, ruin the lives of children, and make the lives of colleagues, friends, and neighbors miserable. The collateral damage of a lack of self-awareness in matters of character is significant. Like the proverbial rock being dropped into a pond, the ripples keep going far and wide for a long time. In families, lack of self-awareness of character can hurt generations of children.

So, how do you become self-aware? The first step is *wanting* to be self-aware. Ask others about your character. This may seem obvious or nonsensical, or perhaps both. It is one thing to ask others about your leadership ability or about your strengths and weaknesses. But your character? Can you imagine?

You: *What are the areas where I have weak character?*

Them: *Well, let's see. There are the obvious deficiencies. You lie. You cheat. You steal. You're arrogant. You take credit for others' successes. You always put yourself first. You do whatever it takes to succeed, irrespective of ethics or others' feelings. You're in love with yourself. In a phrase, you are really a jerk. Now these are the first things that come to mind. I will have to think some more on this to dig beneath the surface . . .*

Asking people to help you understand your character is understandably threatening, both for yourself and for them. To ask someone to describe your character is to ask them to tell you what your soul is like. You are asking them to tell you whether you are a good person or not. It is one of, if not the most, threatening questions you can ask anyone. Who would want to answer such a question honestly?

In reality, most people feel so threatened by talking about a subject like their character that they simply do not want to know. They are too afraid. Again, they can't handle the truth. Why can't we handle the truth? Because if our sense of self and self-worth depend on preserving the illusion we are "good people," we are in trouble. No one is a truly good person—that is, all the time and in all circumstances. We all have our faults and failings.

The Apostle Paul, who was an admirable leader, said about himself that he was the worst of sinners. This was no idle comment. He gave approval for the death of Stephen, a deacon in the early Church who was responsible for distributing food and caring for widows. Stephen was the first Christian martyr, falsely accused of blasphemy. (Acts 8)

Paul continued to make murderous threats against the disciples of Jesus. He was on his way to Damascus, taking Christians there as prisoners, when he had a dramatic encounter with the risen Jesus and his life was changed. (Acts 9) Paul was one of the early Church's bitterest enemies before his conversion on the road to Damascus. After his conversion, he spread the Christian faith throughout the Roman Empire. Paul was not without merit in calling himself the worst of sinners. He did not sugarcoat his past or his character.

Are we willing to demonstrate this same level of self-awareness? Before you ask others about your character, do a gut check. *Do I really want to know? Can I handle the truth?* If your self-worth depends on being perfect (that is, all the time and in all circumstances) or being seen to have good character, you could be in trouble.

Let's assume you can handle the truth. It is still going to be hard to find friends and family who will tell you what they think. It is going to hurt, even if you don't have all your self-worth bound up in your belief that you have good character. We are all human. Your friends and family are going to know this and will be reluctant to tell you the truth. You will have to convince them you want to know and that you will not hold their opinions of your character against them.

Start out asking them something like these questions: "What parts of my character do you value? What are those character traits and why do you value them? Can you give me examples or specific incidents when that character trait was evident?" On the other side, regarding the areas of character you are not so proud of, ask them questions like this: "In which areas of my character can I most improve? I really want to be a better father/mother. I want to be a better husband/wife. I want to be a better friend. I want to be a better employee. I want to be a better boss. Please help me improve." Sincerity and humility will win the day. If you keep probing, people who really care for you will be honest with you.

After someone has shared elements of your character that you are not so proud of, it is vital to affirm them and thank them for what one friend of mine calls "the gift of feedback." You might also tell them it would really help you if they could discreetly point out when you exhibit some of those character traits that you are not proud of.

Having feedback from friends and family, co-workers and colleagues, can be so helpful. Earlier we talked about leadership 360s. Well, what about a character 360? Ask those above you, below you, your peers, and friends and family about your character. Two simple questions could suffice: "What qualities of my character do you admire?" and "What qualities of my character need improvement?" Again, with both of these, ask for examples. By the way, the more self-aware you are, the easier asking these questions will get. You won't be so surprised by the feedback they give. It is like riding a bike. It gets easier!

Putting It All Together

How do we become people of good character, like a Gandhi or a Washington, or biblical figures such as David or Moses? It all comes down to this: we are what we value. We are who we want to be.

It is one thing to say that we are not everything that we wanted to be or that our lives are not everything we had hoped for. What we usually mean by this is our career is not as fulfilling as we wanted it to be. Maybe we don't have the perfect spouse, the perfect kids, or the perfect family. Perhaps we don't have as nice a house as we wanted and can't afford to go on the kind of vacations we always dreamed of. Those things aren't always in our control.

But character? We can be who we want to be. We have control over this. If we want to be kind and honest, or compassionate and giving, or courageous, we can be those things.

Character describes the very essence of who we are, our personhood.

> We can be who we want to be. We have control over this. If we want to be kind and honest, or compassionate and giving, or courageous, we can be those things.

Is character innate or is it learned? Is it nature or is it nurture? I would say both. Whether I value humility more or compassion more on a priority scale might be due to my nature—my design. But the extent to which I cultivate those qualities, that is nurture. I can choose to practice and grow in them. Like many things that go to form who we are, character is formed by both nature and nurture.

What this says is that there's hope. Yes, some elements of character may be formed right out of the gate and early on in childhood; for instance I believe my appreciation of humility and integrity was shaped by my relationship with my father. But other elements are forged, sometimes by crucibles.

Perhaps you have just gone through a crucible. Your business has failed. Your marriage has ended. That is a good time to take stock. Look at yourself in the mirror. Do you like the person you see? If you don't like what you see, there is hope. You have an opportunity to become who you want to be.

Reflection Questions

1. Would you say you are self-aware? If not what steps are you going to take to become more self-aware?
2. What are some shortcomings in your character, and what can you do to get better in those areas?
3. If it's true that we are what we value, write out the top five values that guide your life and leadership. How can these insights help you grow your character?

My great-great-grandfather, John Fairfax, founded the family business in 1841 with a single newspaper and grew it into arguably Australia's most influential, diversified media company.
ALAMY STOCK

My father was married twice before and my mother once before they met each other. Despite their differences in personality, they deeply loved each other.
FAIRFAX FAMILY PHOTO

My parents were very different. My father, Sir Warwick Fairfax, was a thoughtful, reflective intellectual man, who had a sense of fairness and curiosity about opinions different than his. My mother, Lady Mary Fairfax, was a vibrant, outgoing woman, full of passion and perseverance.

FAIRFAX FAMILY PHOTO

My father and I had a very close bond. I always worked hard and did well in school and perhaps he saw some of himself in me.

FAIRFAX FAMILY PHOTO

From an early age, I felt it was my duty to go into the family media business. I loved my father dearly and did not want to disappoint him.

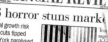

John Fairfax Ltd. had three of the most important newspapers in Australia. *The Sydney Morning Herald*, *The Age*, and *The Australian Financial Review* were the Australian equivalent of *The New York Times*, *The Washington Post* and *The Wall Street Journal*.

After the takeover, when I was in control
of John Fairfax Ltd., as proprietor I was
responsible for a company that held some of
the most influential newspapers in Australia.

As proprietor, I was in charge of a large
company that included, newspapers, TV
stations, radio stations and magazines.
I did feel a bit out of my depth.

When the $2.25 billion takeover bid ended, it was a sad day: 150 years of family history gone.
THE SYDNEY MORNING HERALD, DECEMBER 11, 1990, FAIRFAX SYNDICATION

The Sydney Morning Herald

Late Edition   50 cents*   52 Pages   No 47,819   First Published 1831   Editorial 282 2822; General 282 2833; Classifieds 282 1122   **Tuesday, December 11, 1990**

❝To spare no pains and to spare no money to make the Herald a first-class paper as an organ of commerce, a vehicle of news and a political power.❞
1831: The plans of John Fairfax

❝I have a vision that has been burning a hole in my heart . . . I want John Fairfax to be a company where there is a real sense of leadership and vision.❞
1987: The plans of Warwick Fairfax

❝I have the support of the company and its bankers. It is not my intention to be closing out or phasing back operations. It is business as usual.❞
1990: The plans of receiver Des Nicholl

Banks end the Fairfax era

Receiver appointed, but business as usual

By DEBORAH LIGHT and GLENN BURGE

Warwick Fairfax emerges briefly last night . . . "I have nothing to say." Inset, Lady Fairfax.

The lonely man in the red Toyota

By JOHN LYONS and ALAN DEANS

INSIDE

THE FUTURE
A long haul on road to reconstruction   7
Media ownership rules in doubt   7

THE FAMILY
A mother's love stretched to the limit   7
A very sad day, says James Fairfax   6

❝Warwick Fairfax destroyed his birthright in an ill-advised but essentially noble bid to save it.❞
Editorial   14

THE BIDDERS
The strong contenders   23

THE LAST DAYS
Mark Westfield's Insider column   23

THE ADVISERS
A festival of fees for the advisers   6

Downfall of Crusader Warwick
By VIC CARROLL

While naturally shy and reserved, I have become more comfortable telling my story and the lessons I have learned.

This is a somewhat humorous cartoon, emphasizing how I grew up privileged and suggesting I was foolishly playing around in a situation I didn't fully understand.

GEOFF PRYOR, *THE CANBERRA TIMES*, SEPTEMBER 1987

This cartoon was one that hurt, focusing on my perceived lack of business understanding and how my efforts to save the company greatly diminished it.

PETER COOK, *AUSTRALIAN FINANCIAL REVIEW*, SEPTEMBER 30, 1987

This was a particularly savage editorial cartoon: emphasizing how I destroyed a 150-year-old media dynasty.

GEOFF PRYOR, *THE CANBERRA TIMES*, SEPTEMBER 1987

THE AUSTRALIAN *magazine*
November 12-13 1988

WARWICK FAIRFAX

The man behind the mask

During the takeover of John Fairfax Ltd., I was reticent to do interviews—leading the media to create an impression of me as secretive. In truth, I was shy and felt a bit overwhelmed.

THE AUSTRALIAN MAGAZINE, NOVEMBER 12, 1988. NATIONWIDE NEWS PTY LTD

After the takeover bid ended, the media coverage did not. I was confused about my future, but did find comfort in my young family.

GOOD WEEKEND, *THE AGE MAGAZINE*, NOVEMBER 2, 1991. FAIRFAX SYNDICATION

EXCLUSIVE

YOUNG WARWICK

Picking up the pieces

I am blessed to have a wonderful family: my wife, Gale, and my three children (from left), Robbie, Gracie, and Will.
PATRICK MCNAMARA

A key part of Crucible Leadership is the podcast Beyond the Crucible, which I co-host with Gary Schneeberger. I love being able to interview people who have come back from adversity to lead lives of significance.

BEYOND THE Crucible

Part Three

CRAFT YOUR VISION

Vision is the engine that makes your journey to a life of significance possible. It must be rooted in the values, passions, and gifts you hold dear. Your vision must be your own, not inherited or thrust upon you; additionally, it also must be *bigger* than you. And to make your vision a reality, you'll need to get buy-in from others, including your team.

A key aspect of getting that buy-in, of creating a shared vision, is embracing the art of listening. This means receiving advice—even and especially tough advice—from your team, as well as others around you, including employees, shareholders, suppliers, and customers. Just as important, you'll need to pull a closer group of advisers together to help you get through the rough patches that are sure to come.

In these five chapters, we will explore where the seeds for your vision can be found and how you can broaden it to attract those who can help you achieve it.

Chapter 9

FINDING THE SEEDS OF YOUR VISION WITHIN

A great vision painted by a true visionary is a worthy and compelling cause, a rallying cry, in some sense, to make society a better, more harmonious, more just place.

A leader without vision is like a tennis player without a racquet: powerless. Of course, there is more to leadership than having vision, but having vision is a necessary component of leadership and certainly an indispensable component of great leadership.

My favorite definition of the word "vision" is "a present picture of a future reality." A great vision painted by a true visionary is something that seems so real you can feel it, touch it, and smell it. It is an enticing picture of a preferred future that actually seems possible.

A great vision may seem idealistic, almost naive, yet it stokes the fires within us that yearn to believe the idealistic and the naive are possible after all. It is a worthy and compelling cause, a rallying cry, in some sense, to make society a better, more harmonious, more just place.

We are drawn to this kind of vision as a moth is drawn to light. Deep down, we all want to believe that the world could be a better place, that it *should* be a better place, even that it *will* be a better place. That belief is what keeps us pushing toward a life of significance, even when additional crucibles crop up in our lives.

Vision from the Future

Science fiction is not everyone's cup of tea, but I have always loved it. At its best, science fiction paints a picture of a better tomorrow and often enables us to look at difficult social issues in a less-charged atmosphere. It raises fundamental questions of who we are and who we will become. In short, it casts a strong and resonant vision.

One of my first introductions to science fiction was the movie *2001: A Space Odyssey*, which came out in 1968 and is one of the most influential science fiction movies ever made. The film was directed by the acclaimed director Stanley Kubrick and was based on a novel by best-selling novelist Arthur C. Clarke. The movie affected me, then age seven, on many levels.

The opening sequence, set in the prehistoric era with apes learning how to use bones as tools and weapons, was accompanied by Richard Strauss's "Thus Spake Zarathustra." The scenes with space shuttles moving toward orbiting space stations or landing at a base on the moon had, as their backgrounds, Johann Strauss's "Blue Danube." Ever since that movie, I have been a huge fan of Johann Strauss's music, just as my father was.

Part of what drew you into the film was those long scenes of the spacecraft effortlessly floating along to the beautiful "Blue Danube" music. You felt as if you were actually there. At the same time, the picture of the future Kubrick painted seemed so genuine, you felt you were seeing what would actually happen—not what *might* happen, but what *would* happen. So many small touches made it seem real.

The combination of familiar technologies (such as the inclusion of Pan Am airplanes, one of the most popular airliners at the time) with unfamiliar ones (such as a highly sophisticated talking computer capable of emotion) fostered a unique vision of the future. The significance of this vision was compounded by the presence of so many uncannily accurate predictions of future technology. In-flight entertainment screens, voiceprint identification, artificial intelligence, and other technologies were depicted on-screen decades before they would ever become a reality. The film portrayed many other forms of technology that still do not exist today, but the strength of the vision makes you think that they might someday.

Arthur C. Clarke was one of three great science fiction writers of the time, along with Isaac Asimov and Robert Heinlein. What intrigued me about Clarke was his ability to predict the future, at least in some instances. In 1945, he published an article in a technical publication in Britain, forecasting that there would be telecommunications relays through satellites in geostationary orbits. This was to come about twenty-five years later.

Clarke also formulated three "laws" of prediction. They are all intriguing, but the second one is especially worthy of note: "The only way of discovering the limits of the possible is to venture a little way past them into the impossible." That

> A great vision in some sense makes the impossible seem possible.

is a good description of a great vision. A great vision in some sense makes the impossible seem possible. Certainly, *2001: A Space Odyssey* did that.

Inspirational Vision

I grew up with stories of heroes doing great things, doing the impossible. Whether it was tales of great English heroes such as Lord Horatio Nelson or the Duke of Wellington or stories from Greek mythology, my youth was filled with accounts of great men doing great deeds.

I remember my father reading me a book by Charles Kingsley—*The Heroes*, written in 1856—detailing the stories of three Greek heroes: Perseus, Jason, and Theseus. With the help of the Greek gods Hermes and Athena, Perseus slew the Gorgon Medusa, a snake-haired woman who turned all who saw her into stone. Jason assembled a group of heroes called the Argonauts and sailed on the largest ship ever constructed at the time, the *Argo*, to bring back the Golden Fleece. Theseus, with the help of a young woman, Ariadne, defeated the Minotaur, a monster with the body of a man and the head of a bull, in a huge labyrinth.

For me, it was not just daydreaming about heroes accomplishing great deeds against great odds, or even about what great deeds I would accomplish one day. Vision for me was focused on the part I would play one day in the family newspaper company.

The vision of the company's founder, John Fairfax, was forged in trials. After he was bankrupted in Leamington, he was likely discouraged, but he did not give up hope. The early years in Sydney were not easy, but John's dream did not die. This vision of the great newspaper he wanted to build, a paper "without fear to express opinion . . . without the reproach of self-interest, sworn to no master and free from the narrow interests of sectarianism," had long been in his mind.

Over time, this vision began to take clearer form and became woven into the *Sydney Morning Herald*. After becoming friends at the Australian Subscription Library, John Fairfax and Charles Kemp sat in the library long into the night, discussing newspapers. Their vision was to buy the *Sydney Morning Herald*. John saw that the *Herald* had economic strength with its advertisements. He could envisage how he and Charles would work together: John would handle the business side, while Charles would take care of the news side. Together they would collaborate on editorial policy.

John could see the benefits the *Herald* could offer the nation. He could visualize its growth. He could half close his eyes and see the words he would write fighting for just causes and exposing abuses. Night after night, John and Charles would discuss and plan their future that would become the *Sydney Morning Herald*. John had set ideas on how their partnership would work. There would be no "cross words" or "bitter thoughts" between them. They would do their "utmost for the improvement and growth of the Colony." They might fight for causes they cared about, but, he wrote confidently, ". . . when we are wrong, we will admit it."

If ever there was a vision that was a present picture of a future reality, so real you could almost taste it and touch it, John Fairfax's vision of what the *Sydney Morning Herald* would become was it. His plan to build a great newspaper was an inspirational vision, not an inherited vision. This was not a vision he felt obliged to carry out because of a duty to past generations. This was *his* vision, forged in adversity during his days in England and nurtured in a young colony in Sydney where there was hope and wider possibilities. It was rooted in his deepest passions and talents and aimed to make the world a better place. It was a vision that energized and enabled his pursuit of a life of significance.

Inherited Vision

In contrast, I would not consider my father as a man of vision, per se. He inherited the vision from his father, his grandfather, and his great-grandfather, John Fairfax. Like those before him, my father would carry on the tradition of helping the media company that sprang from the *Sydney Morning Herald* prosper and ensuring that the newspaper's reporting was fair and accurate.

The major business property in 1930, when my father began to lead the company, was the *Sydney Morning Herald*. By the time he died in 1987, the company had grown into a major media company. Truth be told, that growth was due as much to the management my father had under him than it was due to a concrete vision of his. For much of this time, Rupert Henderson was the chief executive. While my father's interest was more in the journalistic and editorial side, Henderson was a man of energy and ambition, providing balance to my father's philosophical and contemplative nature.

As I've described in previous chapters, when I was growing up, I never really considered the question of whether I had a choice in taking on the role (and the vision) I had inherited. I felt it was my mission in life, why I had been put on this earth. It was my destiny, my heritage, and above all, my duty. I did not want to disappoint those who had come before me, and above all, I did not want to let down my father.

Was this vision I had of what John Fairfax Ltd. could be, and what the *Sydney Morning Herald* could be, my own? Or was I merely inheriting the vision of my forefathers? I had lived so long under the John Fairfax legacy, the *Sydney Morning Herald* legacy, the company legacy, and the family legacy. So subsumed was I by the family legacy, I did not really know who I was without this vision.

On reflection, I am fairly certain the vision was not fully mine. I felt, in a sense, I was an actor filling a part. What was needed was the crusading heir to the family legacy who would restore the vision of the founder. That was the *role* in which life had placed me. Later, when my faith deepened while I was at Oxford, I would come to believe that it was also the role that *God* had for me. This made my sense of commitment to the vision all the stronger and all the harder to escape. To not fulfill the vision was not only to let down my father and the family legacy; it was to let down God. That was the ultimate pressure, the ultimate sense of duty. In my mind, how could I not fulfill God's vision for the family media company?

In hindsight, thinking of the family legacy in the way I did—to say that this was "God's vision"—sounds presumptuous. Did God care about whether the John Fairfax legacy was continued or whether John Fairfax Ltd. remained in Fairfax family control? If you believe that God does not allow anything to happen that He does not want to happen, then self-evidently God did, in effect, allow John Fairfax Ltd. to pass from family control. If that were true, saying that it was God's vision to bring John Fairfax Ltd. back to the ideals of the founder is a lot to speculate!

But, theology aside, it is clear to me now that though the vision I had to restore John Fairfax Ltd. to the ideals of the founder was not totally my vision, and it may not have been God's vision either. Nonetheless, it was real to me. How real? Real enough that it was "a present picture of a future reality" in my mind's eye. And so, I pursued the vision I had inherited with everything that I was.

Trying to Make It Work

At the time of the takeover, I wrote a letter to a family member involved in the company, saying that I had "a vision that has been burning a hole in my heart," a vision of a company that cares about its employees and knows where it is going. I had been reared on that vision. I had heard stories about my ancestors—my grandfather, great-grandfather, and great-great-grandfather, the founder. I had read J.F. Fairfax's biography of John Fairfax. And, I had a long-term plan to make that vision become reality. I had always seen myself as one day being the chief executive of John Fairfax Ltd. I had intended to work my way up, probably starting in the marketing department and progressively gaining experience, and hopefully some successes, so that in due course, I would merit the promotion to chief executive. However, in late August 1987, I launched the takeover and everything changed. I felt that I was too young and inexperienced to be the chief executive at that point, so I brought in an outside executive with extensive management experience to fill that role.

Of course, right from the start, my plans to make the vision a reality ran into problems due to the debt load. So many aspects of the vision had to be shelved. For instance, the desire to make the reporting of the newspapers more fair and less sensational was put on hold. We could not afford to make major editorial changes and risk a strike by the journalists, who were unionized. That could endanger profitability at a time when we had no financial margin.

But there was a deeper issue. I made many miscalculations and false assumptions leading up to and during the takeover. But perhaps the biggest miscalculation I made was about myself. Even if the vision was a good and noble one, there was one big problem: *Was I the person to lead that vision, to bring it about? On a deep, personal level, did I even want to make that vision happen?* This was one of the things that most struck me during the first few months of the takeover, and especially after it had "succeeded" in December 1987. I felt wholly inadequate to the task.

While I did participate in the refinancing decision-making, and was actively involved in many ways, I did not fit the picture of what was needed to bring about the vision. There was no walking the hallways to talk to people, to encourage them or reassure them. There were no big speeches laying out the vision and how we would work together to make it a reality. I was either in my office at the company, in meetings, or in refinancing strategy sessions in Australia and other parts of the world. When I went up in the elevator each day to go to my office, I did not know what to say to people. I was so uncomfortable.

I think on some deep level, I realized I did not have the disposition or the desire to head up a large media company. But more than the fact that I did not seem to be the right person for the job, being in control raised additional issues about how passionate I was about the vision. There is a saying, "Be careful what you wish for." Sometimes you think the grass is greener on the other side, to quote another saying, but it is often not.

Facing Reality

Having "succeeded," my sense of duty to try to make the takeover work and ensure the company stayed solvent through refinancing remained high. But my passion for the vision subconsciously was not what it had been. I was overwhelmed by the enormity of the task—how to keep a company with huge debts solvent and at the same time, restore the management to the ideals of the founder. The enormity of the work needed to make the vision a reality tested how much the vision was my vision. And it did not pass that test.

If it was really my vision, wouldn't I relish the challenge, jump into the fray, and do whatever it took to make it become reality? The vision was not just about making the company solvent. In fact, it was not part of the vision at all—it just became a practical necessity after the takeover. The reality of the aftermath of the takeover was that somehow the vision that fueled my actions did not seem so important; or, perhaps if it was still important, it was a vision meant for someone else, not me.

I was filling the shoes of others before me. I was trying to do what my father had not been able to do, either because he didn't have enough control or because he didn't have enough aptitude. Just as my father was not really suited to running a large media company and was living a life out of duty, so was I.

The reality of living a vision that was not really my vision, and of not being the person that was needed for such a monumental task with so many challenges, really hit home. With the multiple crises we went through, I came to understand I was out of my depth. I did not come to work each morning thinking, *Oh, joy! Today we take one more step to making the vision a reality!* I was not thinking "vision" as much as "survival."

People who own their vision seem to turn challenges into opportunities—opportunities to rally people around a noble cause. Franklin Roosevelt gave a speech to a joint session of Congress after the bombing of Pearl Harbor in December 1941. Winston Churchill gave speeches to the British people during the dark days of the Second World War. These leaders relished the challenge of making their visions a reality, and using challenges as rallying point for action. I did not.

The inescapable conclusion is that if the vision of restoring John Fairfax Ltd. to the ideals of the founder had been really mine, surely I would have reacted more like Franklin Roosevelt or Winston Churchill than

Warwick Fairfax. Time and experience (and maturity) have taught me that one of the reasons I was not able to carry this vision to reality, economic challenges notwithstanding, was that it was not a vision rooted in who I was and what I deeply desired to do with my life—to help others and lead a life of significance.

It would only be after the crucible experience of the takeover falling apart that I would fully realize the importance of crafting and making a reality a vision that was truly my own.

Reflection Questions

1. Define "vision" in your own words. Do you have a clear idea of your vision? If not, what can you do today to begin to cast a vision for the life of significance you want to lead?

2. What book or films have you read or seen that have sparked vision in you? What leaders do you most admire? What about them inspired you?

3. What are some building blocks—like your passions, talents, and experience—you can draw on to craft your vision?

Chapter 10

HARNESSING THE POWER OF VISION

A successful vision has to become real. To be a successful visionary, you have to own your vision, combine it with your passions, and be persistent—believing that nothing is impossible.

The experiences and travails during my days at John Fairfax Ltd. have affected me in many ways. They have affected my view of myself, my view of vision, and my understanding of what it takes to make vision a reality. They have also affected how I help others.

At a personal level, my "failure"—which I consider my life's greatest crucible experience—hurt me deeply and has humbled me, but ultimately, I believe it has made me wiser and put me on a better path. What was searing was the repeated thought that I had this great vision, this God-given vision as I believed it was, and I let God down.

John Fairfax Ltd. could have been so great, and I blew it. How did I blew it? Count the ways. Either I blew it by not being the take-charge leader the job needed, or I blew it by being too impatient for change and not really giving other family members involved in the family business a chance to embrace the vision I was trying to make a reality. Perhaps I would have found some commonality between my vision and their visions. I did not ask, so I do not know. Either way, I failed in my mission to bring the vision to reality.

More Lessons Learned

But what was worse, in some ways, was what I learned about myself. That was not fun. I learned that perhaps I had a hero complex, the desire to be the crusading avenger who saves the day.

I had also made assumptions about the rest of my family, who they were and what they were about, based on others' perceptions. I had not tested these assumptions by talking to my relatives myself and listening to them. There was resoluteness there, but there was also the other side of that, which was stubbornness. These reflections about who I was, my character and my motives, were not fun or easy. But part of living life well is learning from your failures and living life in light of these lessons.

So what are some of the lessons learned? You have to be humble. You cannot have this ego complex that you are going to be the savior of the world. That is dangerous and does not often work out well. You can hurt a lot of people while you are trying to save the world. There is another saying, "The path to hell is paved with good intentions." I may have been trying to do the right thing. But a lot of bad things seemed to happen: to me, to others, and to the company. Having a "save the world" ego complex can be dangerous. And it is all-too-often the fuel of a devastating crucible.

You cannot inherit a vision. Just like you cannot inherit your parents' faith, you cannot inherit your parents' vision. I tried it and failed. If it is not your vision, no matter how noble it is, do not try to *make* it your vision. If you do, you risk facing a life-changing crucible of your own creation, causing pain in your own life and the lives of others.

For this reason, it's important to have an accurate assessment of yourself, a healthy self-awareness. As a leader, as a human being, it is not enough to have a great and worthwhile vision. You have to ask yourself, in all humility, *Am I the right person to make that vision happen? Do I have the skills and the gifts, let alone the requisite experience, to bring that vision to reality? How has this experience with vision shaped me and molded me?*

Funnily enough, I am still attracted to vision. These days, though, I am more cautious regarding my own role in a worthy vision. I no longer see myself as always central to the picture. I am happy to help others with their visions. I am older and hopefully wiser. I have a few battle scars. I am more realistic, both about the challenges of making a vision a reality and about who I am and who I am not. But I have not given up on vision.

As I have said, I hate cynicism and defeatism—the sense that it is hopeless, nobody cares, why bother. Fortunately, through God's grace, I have not become world-weary. I am still idealistic. I still have hope. I still believe the impossible is possible. I am committed to the truth that crucible experiences can be overcome if we learn the lessons of them, craft a vision to move beyond them that is rooted in our gifts and passions, and dedicate ourselves to making that vision a reality as we pursue a life of significance.

What It Takes to Find Your Own Vision

In my capacity as a coach and consultant, when people ask me for advice on job transition, or if people who have sold businesses come to me looking for a new direction, I have a paradigm I use. I ask them about their gifts and abilities. I ask them about their passions (that is, what activities or causes they are excited about). If they are Christians, I ask them how their planned new job or activity would advance God's Kingdom. (If they are not believers, I might ask them how that job or activity would fulfil a higher purpose.) So, if that new job or activity is in the center of their gift set, in an arena they are off-the-charts passionate about, and they believe it advances God's Kingdom or fulfils a higher purpose, my belief is that they will feel fulfilled and, I would say, "called" to that position.

In my life, too, I try to live by that model. I believe I am at my best when I am advising, facilitating, and writing. I am passionate about my faith. I want everything I do to advance God's Kingdom. When I advise, my desire is to help people follow a calling that fits them, that draws on their greatest passions and talents. Helping people fulfil their visions gives me as much pleasure and joy as anything else in life.

Sometimes to be the best version of yourself you have to go through some trials and tribulations you do not want to experience—crucibles. Research done by Crucible Leadership has found that 49 percent of business leaders have had crucible experiences, events so painful that they have fundamentally changed their lives. I am certainly among that 49 percent. I have experienced much pain, and much self-reflection and soul-searching. The benefit of coming out on the other side of the failed takeover is that I now have a vision I am truly excited about, one that is truly *my* vision.

> Vision occurs when deep-seated beliefs and character meet circumstances in an area in which the visionary has aptitude.

Where does vision come from? Is it internal or external? It would seem vision is often inspired by external events or comes from sources outside ourselves. Consider John Fairfax's vision of the great newspaper he wanted to build one day. That vision was nurtured while working for a London newspaper and during the trials of working in newspapers in Leamington. His vision was cemented by the crucible of failure and then flourished under the promise of the young colony of New South Wales.

There was much external encouragement, such as that from John's wife, Sarah. Yet that is not to say there was no internal component to John's vision. Perhaps the greatest internal influence was his character, coupled with his aptitudes. John's character made him want to build a newspaper that was fair, would fight for just causes, and help build a young colony. The facets of John's character—fairness, justice, and compassion—were inextricably woven into his vision. Remember:

Vision occurs when deep-seated beliefs and character meet circumstances in an area in which the visionary has aptitude. This was certainly the case for John Fairfax in a way that was not true for me.

Staying True to Your Vision—Walt Disney

Walt Disney was one of the most intriguing visionaries of our time. He saw cartoons as something that could be artistically beautiful but also have compelling stories, such as his then-innovative feature-length film, *Snow White and the Seven Dwarfs*, which was produced in 1937. Additionally, Disney saw amusement parks as places that could provide family entertainment in a clean environment, at a time when the attractions were generally disreputable places where families would not want to go. As Thomas Edison was with inventions, Disney was with visions. He saw what others did not see.

One of Disney's great qualities was perseverance. In 1928, for example, he was returning to California by train from New York with his wife, Lilly. He had gone to New York to ask the distributor of his cartoons to movie theaters for more money for his *Oswald the Lucky Rabbit* cartoons. But when Disney arrived in New York, he found that the distributor had secretly hired away almost all of Disney's animators and had also inserted some fine print in the contracts that said that Oswald belonged to him. Disney was forced to walk away from Oswald.

On the train back to California, rather than being angry and depressed, Disney got out a yellow legal pad and began drawing circles, big ones and small ones. Watching him, Lilly realized he was drawing a mouse. Smiling, Disney said to his wife, "What do you think of the name Mortimer Mouse?"

Lilly replied, "How about Mickey?" Thus, Mickey Mouse was born.

What is amazing about this story is that in the midst of what, at the time, was a potentially crushing blow to his business, Disney did not go away to bemoan how the distributor had swindled him out of Oswald the Lucky Rabbit. Instead, he came up with the best-known cartoon character in history.

But he didn't stop with one or two successes. Disney was always innovating. The first Mickey Mouse cartoon, *Plane Crazy*, came out in 1928, the same year he was swindled out of Oswald. Later that same year, sound was coming on the scene. While many studios took a wait-and-see attitude, Disney embraced the new technology and came out with *Steamboat Willie*, the first Mickey cartoon with synchronized sound. A few years later, during the Great Depression, Walt heard that a new company called Technicolor had made a breakthrough in producing color in movies. Disney convinced Technicolor to give the Disney company two years' exclusive rights to use color in their cartoons. As Lilly Disney later said, "Walt just kept progressing. He was first with sound. He was first with color. Then he wanted to make a feature."

By 1934, Walt Disney had a comfortable life. He owned a large house, he played polo, and his company was successful. But he was not satisfied to sit back and enjoy his success. Walt Disney decided to risk it all by going into debt to create the first full-length cartoon feature. Many in the movie industry thought he had gone crazy.

While it was being made, *Snow White and the Seven Dwarfs* was widely known as "Disney's folly." It took three years of work and two million frames of film. One animator said, "Disney had only one rule. Whatever we did had to be better than anybody else could do it." In December 1937, *Snow White* opened in Los Angeles to a gala premiere. It was a huge success.

Not long afterward, in the early 1940s, when Walt Disney's two daughters were young, he wondered why there was no clean, safe place where parents and children could enjoy themselves at the same time. Back then, amusement parks were typically rundown places with rusty Ferris wheels, creaky merry-go-rounds, and the smell of rotten food in the air. Disney dreamed of a park that was clean and had good food and did not have a Ferris wheel. Charging admission would help keep the park a family place. Drunks and others wanting to accost people would be kept out. Once again, the naysayers were plentiful. Amusement park owners thought Disney was off his rocker.

As with *Snow White*, Walt Disney used much of his own money to finance the park in Southern California that he called Disneyland. To help offset the cost for the park, he used the new medium of television to promote his work. Unlike others in the movie industry, he saw the potential in television. He struck a deal with the ABC TV network to produce a one-hour weekly TV show in return for ABC helping to finance the building of Disneyland. The new show, called *Disneyland,* after the park, came on air in 1954.

Disneyland was the biggest project Walt Disney had ever undertaken. He had committed to building it in less than two years. He had to turn one hundred and eighty acres of orange groves into a Magic Kingdom, complete with a turn-of-the-century Main Street, a castle, a jungle, a riverboat, a railroad line, restaurants, walkways, ticket booths, and restrooms. Slowly, Disneyland emerged. Main Street led to a hub where the Sleeping Beauty Castle was located. The hub, in turn, led to Fantasyland, Adventureland, Frontierland, and Tomorrowland.

Disneyland opened on a Sunday in 1955 and became a great success. Then, in the late 1950s, Disney began to buy up thousands of acres of swampland near Orlando, Florida, for a second theme park. This became known, after Disney's death in 1966, as Walt Disney World. It opened in 1971 and is now made up of four theme parks: Magic Kingdom, Epcot, Hollywood Studios, and Animal Kingdom. A recent report found that the Walt Disney Co. had nine out of the top ten theme and amusement parks in the world.

A True Vision is an Enduring Vision

Walt Disney was a serial visionary. It was said that he did not know the meaning of the word "impossible." In fact, he famously said, "It's kind of fun to do the impossible." That pretty much sums up Disney's life. He had fun doing what others thought was impossible. He was more often than not out in front, seeing things before others saw them.

When Disney faced financial ruin and bankruptcy or business reversals, he picked himself up, dusted himself off, and started all over again. This reminds me of the great song, "Pick Yourself Up" from the 1936 movie *Swing Time* with Fred Astaire and Ginger Rogers.

Disney's characteristic perseverance is another mark of a true visionary—someone who owns a vision that is not borrowed, imposed, or inherited. When he was heading back to California from New York after being swindled out of Oswald the Lucky Rabbit, did Disney mope around? No, he picked himself up, dusted himself off, and started all over again. He moved on and created Mickey Mouse. Who ever heard of Oswald the Lucky Rabbit? The whole world has heard of Mickey Mouse. This song could be an epitaph that fittingly sums up Walt Disney's life.

A successful vision has to become real. To be a successful visionary, you have to own your vision, combine it with your passions, and be persistent—believing that nothing is impossible. And above all, never give up. You have to believe in your vision when no one else does and pursue it even when many think you are crazy.

What is Walt Disney's legacy? A treasure trove of memories that have delighted children and families for generations, from cartoons and movies to theme parks. Who has not gone to Walt Disney World, with its attractions, clean streets, ever-fresh flowers, restaurants and cafes, and thought to themselves, *I wish I could always live here?* Walt Disney World is in some sense a kind of utopia. It is a taste of the way the world could be.

Walt Disney's vision continues to live on, delighting millions of children and families every year. His is a stellar example of what it means to lead a life of significance, not because of the grandness of his accomplishments, but because what he accomplished contributed to the joy of the world and was rooted in a compelling vision that reflected his deepest passions and values.

Reflection Questions

1. Why is it important to follow your own vision, not someone else's?
2. Why is an element of serving others, creating a life of significance, so critical to a successful vision?
3. Why is perseverance so critical to making a vision reality?

Chapter 11

SHARING YOUR VISION WITH OTHERS

Buy-in to the vision is one of the most critical aspects of leadership. To get buy-in from a group of people or an organization, those people must feel they can modify the vision and add to or subtract from it.

One of the hardest areas of leadership is inspiring a group of people with a common vision—that is, a vision they all believe in and embrace, a shared vision. James Kouzes and Barry Posner, two of the leading authorities and researchers in the area of leadership, say that in the many years they have been collecting data, leaders consistently score lowest in the area of inspiring a shared vision. Why is this, and why does it matter?

The typical visionary climbs up Mount Olympus, consults with the oracle, and comes down from the mountain with his or her vision of the future. They have thought, they have reflected, and they now have it! This is the vision that will serve the organization for the next millennium, maybe even beyond! To them this vision is like Michelangelo's statue of David. It is perfect. Every feature, every aspect, is exactly as it was intended and ordained to be. To change even a small part of this vision is to desecrate perfection. The vision needs to be admired, honored, and even worshipped. Recommendations for changes are certainly not welcome. To even suggest a change means you don't truly understand the magnificence of the vision.

That is the problem with some visionaries. They tend to fall in love with their vision, birthed as it is out of their most cherished passions, and are not always open to input that might change it. But herein lies the problem. If no one else is willing to follow the vision, how will it become a reality? The short answer is that it won't. It will be lifeless, empty, doomed to remain in the pages of some vision statement or rattle around the visionary's head until he or she is old and grey. A vision unfulfilled is a vision lost. Few things are more useless than a vision that has died, never communicated and shared by others.

Getting Buy-In

One of the hardest things a visionary has to learn is that to inspire a group of people with a shared vision, he or she must give up the proverbial "keys to the kingdom." To return to the metaphor of Michelangelo's David, the visionary has to be willing to give a hammer and chisel to people in the group or organization and say, "This is my vision of the future, but I would like you to add to or subtract from it. This vision has to be our vision, not just my vision."

As others cautiously approach the statue of David, the visionary has to gently prod them and reassure them as they decide whether to lightly hammer away or take a big chunk out of it, and then what part of the vision to hammer into. The price of getting a group of people on the same page, inspired by a shared vision, is allowing them to contribute to the vision and how that vision is implemented. That is another test of leadership. Are you willing to share the vision—and the credit—with others?

Buy-in to the vision is one of the most critical aspects of leadership. To get buy-in from a group of people or an organization, those people must feel they can modify the vision and add to or subtract from it. When given the opportunity, many people may decide upon reflection that the vision is so good, they can think of hardly anything to change. But the mere exercise of inviting people to influence the vision, "Please go ahead and chip away," even if they end up not changing a thing, creates buy-in. By allowing people to have input and truly listening to them, you create a sense of shared vision.

Now, that does not mean you have to include input from everyone. The need of people to be heard and to give input is deeper than the need for their input to necessarily be deemed right. In other words, people can accept a vision that may not be their own if they feel they have truly been heard. But a leader must genuinely listen to others' input. If the leader says he or she is listening, and yet no one else's input makes it into the final vision, then the assertion that they are listening will sound a little hollow.

I have a saying: One hundred percent buy-in to 80 percent of the leader's vision is better than zero percent buy-in to 100 percent of the leader's vision. In other words, which is better: the "perfect" vision that seems like Michelangelo's David to the leader but which never becomes reality or a vision that is 80 percent the same as the leader's original vision but becomes reality? To me the choice is clear. A modified vision that becomes reality is better than an intact vision that gathers dust and goes nowhere. This is so important for a leader who wants to lead a life of significance, who believes his or her vision is the key to that happening.

Inspiring Others with a Shared Vision

Inspiring people with a shared vision is a lot easier if you live what you believe and you are a man or woman people can count on.

Throughout his life, John Fairfax inspired people with his integrity, faith, passion, and ideals. His wife and children admired and fully supported the vision he pursued of doing "good on a large scale." Another testimony to the extent his vision was shared is shown by the longevity of family control of the family newspaper business he founded. The Fairfax family controlled the company for almost 150 years, making John Fairfax Ltd. one of the oldest family newspaper companies in the world. The vision he had for the *Sydney Morning Herald*, and subsequently for other publications the company acquired, as "a free, hard-fighting, vigorous newspaper . . . sworn to no master and free from the narrow channels of sectarianism," endured through five generations.

It's hard to say to what degree my father inspired a shared vision within the company. He did have strong views on the role of the *Sydney Morning Herald*—views that coalesced into a vision for the way the paper covered the news that was very much like John Fairfax's. Some of his articles were contained in a book published after the 1943 Australian federal election called *Men, Parties, and Politics*. In it, he wrote, "A party paper, like a party man, is one which, once a party decision has been made, supports, explains and justifies it loyally against all opposition; and such papers have existed. But the *Herald* has always criticized any and every party whenever it thought them wrong." In the book's foreword, my father wrote that the paper's present policy was one of "aggressive moderation," a phrase that recalled the *Herald*'s former motto, "In moderation placing all my glory."

My father was clearly a gifted writer and was regarded as such. In one memorandum to the reporting staff in 1940, he wrote that no matter what happens in other departments, "all newspapers stand or fall by their news . . . In other words, they stand or fall by the skill and devotion of their reporting staffs." He stated that headlines should clearly convey what the story was about and not be vague. Articles should be written in short, crisp sentences with short, simple words, rather than long-winded sentences.

Through his direction to his staff in the 1930s and 1940s, and the way he encouraged his reporters to write, my father clarified his vision for the company and communicated it to his employees and others.

A Personal Lesson

I have said that crucial to inspiring a shared vision is listening to the visions of others in the organization, telling them what your vision is, and then being willing to adjust it, at least to a degree. I am not aware of my father asking his cousin or my older brother what their visions were and having this discussion. I don't believe he asked questions, such as, "What are we doing well? Where could we improve?" This would have required real listening. While my father did like to learn, he also, at times, liked to tell others the way things should be. I wonder whether, had my father listened more to the visions of his cousin and older son, the incidents of 1961 and 1976 would have happened.

It is difficult to write about this topic as it pertains to me. When I think back to my involvement with John Fairfax Ltd. in the area of shared vision, it is painful. I consider my inability to inspire a shared vision of what was on my heart for the company to be one of my biggest areas of failure. I did not inspire a shared vision in those members of my family involved in the company; I did not inspire a shared vision among the senior leadership team of the company, nor did I inspire a shared vision among the company's employees. My inability to do so was certainly a factor in the crucible experience my takeover bid turned into.

Was it clear to people what the takeover was all about, what my vision was? I did not talk to family members about this, at least not much. There were brief conversations with some family about my vision the day before I launched the takeover. But all that was too little, too late. As I look back, I never sat down with my family, both those involved in the business and others, to explain what my vision was. I never discussed with the Fairfax board what my vision was. I had begun to sit in on board meetings in the first half of 1987, so either at these meetings or informally, I probably could have found some way to share my vision.

I did not gather the new executive team that came on board after the takeover and tell them what my vision was. I did have one-on-one conversations with a couple of them, particularly the new chief executive. But there were no sustained "rally round the flag" gatherings to remind the senior leadership team of why we were doing what we were doing. Still less did I give speeches to all the employees of the company or smaller gatherings of various departments (journalists, printers, marketing and sales staff, circulation staff, etc.) to tell them what the takeover was all about.

There was no managing by walking around. I also never really sat down with the business partners of the company, such as our bankers, suppliers, newsagents, or unions (printers and journalists, for instance) to explain my vision. I did not give interviews to any media. The only interviews I gave were after the takeover had failed, and the company had gone into receivership.

How could anyone else have shared my vision? I did not tell them what it was! People cannot embrace a vision if you will not tell them what it is. People cannot just ingest your vision by osmosis or through some psychic connection. It does not work that way. To get others on board with what you're doing, you must be intentional about sharing what you're thinking, planning, and doing.

There was much interest in the Australian media about who I was, why I launched the takeover, what I wanted. While I would not give interviews, that did not stop the media from writing stories about me. One article in the Saturday edition of *The Australian* newspaper was titled, "Warwick Fairfax, the Man Behind the Mask." *The Australian* is a national daily newspaper published by Rupert Murdoch's company, News Ltd. The article asked all sorts of questions: Who is Warwick? What is his vision for John Fairfax Ltd? What does he believe? Since I would not talk to journalists, the writer put the questions to others. One participant in the takeover described me as "the most secretive person I've ever met . . .

He doesn't like people to have any insights into him or understanding of what he is up to or why."

Whether this was true or whether my reticence was a result of my youth, feeling overwhelmed by the situation and inadequate to the task, coupled with my innate reserve, is another question. At the time I did not grasp the importance of inspiring a shared vision in other people. Somehow, I believed that if I picked the right people then the company would be well led and the newspapers would be run in line with the ideals of the founder. Of course, that is part of it, but you still have to tell people what your vision is. They need to know what you expect of them as you lead them.

In hindsight, all this seems obvious. But to me at the time of the takeover, aged twenty-six, it was not. Clearly, I was unprepared for doing some of the critical things a leader needs to do to head up an organization, including inspiring all those involved with a shared vision.

The Importance of Listening to Shared Vision

Not only did I not tell people what my vision was for the company, I also did not listen. If there is another thing I can point to as one of my biggest failures, it is the unwillingness to listen to others. I did not ask other members of my family, whether or not they were involved in the family business, what *their* vision for the company was. What did they think the ideals of the founder were and what did they think his vision was? Did this vision have relevance for the company now? What was their vision? What part did they see themselves having in fulfilling this vision?

It is often better to listen before you speak and share your vision. You will have a much greater chance of being heard. You might actually find out that others share at least part of your vision. But how will you know if you don't ask? The same was true of the board at John Fairfax Ltd, the senior executive team, the employees, and our business partners. I asked none of them what their vision was. If I had done this over several months or years on coming back to Australia in 1987 after several years away, I might have learned a lot.

I would have done well to listen to what I shared earlier: 100 percent buy-in to 80 percent of the leader's vision is better than zero percent buy-in to 100 percent of the leader's vision. Could it have been possible that the family, the board, and existing executives and employees all could have had 100 percent buy-in to 80 percent of my vision? Because I did not ask and did not listen, we will never know. It was a huge mistake on my part.

> It is often better to listen before you speak and share your vision. You will have a much greater chance of being heard.

Part of the problem of having a Mount Olympus approach—that is, going up the mountain and coming back with an unalterable vision—is that you think you don't really need to listen to other people. You think you know what the vision should be, who needs to go, and who needs to come in. People just have to get in line with your vision, and if they won't, they need to get off the bus. This can come across as a pretty arrogant approach! That's because it *is* an arrogant approach.

And, there was some of that in me. I was so certain of what that vision was and what needed to change. I had made up my mind about where the company had been heading, and where the people in charge (both family members and management) wanted to take it. I felt certain that I wanted the company to go in a different direction.

My vision was grounded in the history and the "truth" I had grown up with. I heard my parents' version of 1961 and 1976. I heard my parents' opinion of other family members and the management and the direction of the company. This, of course, heavily influenced my opinion of where the company was going. This was the lens through which I saw the company.

If I had been wiser—I dare say older and wiser—I would have asked myself whether the "truth" I had grown up with was really the complete truth, whether the lens I looked through in coming up with my vision was really an accurate lens. If I had been wiser, I would have realized that my parents' perspective, and indeed my own view at the time, was just one version of history and events.

Getting It Right

So what are the lessons from this in inspiring a shared vision? First, don't assume your version of the "truth" is the truth. Don't assume that your version of history and the players involved (in my case, family and management) is accurate. Test your assumptions. Speak to other people involved (in my case, family and current and former management). Get their take on events and the players involved. Ask them to be honest and forthright. (In my case, I know they would have been giving opinions about my parents, in particular my father.)

Reassure them that you really want their honest thoughts. Keep prob-ing. Encourage them to tell you their "truth." Then go away and think and reflect on what you have learned. If you have some trusted advisers, ask them for their take on what you have heard. If you can manage it, ask those on "your side" how they react to the information you have gathered. (In my case, it would have meant asking my parents for their reaction, and possibly their advisers as well.) Then go away and do a gut check. Do some heavy-duty reflecting. (In my case, I would have also wanted to pray.)

In order to get it right, your vision must be based on an accurate, objective view of reality. It must be based on an objective view of history and the people involved. If it is not, you will have little chance of inspiring a shared vision. Your version of events, and thus the reason for your vision, will seem hollow and off-key. Your vision will likely go nowhere, or, if it does take effect, it may do more harm than good.

At the same time, be listening to those around you, including those with different opinions than yours. In doing this, you will both test your version of events and the people involved and help formulate a shared vision. Ask people what they think the vision of the company should be. How close is the company to living that vision? Do we have the right people on board to carry out that vision? What changes do we need to make, if any, to people or strategies to see that vision become a reality? Just asking people the right questions can help them think along useful lines. Half the battle is getting people to reflect on these kinds of questions.

Going back to Australia from the U.S., after I finished up at Harvard Business School, I was viewed as having somewhat of a clean slate. Family members, and I believe management, thought I was intelligent and probably capable, given my education and training. I don't think they thought I would reflexively believe everything I had heard from my parents. I am sure they thought I would be influenced by my parents, but I imagine they thought that, over time, I would form my own views and would be an asset to the company. All this may have been true if I had waited, listened, and learned. But I didn't. It is easy to remember the urgency I felt in 1987, my belief that the company was not being well run. All this made it seem urgent that something needed to be done.

In hindsight, we will never know whether events were as urgent as I thought they were. You may well ask whether the cure was worse than the disease. What I was trying to avoid—the company being taken over—ended up happening because of the takeover. The company passed out of family control. You could say that what I did not want to happen happened, in part, because of what I did.

So another lesson from this is that sometimes things may not be as urgent and dire as we think. There is a place for quick and decisive action, and there is a place for waiting, learning, assessing, and reflecting. Clearly, it requires much wisdom to know when to take decisive action and when to stop and reflect.

Having inspired those in your organization with a shared vision, your task is a bit like gardening. Just because you planted your flowers well, fertilized, and watered them, it does not mean you never have to water them again. It is the same with vision. Just because you think you have achieved a shared vision, it does not mean you don't have to continually share what that vision is and continually engage with people to reinforce that shared vision. That means using all the tools available to communicate that shared vision.

The Leadership Lessons of Jesus

I believe one of the most dramatic examples of shared vision is the rise of the Christian faith from an obscure religion in Palestine to the dominant spiritual movement of the Roman Empire and ultimately, the dominant faith in Western civilization. Some would say the Christian faith was a significant factor in the growth of Western civilization itself.

In his book *The Rise of Christianity*, Rodney Stark states that the number of Christians in 40 AD, just a few years after Jesus' death, is estimated to have been around 1,000. By 350 AD, it is estimated that just more than half of the sixty million people within the Roman Empire were Christians. That adds up to a growth rate of the Christian population of 40 percent per decade. What accounts for this dramatic growth in the Christian faith from nothing in the mid- to late- '20s AD, when Jesus started His ministry, to the majority faith in the Roman Empire by 350 AD? There were a number of factors, but one key was the strength of the vision Jesus shared with His disciples and the early believers.

Jesus was truly authentic to the vision He shared—a critical factor in implementing a vision effectively. In the Sermon on the Mount, He taught that the poor in spirit (that is, the humble), the meek, and the merciful are blessed. Jesus was all of those things. Jesus, God made flesh, did not come to earth as a conquering hero, some earthly prince, or king:

He came as the son of a carpenter. He recognized that He was under the authority of God, the Father. In that authority, Jesus healed people who had leprosy, cured the crippled, and raised the dead back to life. Ultimately, Jesus' mercy for us was shown by His death on the cross to secure the forgiveness of our sins.

Look at how Jesus shared His vision with His team, His disciples. The disciples saw Him embody love, preach the good news of the forgiveness of sins, and challenge the hypocrisy of the religious leaders of the time (who tended to say one thing but do another; needless to say, hypocrisy among leaders has existed in all times to this day).

Jesus was a servant leader, as illustrated by His washing His disciples' feet. It is worth revisiting this powerful image. In John 13, shortly before He was arrested, Jesus gave His farewell address during the Last Supper. He knew He would soon be returning to the Father, and wanted to show His disciples the love He had for them, and to show them the love they should have for others. So He got up from the meal, took off His outer clothing, and wrapped a towel around His waist. Then He poured water into a basin, washed His disciples' feet, and dried them with the towel. After He had finished, He said: "Now that I, your Lord and Teacher, have washed your feet, you also should wash one another's feet. I have set you an example that you should do as I have done for you." (John 13:14–15)

In this way, and many others, Jesus truly lived His vision. He preached it. He taught it. He embodied it. He also entrusted the vision to a faithful few—a critical act for a successful leader. Jesus focused so much of His energy on sharing the Good News of the Gospel, not with thousands, but with a few, His disciples, and particularly Peter, James, and John.

Finding a loyal, faithful team that truly embraces the vision and passes it on is not easy. Even Jesus found this tough. But in the end, His perseverance paid off. The last words Jesus gave to His disciples after the resurrection and before He ascended to heaven are contained in the beginning of Acts: "But you will receive power when the Holy Spirit comes on you;

and you will be my witnesses in Jerusalem, and in all Judea and Samaria, and to the ends of the earth." (Acts 1:8)

Jesus' instructions were clear: *You know the vision. Spread the vision everywhere, even to the ends of the earth. And by the way, I know you can do it.*

In the next chapter in Acts, Peter speaks to a crowd in Jerusalem and gives them the gospel message. So powerful was this message, and indeed so powerful was the hand of God in this, that the Bible tells us: "Those who accepted his [Peter's] message were baptized, and about three thousand were added to their number that day." (Acts 2:41) Peter may not have been the perfect embodiment of the vision—like all of us, he had his issues—but he was a powerful force for Jesus' vision in word and deed, as were many other disciples. The vision lived on and spread rapidly.

As Jesus modeled for them, one key was that His disciples and those that came after them not only taught the vision; they lived it. The extent to which they did this, and its effect on sharing the vision, can be illustrated by two great epidemics that devastated the Roman Empire. One occurred in 165 AD and lasted fifteen years. It is estimated that a quarter to a third of the population died in this epidemic. The second epidemic occurred in 251 AD and was equally devastating.

Caring for those with the disease was very risky, but Christian communities had been taught Jesus' values of love and charity. They were also taught that they were headed to a better place, so the prospect of death actually brought joy. In times of disaster such as these, Christian communities cared for each other and also for those in their vicinity who were not part of their Christian community. Many Christians died by caring for those who were sick, but this caring for each other led to higher survival rates within and around their communities. Christians caring for others, even without modern medical tools or understanding, actually saved lives.

It is estimated that conscientious nursing without any medication would have cut the mortality rate by two-thirds or more. One contemporary observer during the 251 AD epidemic noted that Christians' treatment of the sick was in marked contrast to that of other people. Other people, when faced with those suffering disease, fled, even if those suffering were their loved ones, literally "throwing them into the roads before they were dead."

Then there were those who were killed for their faith. One account of a Christian martyr who was tortured and executed tells how he cheerfully received the sentence and was tied to a stake to be burned alive. As the wood was being heaped around him, he exclaimed, "Where then is the fire?" The combination of steadfastness, joy, and bravery of these Christian martyrs not only struck other Christians, but it made an impact on unbelievers as well. While the number of Christians who were martyred for their faith was not great, it became a dynamic force behind the growth of the Christian faith. Many of the early disciples of Jesus died for their faith, including James, the brother of Jesus, Paul, and Peter.

The central vision of the Christian faith was (and still is) extraordinary. The offer of forgiveness for our sins because of Jesus' death on the cross, requiring merely repentance and acceptance of this forgiveness, sounded almost too good to be true. The notions that God so loved the world that He gave up His own son for us and that we should love each other as Jesus loved us were also extraordinary. This was so different to the prevailing culture at the time of gods who were mercurial and not always moral. Classical philosophers believed that mercy was not rational, and humans must learn "to curb the impulse." Pity was deemed to be a defect of character "unworthy of the wise." Christians brought to their world a new concept of humanity.

But what really made the vision of the Christian faith so extraordinary was the way its followers lived and preached it. The followers of the Christian faith, from Jesus' early core team of disciples down to later followers in the first few hundred years, were passionate about the vision Jesus had given them. They were willing to be tortured and martyred for their faith.

They died, not with some grim determination on their faces, but with joy. They were going to a better place, and clearly, they believed that.

The early Christians did not just parrot empty words about caring for each other, as many modern organizations do. The early Christians truly lived the vision. Acts 2 talks about the fellowship they had: "All the believers were together and had everything in common. They sold property and possessions to give to anyone who had need." (Acts 2: 44–45)

These early believers were not perfect. They had their flaws. But the prevailing culture within the Christian community was of living Jesus' command to love one another, and that is what they did. It is no wonder that the Christian faith grew so rapidly in its first three hundred and fifty years. It is hard to know what Western civilization and much of the world's history these last two thousand years would have been like without the rise and growth of the Christian faith. I, for one, am glad we will never know.

Reflection Questions

1. What, in your own words, are the benefits of creating a shared vision?
2. Why do you think it's hard for leaders to inspire a shared vision?
3. How would you rate yourself in inspiring a shared vision for your leadership goals? How might you do better?

Chapter 12

LISTENING FIRST TO ACT EFFECTIVELY LATER

Good listening allows leaders to hear ideas that will make their visions better and their plans to implement those visions more likely to succeed. Good listening allows leaders to learn of potential pitfalls and roadblocks that enable them to cast their vision in ways that increase the likelihood of success.

O ne key principle of good leadership is that people do not so much need you to agree with them as they need you to listen to them. If people feel heard, more often than not, they will go along with the direction you advocate. They will feel that if they have been really heard, and yet you still decide to go in a different direction, you must know what you are doing. Listening, real listening, is the key to buy-in.

In 1841, Australia was hit by the worst depression in its history up till that point. The price of wool and land values fell, and it was said that one adult male in every twelve was bankrupt. John Fairfax had only taken over the *Sydney Morning Herald* earlier that year, along with his friend Charles Kemp. Now, in the very same year that he had finally achieved his dream of owning his own newspaper, John's dream seemed once again on the brink of ruin. Another newspaper venture ended, probably reminding him of those dark days in Leamington when he had been bankrupted.

How did he respond? Amid the turmoil, he acted. He raised subscription and advertising rates to increase revenue. Then John met with his employees and told them about the severity of the paper's situation. He told them their wages would have to be lowered. They were understandably unhappy.

John knew these men, and they knew and respected him. As recorded in John Fitzgerald Fairfax's 1941 biography of him, John looked out at their faces and said:

You tell me, lads, that you cannot accept the terms we have offered. Well, I can see your argument and I can feel nothing but sympathy for you when the price of bread and board is rising and there are mouths to feed at home and friends and relatives thrown out of work. My partner and I would not suggest this cut in your wages were times normal and the receipts of the business satisfactory. But times are not normal and receipts are not satisfactory, and I tell you, and I know, that unless the heavy drain of expenditure is eased for a while, that your jobs and Mr. Kemp's job and my job will be in the greatest peril. We do not want the Herald to go the way of those other newspapers which have foundered in the storm. We, you and I, want this paper to grow great and strong, so that in time the Herald may be a name to conjure with, so that a man may be proud to be a Herald man. If you accept my proposal, I know that, in a short time, when this financial depression reaches its depth, you will be glad, very glad, to be a Herald man. I propose that at the end of each week we draw our wages pro rata, you and I, as the receipts, offset by expenditure, are shown by the books. In this way, and this way only, can we ride out the storm. Here is the proposal, lads. I will leave it with you.

The next day, the employees accepted John's terms. As it happened, his prediction about the economy worsening proved to be accurate. While other printers were getting paid a lot less, if they had jobs at all, the *Herald* employees had jobs and—relative to others at the time—decent wages. While the men were paid, John and his partner, Charles Kemp, often did not have much left over for themselves. There was no scene of profits going downhill and wages being cut while the CEO gets a multimillion-dollar bonus, which we see all too often today.

So what does this story from the life of John Fairfax in 1841 have to do with listening? During one of the key moments in his professional life, listening is exactly what he did. It is worth looking in some detail at the speech he gave his employees. Notice how clear it is that he has already been listening to them, to their needs and concerns. He starts out by acknowledging the very real hardships his employees are going through. He shows genuine understanding of their situation. Food prices are rising, as is the price of lodging. They have families to provide for. Many of their friends and family members are out of work. He has heard them, and he feels empathy for them.

But then he tells them what they do not want to hear but need to hear. He tells them that unless costs are lowered, including wages, all their jobs, including his, will be gone. He encourages them by reminding them of the vision they are all working toward: "We, you and I, want this paper to grow great and strong." He then tells them that he is going to be fair. At the end of each week, they will share in what is left and together they will "ride out the storm."

This is such a great lesson in leadership. It is no wonder that John Fairfax's employees loved and admired him so much. He truly listened to them. He really did feel their pain and acknowledged it. He did not sugarcoat the situation, but he gave them hope. He painted a picture of the vision that, together, they were working to achieve.

History proves the respect and admiration that John's staff had for him, judging by the fact that there was a record among his employees of long service. Few left the *Herald* and few were dismissed. Their respect and admiration for him can also be seen in the words of the tribute paid to him on his death in 1877. They praised his insight and "his conscientious desire to aim at the realization of a high ideal." They referred to him as "the mainspring of the leading journal of the Colony" and noted that he desired the prosperity of the colony and "held an elevated view of the functions of journalism." They ultimately concluded: "We feel that in his departure we have lost a kind employer and a valued friend."

Great Leaders Are Good Listeners

Many leaders know what they want to do. They have a clear picture of where they want to go. Some know who they are, have faith and character, and have been battle-tested in life's crucibles. But still they fail. Why? I believe it is because many leaders—I would almost say most—don't listen.

To an extent, this is understandable. It is tough to be a strong leader who knows where he or she wants to go, and what he or she wants to do, and yet stop to listen. After all, you might say, "Why do I need to listen? I know what I want to do. Time's moving on. Now is the time for action, not for sitting around and endlessly talking. Less talk, more action. What we need is action and action now."

What this all-too-common attitude misses is that unless we listen, we will not be able to act effectively. To act well, your whole team, your whole organization, must be on the same page, united behind a common vision, a common cause. That does not happen without dialogue. That does not happen without listening. Until people have been heard, they will not wholeheartedly buy in to your vision. Listening is the price of your team's commitment.

Some leaders understand that good listening is crucial to their success. Good listening allows leaders to better understand what is going on in their organizations and, for that matter, in the world around them. Good listening allows leaders to hear ideas that will make their visions better and their plans to implement those visions more likely to succeed. Good listening allows leaders to learn of potential pitfalls and roadblocks that enable them to cast their vision in ways that increase the likelihood of success.

> Until people have been heard, they will not wholeheartedly buy in to your vision. Listening is the price of your team's commitment.

So why is listening so hard? There are certain skills that help make people good listeners, such as being able to read nonverbal cues, listening as much for what is not said as what is said, and listening for how things are said. But while natural aptitude and skills may play a part, the secret to being a good listener comes down to one simple point. Most people do not want to be good listeners. Most people would rather talk than listen. It's that simple. They may realize they *should* listen, that it might help them in their leadership, but in their heart of hearts, they don't *want to* listen.

In part, it comes down to ego. Many people who would rather talk than listen often have big egos. They love the sound of their own voices. They love to pontificate on the issues of the day or the current state of their organizations. They will happily interrupt others to offer yet another pearl of wisdom but become incensed if others interrupt them and disturb their flow of thought amid a great discourse.

It also comes down to a lack of curiosity. Many people would rather teach than learn. Many of us would rather lecture and be the expert than learn from others. Lack of curiosity about the world, other people, and subjects beyond our training are all too prevalent. The consequences of this lack of curiosity are huge, leading to misunderstandings, conflicts, and even wars.

Related to a lack of curiosity is a lack of desire to truly understand other people. You could also call this a lack of empathy. The desire to put yourself in someone else's position is all too rare. Think of what the world would be like if all its leaders truly desired to understand what it would be like to walk in the other leaders' shoes. How easy is it to have a conflict with another leader whom you desire to truly understand? Once you start to understand another leader, understand his or her background and perspectives, empathy can grow. Even more revolutionary, friendship may blossom. It is tough to have conflict with someone you understand and for whom you have empathy.

At the risk of saying something controversial, I would also suggest that one reason listening is so hard for many leaders is that to this day (although this is changing), more leaders are men. There is the stereotype that women are better listeners than men. There may be some truth in this. I am a certified member of the International Coach Federation (ICF), the world's leading professional coaching organization. More than 70 percent of ICF member coaches are women. To be a great coach, you have to be a great listener. Many men are not good listeners. Therefore, not many men have the qualities required to be a great coach, or perhaps even want to be one. Many would rather act than coach or lead than listen. But to lead well, you have to listen.

So in essence, while the ability to listen is helped by aptitude, it is in large part a matter of will. We do well, in many cases, at those things we want to do well at. And many people simply don't want to listen. Irrespective of what the good leadership manual might say, they just don't want to do it. Unfortunately, there are consequences for not doing those things you know you should do but just don't want to do.

The Perils of Not Listening

I like to think that I have a natural aptitude for listening, and I have made a concerted effort to develop it. I believe this is one of the stronger points in my leadership. (Some of the time with my family I listen, but not all the time, I'm afraid. There have been times I have not listened so well.)

I love learning about the world, other cultures, different aspects of history, and other points of view. I feel like every person has something to teach me. It may be in their life stories, their experiences, or a particular point of view. I also love understanding where a person is coming from and why. These interests led me to start hosting my podcast, *Beyond the Crucible*. I am fascinated by the stories of the men and women, coming from all walks of life, as they discuss the crucibles they've endured and how they've bounced back from them to lead lives of significance. I like to listen intently enough to their descriptions of their experiences so that when I ask them questions, they often discuss what they've been through with more detail and emotion than they ever have before.

But, even if you have a natural aptitude for listening, it does not mean that you will always listen in all situations. Sometimes, your mind is already made up about how things are and you just do not listen. You almost purposely decide not to listen and to tune out discordant voices.

That may be part of what happened to me during the takeover of John Fairfax Ltd.

When I was growing up, the view I had of what was going on in my family and the family business was largely (if not exclusively) formed from one side. I loved my father deeply, so when he or my mother told me their perspective on what other family members had done to him, I naturally accepted what they said as the truth.

It may have been the truth from their perspective, but that is not the same as the absolute truth. When the other members of my family forced my father to resign as chairman in 1976, the image I had in my mind was of a great man wronged by an ungrateful family. This was a man who had dedicated his life to the family company and its newspapers—in particular, the *Sydney Morning Herald*. It felt as though my parents were a vanguard trying to keep the company true to the traditions of the founder in its approach to journalism, while at the same time, modernize and improve its management. My father's was a voice for change, for keeping up with the times, amid a sea of conservatism.

This was my parents' view. But it was only one view. Did I really understand what the views of other family members were? Did I really understand the reasons why they forced my father to resign as chairman? I did not know what their perspective was because I did not ask; I did not listen. (In fairness, in 1976, it would have been asking a lot to expect me to go to these other family members and ask them why they had done that to my father. They might not have wanted to get into it with a fifteen-year-old boy, particularly if what they said might be seen as denigrating his father.) However, this view of the rest of my family colored my attitude leading up to the takeover in 1987.

Listening should have taken place in the months beforehand, along with expressing my concerns. That would have meant telling them that I was concerned the company might be taken over, given the rapid rise in the share price in the first half of 1987. I could have expressed my concern that there was too much sensational journalism, too much editorializing in the news columns instead of straight reporting. I could have expressed my concerns about management, both in their (from my perspective) ill-thought-out capital-raising schemes and in how they mishandled the *Herald* and *Weekly Times* episode, which ended up leading to the sale of our television stations. But did I express these concerns to my family? No. In part, it was because I thought these other family members would not listen. But did I give them the chance to respond? After all, sometimes our assumptions can be wrong. And in assuming they wouldn't listen, I ensured that I wouldn't listen.

Frankly, I am not sure how open I would have been to the answers. In hindsight, I was only open to what I *wanted* to hear. When in 1987 I came to believe that a takeover of the family company was necessary, I sought advice from a prestigious corporate advisory firm. They analyzed the situation and advised me it would not be prudent to attempt a takeover at this time. That was not advice I wanted to hear.

So, I sought advice elsewhere. I ended up going to advisers who were more unconventional and that had some success. They told me that the takeover was possible and ended up helping me formulate a plan to launch the takeover. But, once the takeover was completed, the debt load ended up being too much for the company to handle. The takeover also led to hurt feelings within the family, which lasted for many years. Did I truly take account of all these possibilities? Not really because my mind had been made up. The takeover was necessary, and we were going to push through, come what may.

I learned some powerful lessons during those times. Do not get your information from only one side, one point of view. Do not assume you are getting the whole story without bias from only one side. Rarely will that be true. Get input from many sides and many different points of view. Be slow to make up your mind. Be quick to challenge your assumptions and presuppositions. They may be wrong. You may be wrong. Listen more; assume less. Do not be so resolute so fast. Be willing to change your opinion if new information comes in.

Another compelling lesson is that we should not just listen to those who are telling us what we want to hear, ignoring and discounting advice from those who are not telling us what we want to hear. That, I am afraid, is what happened to me. I listened to the siren songs of those who said the takeover would work, and I was the one to lead the charge. I ignored the advice of those who might have sympathized with my reasons for wanting to do the takeover but felt it was too risky at that time and to wait, either to do the takeover later or look for other potential solutions. The latter course of action would have been the prudent, sensible thing to do. I, to my great cost, emotionally and financially, did not take that advice.

Let the Wise Listen

The Bible has a lot to say about listening. Often, it is about the importance of listening to God, or those whom God sends to speak to His people, such as prophets. Typically, the message they bring is to repent and turn back to God and His ways. We as people are often stubborn and want to do things our way instead of God's way, even if God's way would lead to greater fulfillment and happiness.

More broadly there are some great Scriptures that talk about the importance of listening. Here are two good ones from Proverbs:

Let the wise listen and add to their learning, and let the discerning get guidance.

—Proverbs 1:5

To answer before listening—that is folly and shame.

—Proverbs 18:13

These two Scriptures give us some great insights into why listening is important to life and leadership. It is the wise that listen to those all around them: people above them and below them in the organization and people they work alongside. They listen to their customers and those in the marketplace, in general. All this listening adds to our learning. Similarly, what sense does it make to just spout out your thoughts and opinions before listening, really listening, to what others have to say? Not listening is certainly a good way to make you seem foolish.

The book of James has two good passages on listening, as well:

My dear brothers and sisters, take note of this: everyone should be quick to listen, slow to speak and slow to become angry.

—James 1:19

Do not merely listen to the word, and so deceive yourselves. Do what it says.

—James 1:22

The message from these two verses is profound but not always easy to put into practice. As the first verse points out, it is important to listen first rather than jump in with our opinions or become angry. Maybe we became angry because we did not understand where the other person was really coming from. We reacted without giving them a chance to explain. It is good practice to take a breath and listen, really listen, then as appropriate speak, and do not become angry. It is rare that anger is appropriate or helpful.

The second verse points out that, deep down, we all know we should listen rather than jump to conclusions. But, just because we know this is important does not mean we will always do it. It is hard to do. We get impatient and overwhelmed. We can't take it anymore and someone just happens to be in the wrong place at the wrong time, and we let them have it.

For me, that is where I find prayer really helps. When I find myself about to react, I try to pray to calm down. Because I am human, I don't always manage to do it, but in my better moments, I do. Others might meditate or take their minds to a memory of a tranquil place to calm themselves down. However you get there, it is essential to find a way to listen from a calm and open place. Great leadership depends on it.

A Leader Who Listened—George Washington

A great example of a leader who listened was George Washington. In 1775, he was offered the command of the Continental Army of the American colonies fighting the British in the War of Independence. At this time, the British forces were under siege in Boston.

Washington came to the area in July. At the time, Boston was almost an island, connected to the mainland by a narrow causeway or neck. American troops were barricading the neck, but the British were in something of an impregnable fortress. The problem of how to take Boston and force the British out would consume Washington for months to come. He had 20,000 men, but with absences and those sick, the number fit for duty was fewer than 14,000.

While there had been patriotic fervor in April and May 1775, during the early days of the war, that spirit had waned. The troops had signed on only till the end of the year. Supplies of blankets, tents, and clothing were low, and winter was approaching. It was assumed that many soldiers would disappear when their enlistment was up at the end of the year. The situation was not good.

Washington was a realist and saw things as they were, not as he wished them to be. He was also realistic about his own abilities and his relative lack of military experience. Nonetheless, he would do his best and was no pessimist. He declared that the army should never lose sight of "the goodness of our cause," and difficulties were not insurmountable, that "Perseverance and spirit have done wonders in all ages."

On September 11, Washington convened the first of what was to be a number of councils of war. This council included three major generals and four brigadiers. The only professional soldier present was Major General Charles Lee, Washington's second-in-command and a former British officer. At the meeting, Washington made his case for an all-out amphibious attack on Boston. He reminded the council that winter was approaching, the troops did not have barracks or firewood, and they would be eager to go home once their enlistment expired at the end of the year. There was discussion of all this, including the enemy's defenses, which were fairly impregnable. The council unanimously agreed not to attack. This was a good decision. The chance of disastrous failure was high. Unless they caught the tide just right, the men in the boats could have been stranded in the mudflats with British fire bearing down on them. Casualties would have been enormous. But Washington was still impatient for some decisive stroke.

On October 18, another council of war was convened. This time, Brigadier General Horatio Gates, who had been absent from the previous meeting, was present. Like Lee, Gates was an experienced former British officer. As with the previous council of war, this council decided that the risks were too great to attack, "under the circumstances."

On January 16, 1776, Washington again convened a council of war, speaking of the "indispensable necessity of making a bold attempt" on

Boston. The council again listened, voiced agreement that a "vigorous attempt" should be made, but only when "practicable."

On February 16, Washington convened his fourth council of war calling for approval of an attack on Boston. This time, he had the addition of fifty-eight mortars and cannon that Colonel Henry Knox had captured from the British at Fort Ticonderoga on Lake Champlain. Knox had brought these guns quite a distance to the Boston area. Washington convened this council probably hoping that, with the addition of these guns, there would be unanimous agreement that the time had come to attack.

Once again, however, the generals wisely said no. Instead of agreeing to Washington's plan to attack the British in Boston where they were well fortified, there was agreement on another plan—to occupy the heights of the Dorchester Peninsula with troops and their newly acquired cannon. Placing these cannon on Dorchester Heights, overlooking Boston, would put the British in a very difficult situation, the council thought, and would force them to come out to attack. Washington was upset over the decision not to attack. But he conceded that perhaps he had been wrong: "Perhaps the irksomeness of my situation led me to undertake more than could be warranted by prudence." Washington had moved on. The issue was "now at an end, and I am preparing to take post on Dorchester."

The plan was to occupy the heights of the Dorchester peninsula on a single night. After dark on March 4th, the troops and guns moved in. By dawn the next day, over 3,000 men were on Dorchester Heights with at least twenty cannon in place. During the night, the Americans had sent wagons loaded with hay bales, barrels, and other portable defense works near enough to Boston that had the British been alert, they might have discovered what was going on.

When he saw what had been achieved, British General William Howe declared, "My God, these fellows have done more work in one night than I could make my army do in three months." The British tried to fire on the Dorchester Heights positions, but their guns could not be elevated enough to strike such a high target. The British naval officers whose ships were in Boston Harbor felt the Americans' cannon might be in range of their ships and said they would not remain unless the cannon were removed. General Howe decided to attack Dorchester Heights. His pride and honor demanded it.

Before the British could launch an attack, however, the wind picked up and a storm raged, making an amphibious attack on Dorchester Heights impossible. This was fortuitous, as a number of British officers believed that an attack against such a strong position was doomed to failure. On Sunday, March 17, 120 ships with more than 11,000 British troops, Loyalists, and family members left Boston bound for Nova Scotia in Canada. One British officer wrote, "Never were troops in so disgraceful a situation. I pity General Howe from my soul." General Howe had been outsmarted by some colonial rebels, led by a man, George Washington, who did not have nearly the same military experience he did. Howe and his troops were unable to mount an effective counterattack and had to leave Boston. It is no wonder the British officer felt Howe was to be pitied.

What accounted for this great victory the Americans enjoyed over the British? It was that Washington listened to the team around him. By nature, Washington was an impatient man with a fiery temper. But, he controlled both his impatience and his temper with iron self-discipline. Self-mastery was one of his highest goals. He strove to do what was right, not what was convenient or pleasant. Washington wanted to press on, to take the fight to the enemy. But where he had never led an army in battle, he was up against British generals like Howe, who, while complacent, was an able and courageous leader. Washington was up against seasoned and able opponents. He needed to be at his best with the best thinking around him.

Four times from September 1775 to February 1776, Washington convened a council of war. Each time, he asked the council to approve a bold attack on Boston. Each time, he was rebuffed. Each time, he listened and accepted the council's advice, albeit reluctantly and not always with good humor. Washington was the commander of the American Army in

Boston. He did not have to listen to the wisdom of the council. But he did. Washington knew his limitations both in ability and experience. He would not let his natural impatience lead him to make an impetuous, rash decision. When advised by seasoned generals, such as Charles Lee and Horatio Gates, and young officers of promise such as Henry Knox, Washington listened.

There were many qualities that made George Washington a great man. One was the ability to listen to his key commanders when every ounce of his being wanted to do the opposite of what they suggested.

Reflection Questions

1. Why is listening such a critical skill for leaders who want to make their vision a reality?
2. Think back to a time when you listened well and a time when maybe you didn't. What differences were there in the outcomes of those events?
3. Think back to a time when you felt you were truly listened to. What did it feel like to be heard?

Chapter 13

SEEKING ADVICE FROM A FEW

True leaders seek advice to try to clear away the confusion and cobwebs and bring clarity. Great leaders have a core of key advisers.

Listening to people around you is helpful, but listening to a select few can be particularly helpful—a select few who really know you, who have particular wisdom, and who have an ability to impart that wisdom in often subtle ways. It takes a strong leader to recognize they can't do it all alone, they don't have all the answers, and they need help.

Many leaders do not have the self-confidence to realize it is okay to admit that, at times, they may feel clueless or all at sea. Sometimes as leaders, we are too close to the situation or are too emotionally involved to see things clearly or make good decisions without help.

Feeling lost and even helpless at times is part of being human. What separates true leaders is what they do about it. True leaders seek advice to try to clear away the confusion and cobwebs and bring clarity. They have a core of key advisers. Depending on the situation at hand or the expertise needed, this may be one person, or it may be a few different people.

> It takes a strong leader to recognize they can't do it all alone, they don't have all the answers, and they need help.

Great leaders realize the issues at hand are too important to be held up by their own blind spots and insecurities. Bad decisions happen that way. Great leaders realize that they can't afford to make bad decisions, or, more accurately, that they can't afford to make too many of them. Great leaders choose advisers who will help them avoid making bad decisions.

Hallmarks of a Great Adviser

So, what should we look for in an adviser? The answer to this question is crucial for leaders. Leaders sometimes choose the wrong advisers, which can greatly increase the probability of making bad decisions. The wrong advisers may not have the right skills to be an adviser or, worse, they may have a hidden agenda to manipulate the leader for their own ends.

There are different types of advisers, but great advisers have some common characteristics. They have no ulterior motives. Their only agenda is to help the leader accomplish his or her objectives. In other words, they have integrity. They are selfless. They are not trying to use the leader or gain indirect power by being seen as the power behind the throne. That is one reason good advisers are hard to find. There are many that would be our advisers to get into the "inner circle," to curry favor, to influence policy, and to further their own position. Those kinds of "advisers" are easy to find. It is harder to find advisers who want nothing from you and only want to help you achieve your objectives.

They are great listeners. They listen before they speak. They actively listen, probe, and ask follow-up questions to ensure they understand the whole picture before they give advice. And when they do give advice, it often comes in the form of a question rather than an answer. I believe the best advice often comes in the form of a question. Ask me ten great questions, and it will take me much further than giving me ten great answers! Great questions can be challenging because they force us to ponder subjects we may not want to think about.

Why are we going to take a particular step? Is this something we are doing because we believe in it or because it is expected of us? What does our team think? Do they believe in it? What will be the consequences of the decision? Are we prepared for this? What do we think is the right thing to do?

Answering these questions may not be easy, but it is vital. That is what good advisers do. They ask questions we may be afraid or unwilling to ask ourselves but which must be asked, and the answers squarely faced, before any action is taken.

They are unintimidated. They are unafraid of speaking truth to power. Since they have no hidden agenda and only want the leader to achieve his or her objectives, they have nothing to fear. This means a great adviser has to be willing to lose it all. They have to be willing to lose contact with the leader, to offend them, and even to endanger the relationship. Sometimes, asking tough questions or giving tough answers will force the leader to consider things they don't want to consider. It will force the leader to confront his or her inadequacies or failings. Speaking truth to power is often fraught with danger and few are willing to do it.

The famous children's story, *The Emperor's New Clothes*, written by Hans Christian Andersen, was a sort of parable whereby Andersen intended to expose the hypocrisy and snobbery of nineteenth-century

Danish society. Along the way, he made powerful points about the need for advisers who will speak truth to power.

As the story goes, there was a vain emperor who cared excessively about dressing in elegant clothes. One day, two scoundrels—who had heard of the emperor's vanity—came to the gates of the palace, boasting that they had invented an extraordinary method of weaving a cloth so fine, it was invisible to anyone who was "too stupid and incompetent to appreciate its quality." The vain emperor immediately hired the men to make the clothes, thinking they would enable him to tell the wise men from the fools and thus determine which men were unfit to work for him.

At one point, the prime minister went to see how the work was proceeding. He was old and considered by everyone to be a man of common sense. When he saw the scoundrels working on the cloth, he could not see anything, but, fearing he would be fired if he told what he really saw, the prime minister said he thought the fabric was marvelous.

When the scoundrels presented the "new clothes" to the emperor, the emperor panicked and almost fainted because he could not see anything. But, fearing that people would find out that he was stupid and incompetent, he took off his clothes and "put on" the new ones. He then paraded in his new (invisible) clothes in front of the people!

His dignitaries preceded him in the procession, proclaiming, "Look at the emperor's new clothes. They're beautiful!" However, a child who was watching the procession shouted out the truth: "The emperor has no clothes!" Eventually, others in the crowd picked up on the boy's cry and repeated it. But, even though the emperor realized the people were right, he could not admit it. He continued the procession and persisted in believing in the illusion that anyone who could not see his clothes was stupid and incompetent.

This parable illustrates the truth that often, the problem with our advisers is less that they lack wisdom and experience than that they lack courage—the courage to speak their minds and give us the advice we may not want but need to hear. The courage to risk their position and influence—in a sense, to risk it all—for our good. This reminds me of a quote often attributed to Edmund Burke, the great Irish political philosopher and eighteenth-century British politician: "The only thing necessary for the triumph of evil is for good men to do nothing."

Good advisers are wise. Even though, at the heart of great advising is asking great questions—not just giving answers—wisdom and experience matter. There is a link between the two. Experience gives you the opportunity of reflecting on and learning from your successes and especially your mistakes, as well as learning from others. Those who do so gain wisdom.

The two post-secondary institutions I attended had professors who asked great questions. At both Oxford University and Harvard Business School, the professors do little lecturing as the primary teaching vehicle; instead, they teach through asking questions. It is, in some sense, the Socratic method, probing the student with further questions to test their knowledge and help them think more deeply. You may ask why anyone would spend a considerable amount of money to be asked a bunch of questions. But what makes the questions so valuable in helping the students learn is the wisdom and experience on which the questions are based. Wisdom and experience matter.

It is no coincidence that International Coach Federation (ICF) coaches, of which I am one, are not that young. In a 2007 ICF global survey, in which nearly six thousand coaches in seventy-four countries participated, it was found that more than 60 percent of coaches were aged over forty-five, and 90 percent were over thirty-five. More than 50 percent of coaches have a master's degree or higher, and coaches on average have five to ten years of coaching experience.

Finding a Good Adviser

Advisers come in different shapes and sizes. Some are mentors. Some are colleagues. Some may be trusted lieutenants or subordinates. Some are peers. Some are coaches.

Advisers can serve different purposes. You may have one set of advisers early in your career and a different set later. As your needs for advice change, depending on where you are in your career and the type of job you are doing, so may your advisers. As your needs change over time, your advisers may vary in the type and level of experience they have.

In some cases, having advisers with a particular industry, skill set, or life experience can be helpful. You may have some advisers who can help you with sales challenges, others with boardroom challenges, and still others with strategy challenges. I am not advocating having dozens of different counselors depending on your precise needs, or even that you have to change advisers as you progress in your career, just that you be open to matching your needs with the qualities needed in your advisers. There are some qualities that all advisers need, irrespective of the type of adviser (mentor, peer, coach, colleague, subordinate) or their function (for example, sales, strategy).

I have quite a bit of experience with the role of adviser, from both sides of the fence. I have had advisers, and I have been an adviser. I know a lot more now about what to look for in an adviser than I did in my newspaper days. Being an adviser and having had some good advisers over the years help give you a greater appreciation and understanding of what good advising is all about.

At the time of the takeover, there were some people around me who were encouraging me to do the takeover, fueling my desire to see that the company be well run and made safe from an external takeover. Then there were some, like the prestigious corporate advisory firm I first saw, and my lawyer at the time, which advised against it. It was too risky.

Whose advice did I end up listening to? The advice I wanted to hear. Did they say it might be difficult, did they say there were risks involved? Perhaps. All I heard was that it was possible, and they were willing to help me. I was focused but perhaps with blinders on to the consequences for the company, the rest of my family, or me. I had set my course, and there was no turning back.

As I look back at my determination to follow through with the take-over, I am reminded of the famous poem of Alfred Lord Tennyson, "The Charge of the Light Brigade." The Charge of the Light Brigade occurred in 1854 during the Crimean War, which was fought between Russia and Britain and her allies in Russia's Crimean Peninsula. Due to a miscom-munication of orders, six hundred horsemen charged into a valley ringed on three sides with Russian infantry and artillery. The result was disas-trous, with over two hundred and seventy-five horsemen killed. Some lines of this poem echo through the ages:

"Forward the Light Brigade!

"Theirs is not to make reply, theirs not to reason why, theirs but to do or die: into the Valley of Death rode the six hundred . . .

"Cannon to right of them, cannon to left of them, cannon in front of them."

The poem is epic in its ability to communicate misplaced heroism and resoluteness to go forward into certain death. There was some of this air of heroism in my determination to do my duty, to protect the company and restore it to the ideals of the founder. *Despite the risks, let's charge onward,* I thought. Once I had started the charge, even if there were "cannon to right of me, cannon to left of me, cannon in front of me," it was not going to be easy for me to stop.

I needed someone, or a group of people, to ask me some tough ques-tions. Someone to ask me questions that might risk their relationship with me, and yes, possibly give up any access to power that might be gained. I needed someone to ask me why I was doing the takeover. Was it because I wanted to do it or was it because I wanted to fulfill some misguided sense of duty to my father and the founder? Did I really want to be in charge of a large media company? Did that fit my gifts? Was this my dream or was it just blind obedience to dreams of others? I would like to believe that if someone had asked me these crucial questions about my motives and the possible effects of my actions, I would have listened. Perhaps I would have stepped back from the precipice and reconsidered. We will never know.

Speaking Truth to Power

I love being an adviser. As I have mentioned, in addition to being an executive coach, I have been on two boards, the elder board of my church, Bay Area Community Church, and the board of my children's school, Annapolis Area Christian School. With Crucible Leadership, I also give advice through my blogs and the podcast I host, when I'm reflecting with my audience and guests on how to move beyond a crucible experience.

While the roles of being an adviser and a board member are different, there are some similarities in how I approach them. In each case, if there is something that needs to be said, I say it. When I am functioning as an adviser, I tend to ask questions to get to the key issue. As a board member, I may ask a question to get at the same issue, but I also do not hesitate in giving my opinion. It is my duty as a board member. If others disagree or the consensus of the board on an issue is different from my viewpoint, that is fine. My duty is to be clear about what I think on a given issue.

The same holds true when I am functioning as an adviser. My duty is to ask the questions that need to be asked. The response is up to the leader I am advising, as are the consequences. So long as I have done my best to ensure that I am asking the leader the tough questions and that I have tried to make them see the consequences of a decision and possible alternatives, then I have done my job.

One thing I have learned, which has not always been easy for me, is that in the end, it is the leader's life and the leader's decision, not yours as the adviser. Whatever questions or doubts you have about the decision the leader is about to make, it is the leader's life, not yours. To be a great adviser, you in some sense have to park your own viewpoints at the door as to what decision the leader should make. I try to treat other people the way I would like to be treated. This reminds me of what has become known as the Golden Rule: "Do to others what you would have them do to you."

The Bible contains many thoughts on the wisdom of taking advice and the folly of ignoring it, many of which are found in Proverbs. Here are a few great ones:

For lack of guidance a nation falls, but victory is won through many advisers.

—Proverbs 11:14

The way of fools seems right to them, but the wise listen to advice.

—Proverbs 12:15

Plans fail for lack of counsel, but with many advisers they succeed.

—Proverbs 15:22

The theme of these verses is clear. The first half of each verse tells us what *not* to do. Nations fall through lack of guidance. Fools only listen to themselves. Our plans will fail for lack of good input and counsel.

The second half of the verse shows us what we *should* do. Many advisers ensure victory. Wise people listen to advice. Many advisers help our plans succeed. When we only listen to ourselves, we often miss the bigger picture. We are seeing the world through only one lens. It is folly to make big decisions without seeking wise counsel. Wise counsel greatly increases the chances of our plans succeeding. This may seem obvious, but such are the temptations of arrogance, ego, and self-sufficiency—that many leaders do not seek advice. They don't want to share success. They want to say, "It was all me!"

To Listen or Not to Listen?

The Bible gives us several examples of leaders who listened to advice and of some leaders who did not listen to advice and the consequences they faced because of it. One biblical leader who did not listen to wise counsel, with far-reaching consequences, was Rehoboam.

Rehoboam became king of Israel after the death of his father, Solomon. Ironically, it was Solomon who wrote most of the book of Proverbs, which is full of good advice. Sadly, Rehoboam ignored much of the wisdom his father had written.

After Solomon's death, several people, including Jeroboam, who had been an effective administrator under Solomon, went to Rehoboam. They told him that Solomon had put a heavy yoke on them with oppressive taxation and conscription of labor. They asked him to lighten the load on them and said they would serve him.

Rehoboam first consulted with his father's advisers, the elders who were part of Solomon's government. The elders told Rehoboam that if he would be a servant to these people, they would always be his servants. Basically, they said that if he listened to these people's requests and was amenable to them, these people would be loyal to him.

Rehoboam then asked some young men with whom he had grown up what they thought. They told him the opposite. The young men told Rehoboam that he should make the yoke on these people even heavier. They told him to tell these people, "My father scourged you with whips; I will scourge you with scorpions." (1 Kings 12:11)

Rehoboam rejected the advice of the elders who had counseled his father and took the advice of the young men. He told Jeroboam and the others with him what the young men had advised him to say. When the Israelites heard that Rehoboam would not listen, they made Jeroboam king over Israel. Israel was now split in two, the northern kingdom of Israel under Jeroboam and the southern kingdom of Judah under Rehoboam.

The young king had consulted with two sets of advisers. One set was older and more experienced and had served in his father's government, and they told him what he did not want to hear. They spoke truth to power. The younger, inexperienced advisers told Rehoboam what he wanted to hear, ensuring they would be part of his inner circle. They chose influence over truth.

Rehoboam made the wrong choice. He chose advice from the wrong advisers, and he paid a big price. Israel and Judah would remain divided for hundreds of years, later conquered by the Babylonians and others. Rehoboam's decision to take advice from the wrong advisers would have lasting consequences for his kingdom and all of Israel. This story sadly shows how often good advice is ignored because it is inconvenient or not what we want to hear.

Franklin Roosevelt's Right-Hand Man—Louis Howe

Louis Howe was one of President Franklin Roosevelt's closest advisers for much of Roosevelt's political career, including the first years of his presidency during the Great Depression in the 1930s.

When Howe first met him, in 1911, Roosevelt was a member of the New York State Senate. Howe was so impressed with Roosevelt that he felt he had the potential to become president. Howe himself would play no small part in helping make this happen. He realized that his experience and maturity, combined with Roosevelt's enthusiasm and charisma, could produce a powerful political force. He helped guide Roosevelt in 1913 when he was appointed assistant secretary of the Navy in President Wilson's administration. Later, Howe worked as Roosevelt's campaign manager during the 1920 presidential campaign, when Roosevelt was the Democratic nominee for vice president, alongside James Cox. (Cox lost in a landslide to Republican Warren Harding.)

When Roosevelt was stricken with polio in 1921, it seemed his political career was over. At that time, such a disability was seen by many as a political death sentence. During this time, Howe sought to boost the spirits of both Roosevelt and his wife, Eleanor. He kept Roosevelt's name in the public eye by encouraging him to issue statements on public issues, write magazine articles, and appear at the 1924 Democratic Convention. At Howe's urging, Eleanor Roosevelt also spoke across New York State to ensure that her husband remained in the public eye. Howe mentored Eleanor, helping her to become a more confident and effective public speaker.

Howe's campaign to keep Roosevelt's name before the public was a success. In 1928, Governor Alfred Smith of New York, then the Democratic nominee for president for the 1928 election, urged Roosevelt to run for governor of New York. Although the Republican Herbert Hoover beat Smith in the presidential election, Roosevelt won the election for governor of New York. The culmination of Howe's advisory role with Franklin Roosevelt came in 1932, when he was elected president of the United States. After Roosevelt's election, Howe was appointed secretary to the president, a role equivalent to the current White House chief of staff.

Howe's influence on Roosevelt was profound. Even after Roosevelt became president, Howe would continue to speak to him bluntly and frankly. He refused to let the aura of the presidency prevent him from offering honest advice. He was known by some as "the man behind Roosevelt." The *New York Times* described him as "The President's Other I." The *New York Herald Tribune* said of Howe, "His loyalty is not to himself, or to an abstract ideal of government, but solely to Franklin D. Roosevelt."

Unfortunately, Howe's health declined, and he died in 1936. The man known as the "man who put Franklin D. Roosevelt in the White House" was gone. For the first time in his political life, in some sense, Roosevelt was now alone. The morning after Howe died, Roosevelt personally ordered the White House flag fly at half-mast. He canceled all of his appointments and activities for at least the next two days and remained in seclusion the rest of that day. Some historians have said the political mistakes of the Roosevelt administration in the years after Howe's death were due to the absence of Howe's incessant criticism and his accurate assessment of public opinion.

Howe's devotion and loyalty to Franklin Roosevelt were remarkable. It is hard to believe Roosevelt ever would have become president without him. When Roosevelt was lying in bed as an invalid in 1921, his political career finished, it was Louis Howe who found a practical way to help Eleanor and Franklin Roosevelt resurrect Roosevelt's political career. One of the greatest tributes to Howe was given by Roosevelt's son Elliott: "The person who was most responsible for the development of my mother's personality was Louis Howe, as he was of my father. He was a man that gave my father the iron will and the ability to move ahead politically, which I don't think he would have ever done on his own. Louis Howe was probably the greatest influence on both my father and my mother's lives." *Time* magazine wrote after Howe's death, "Admirers he (Roosevelt) had by the millions, acquaintances by the thousands, advisers by the hundreds, friends by the score, but of intimates such as Louis Howe he had only one."

Our own leadership journeys will almost certainly not look like Franklin Roosevelt's—at least not in specifics. But like so many of us, the president endured a painful crucible experience. He was only able to move beyond by harnessing the motivation of his vision that drew on his passions and talents to contribute to his state and his country. Having an adviser like Louis Howe, and the wisdom to take his counsel to heart, was pivotal to Roosevelt living a life of significance. Our own path to making our vision a reality is paved with similar stones.

Reflection Questions

1. What do you believe to be the number one quality a leader should look for in choosing an adviser?
2. Think back to the advisers you've had in your life and career. How did they help you achieve your goals?
3. How would you rate yourself as an adviser to others? Be specific.

Part Four

LEAD AND LIVE WITH IMPACT

A vision is only fulfilling if it becomes reality. Whether you are leading a large business, a non-profit, or a small team in your neighborhood, a critical component of success will be hiring the right people and creating an environment for them to succeed.

You will need to do well at all the things we have been talking about: learning from your crucible experiences, being authentically who you are and who you were wired to be, being grounded in your values and beliefs, and living them out day to day. You will need to inspire your team with a vision they can believe in, while being open to refining it through listening to them and to your advisers. You will also need to persevere when the inevitable setbacks come along. All these will be key to moving beyond your crucible experiences to living a life of significance.

In these final four chapters, we will explore how to build a healthy organization, how to make your vision a reality, and how to be resilient in the face of challenges.

Chapter 14

CULTIVATING A THRIVING ORGANIZATIONAL ENVIRONMENT

In some ways, one of the most important jobs of a leader is to be the chief gardener of the organization. Day to day, the leader needs to be looking for weeds and other threats to the culture of the company.

We have looked at several different areas of leadership, some internal, such as character, and some external, such as shared vision. We have talked of the "being" of a leader. But what about the "doing" of a leader—the essential steps that turn your vision into reality?

Human beings, by nature, like order and structure in some form and tend to want to be part of something. Certainly, coming up with a vision and inspiring others to follow a shared vision are critical components of what a leader actually does. That is where, and why, organizational leadership is so important. So much of the day-to-day job of a leader is in this area. To me, the key parts of organizational leadership are finding the right people and creating an environment in which those people can flourish and succeed.

But while it sounds clear, it is certainly not simple. Why? For one reason: leaders are continually distracted. They are constantly in firefighting mode. Every day there is a new crisis they have to deal with and a new blaze they have to put out. Long-term thinking can go out the window. It is the tyranny of the urgent, but even worse than that. Too few leaders realize that along with having a vision for their organization and inspiring their people with that shared vision, organizational leadership (finding the right people and creating an environment where they can succeed) is an essential part of their job description.

What a Leader Does

The role of a leader is not to make every decision or even every key decision in the organization. Once the right people are found and are in an environment for them to succeed, an amazing thing happens. The leader now has the time to think long-term, to envision the future, and to consider how to make that vision become a reality. The day-to-day work is now being done well by a great team.

So what does picking the right people involve? It starts with knowing who you are as a leader—as we say in Crucible Leadership, understanding "how you are wired." What are your strengths, what are your weaknesses, what is your personality (outgoing, introverted, a bomb-thrower, reflective)? Given who you are, what sort of people do you need around you to accomplish the goals of the organization and help make the vision a reality?

Next, how do you create an environment in which these people can succeed? In part, it involves creating a culture in the organization that supports the values you desire the organization to have. Too often, a company's stated values have little to do with how it really functions.

The culture of the organization must support and really live its values. This means ensuring that all the organization's systems—such as hiring and retention, promotion, compensation and benefits, evaluation and professional development—are in tune with its values and help enable the organization's vision become reality. It also involves creating an organizational structure that is in tune with the organization's goals and vision. Is the organizational structure helping or hindering the mission?

Lastly, is the leader running the organization in a way that is in harmony with its vision and values? For instance, if the values of the organization include respect and regarding its people as its most important asset, what kind of people are being hired? Are they yes men and yes women who will agree with the boss all the time, or are they people who will tell the leader what they really think? Will they say the things the leader *needs* to hear, not just what he or she *wants* to hear? Is the leader dictating to his or her team what to do, instead of empowering them to make their own decisions and even their own mistakes?

Creating an environment in which people can succeed is not easy. To use a common analogy, it is like creating a beautiful garden. It may look natural and beautiful, but it does not happen by accident. It requires a lot of intentionality and effort: weeding, pruning, fertilizing, replanting, and keeping away animals that will eat the plants. In some ways, one of the most important jobs of a leader is to be the chief gardener of the organization. Day to day, the leader needs to be looking for weeds and other threats to the culture of the company. Is there a new hire who is not fitting in and upsetting a lot of people? That needs to be dealt with quickly.

Another critical aspect of finding the right people is diversity. When we think of diversity, we often think of race and/or gender. That is certainly an important part, but meaningful diversity is more than that. It means finding for your organization, and in particular for your senior leadership team, people of diverse backgrounds (race, gender, nationality, upbringing, life experience), skills, personalities, and ways of thinking. Is everybody on your leadership team button-down-shirt types? Maybe a few people with T-shirts and jeans might help.

Thinking Outside the Box

Now, granted, it might be hard to make a harmonious culture out of a mix of Wall Street accountants and San Francisco software developers. But, there are core sets of values that many diverse people can agree on, such as honesty, humility, and integrity. You can have honest, humble Wall Street accountants who live lives of integrity, just as you can have San Francisco software developers with the same qualities. Too often, we fall back on excuses, including, "Well, they just wouldn't fit in. They're not our kind of people. They wouldn't be comfortable." Such statements reveal more about the group saying this than the people not being let in.

There was a time when to fit into some areas of the business community, you needed to have come from a certain background. In the U.S., maybe you had to go to Harvard or Yale, with perhaps a good prep school thrown in, such as Phillips Exeter or Groton. In the U.K., maybe you needed to go to Oxford or Cambridge, as well as a good private school such as Eton or Harrow. It is natural for people to want to mix with those they feel comfortable with—people with whom they can reminisce about those good old traditions at Eton or Groton and those eccentric professors at Oxford or Yale. It is so much easier and more enjoyable, they think, to work with people who have similar backgrounds to them and just intuitively understand where they are coming from. It makes communication so much easier and thus the working environment so much simpler—at least on the surface.

> Diversity helps create an environment of greater innovation, of looking at things in different ways.

But it also makes the working environment so much staler and less rich. Diversity helps create an environment of greater innovation, of looking at things in different ways. It can also be the richest environment for ensuring a company can weather the stresses and setbacks of a crucible experience. People who attack problems from different perspectives, informed by different life experiences, offer a wider array of potential solutions to problems when the inevitable crisis hits.

Yes, it is harder in some ways to have a senior leadership team from diverse genders, races, and backgrounds, in addition to diverse skill sets. Yes, it is hard to meld such diversity into a united team committed to the organization's mission. But when such a team comes together, the benefits of such diversity, and the ability to build unity amid diversity, is a very powerful engine that can drive the organization to achieve its vision, in good times and bad. In short, there is great strength and resilience in diversity.

Learning Firsthand

I did not experience much diversity growing up. My father came from a "blue-blood" Anglo-Australian background and was educated at Geelong Grammar School outside of Melbourne, and then at Oxford in England. In a sense, this was the equivalent of the Eton-then-Oxford scenario in the U.K., or the Groton-then-Yale scenario in the U.S. My mother was Jewish, but her parents were not particularly religious, and when she married my father she became Anglican. So, I was raised more within the heritage of my father.

I have always been intrigued by, and have loved learning from, people who are different from me. Perhaps that is because I never felt that I really fit in anywhere. Compared to other countries, in Australia there are relatively few poor people or rich people, with a lot of people in the middle. There is an ethos of "mateship" that values everyone being equal. People who put on airs of superiority are frowned on.

Even though I went to a good private school, it seemed there was no one else there who was like me. There were many kids from fairly well-off backgrounds, but their parents did not own a large influential media company. My family seemed to be at the top of the social spectrum, the blue bloods of Sydney—old money, members of good clubs. I did not worry about such differences. I just wanted to fit in. But it was clear that the other kids in school felt there was a difference.

At Balliol College, Oxford, I came across quite a bit of diversity. When I was there, Balliol was probably the most left-wing college in Oxford. That was a new experience and a new worldview for me. The fact that most of my fellow Philosophy, Politics, and Economics (PPE) students had different political leanings than I was brought up with was fine. I was happy to try to understand their point of view. I used to joke that you didn't ask PPE students at Balliol what political views they had; you asked them if they were Marxist, Stalinist, Leninist, Trotskyist, or Fascist. From a left-wing point of view at Balliol, if you were not Marxist, Stalinist, Leninist, or Trotskyist, you were by definition a Fascist.

But diversity at Balliol went beyond political viewpoints. Balliol actively encouraged students from poorer backgrounds to apply. It also had a lot of overseas students. As it happened, the year I started there, 1979, was the first year Balliol admitted women. Previously, there were men's colleges and women's colleges at Oxford. Beginning in 1979, the men's colleges admitted women and the women's colleges admitted men.

So, the students at Balliol were a diverse lot. I had friends from all different backgrounds and different countries. There were people who were from poor backgrounds in the north of England who had attended state schools. Their attitude on applying to Balliol was almost one of "I didn't know Oxford allowed people like us in." At the time, for U.K. students, the education at Oxford was virtually free. The government paid their fees, and even, I believe, some other expenses, such as room and board. So lack of money did not seem to be an insurmountable barrier to coming to Oxford. If you were smart enough, you could get in.

While there were some students from upper-class English backgrounds at Balliol and certainly at Oxford as a whole, I never really fit in with that group, either. One Balliol student would shout, "Ah, Colonial!" whenever he saw me walking through the college. He was just having fun, but that was his regular greeting to me. I had this sense that in the English social spectrum, you had the upper classes, the middle classes, and the lower classes. Australians and convicts (much the same thing from an English point of view) fell somewhere in the lower classes. This meant that while I didn't really fit in anywhere, in some senses, I could mix anywhere. Since I was not part of the English social spectrum, it was not hard to mix with different people.

However, while Balliol may have welcomed people from different backgrounds, toward the end of my time at Oxford I learned this didn't mean there was equal opportunity for its graduates. This was a sobering experience for me. At the time, most students were looking for jobs and interviewing. Balliol College was considered one of the best colleges academically at Oxford, and, in theory, many doors should have been open to its graduates. But even going to Balliol did not guarantee that you could get a top job in the U.K. at the time. If you came from the "wrong" background, and particularly if you had a lower-class accent, that was a barrier. It was one of those things I never forgot.

The other thing was, at Oxford, there was a tendency for people of different classes to separate themselves from one another, despite the fact they had many things in common: same college, same course, and being highly intelligent. I found it hard to understand why people who had so much in common could not socialize with each other. I experienced the *positive* aspects of diversity: diversity in race, gender, income level, and political viewpoint. I also saw the *negative* reactions society can have to diversity, with different groups not tending to mix and job opportunities not being open to all. These experiences, both the positive and the negative, made me realize how important it is to have a diverse team: diverse in gender, race, and background.

Diversity, Leadership Selection, and Team Building

After Oxford, I went on to Harvard Business School in America, then back to Australia. At that time, I went around to the different state offices and various areas of the John Fairfax Ltd. company (newspapers, TV, radio, magazines). My impression at that time was that the environment within the company was not good. People almost seemed to be afraid and did not appear to like management. But, they seemed to be willing to talk to me.

I have always loved listening and trying to understand where others are coming from. Perhaps because of that, I have often found people will tell me things they will not always tell others. I wonder if because I was part of the Fairfax family, whom people within the company respected, and I was the young "new kid on the block," people felt they could confide in me. This only reinforced my sense that something had to be done about the way I perceived the company was being run.

So, how did that work out? After the takeover, how did the management of the company and the environment in which the employees worked change? I would have to say the record is mixed.

I did bring in a new team, at least in part, to head up the company after the takeover. In particular, I wanted to bring in a chief executive to run things while I gained experience in another role. I did not want to be known as chairman or president of the company, so someone thought of the title of "proprietor," which had been used by family members before me. So that was my title: proprietor.

I wanted to pick a chief executive who had a superb record as a general manager. I believed media companies, at least in Australia, were not run well, and it would not be easy to find a great manager from the ranks of senior managers within Australian media companies. It was also my belief that a great general manager could run anything, that the specific product did not matter as much as the general manager's expertise. So I chose a chief executive, Peter King, who had an exceptional record as a senior executive with a career that had taken him to many countries around the world.

Peter King did a great job, increasing operating profits by 80 percent. This seemed to vindicate my sense that the company had not been managed as well as it could have been. However, not all my choices were as good. The senior team around Peter was not on the same level. Some did not work out. There was not a cohesive senior leadership team, at least among the top few, who were all united behind a common vision and who had a common purpose. I hasten to add, this was more my doing than Peter's. Many of the new senior leadership team members were in place before Peter came on board.

The environment within the company after the takeover was also not good. In some sense, it may even have been worse than before. Before the takeover, John Fairfax Ltd. was financially stable under the control of the Fairfax family. There may have been issues with management before the takeover, but the level of stability after the takeover was a lot less, largely because of the debt. The huge debt we had taken on meant that for the company to survive, at least in my control, a lot had to go right. There was a lot of uncertainty.

There were many questions about this new young proprietor, Warwick Fairfax. *Why did he launch the takeover? What did he want to do with the company?* Since I never gave interviews at the time and pretty much never made speeches, or even spoke to employees after the takeover, it was hard for them to know what my vision was and where I was going to take the company. I did not do much to allay their concerns about the future. I did not do enough to foster the shared vision I have spoken about as being so critical to effective leadership.

The situation was difficult. We were so consumed by day-to-day crises that we had little room to think of the long term. Due to the financial instability of the company after the takeover, if we did believe some managers needed to be replaced, it was very difficult to do anything.

Sometimes, you need to replace people for the good of the organization as a whole to ensure the vision succeeds. But when the organization rests on a knife edge between solvency and insolvency, it is very hard to make many changes.

In short, from the get-go, I learned that creating a healthy organization led by great people with a great environment was not easy. If I desired to bring the company back to the ideals of my great-great-grandfather, the decisions I made and the subsequent events rendered that impossible. Whatever I may have thought of the management team that was in place before the takeover and the environment of the company, my actions, if anything, made things worse.

Organizational Leadership Lessons from My Great-Great-Grandfather

John Fairfax had a strong sense of how to assemble a great team and create an environment where people could prosper and succeed. His success in organizational leadership was anchored by the clarity of his vision. He knew what he was trying to accomplish, he knew where he was going, and he intuitively knew the type of people he was looking to recruit.

In 1853, his long and successful partnership with Charles Kemp was dissolved when Charles decided to retire from the business. The manner of his retirement is testimony to the good working relations between the partners; it is not often that a partnership ends as amicably as that of John Fairfax and Charles Kemp. John valued the working relationship between him and his partner and tried to dissuade Charles from retiring. But he would not be dissuaded.

There were others who could step in. Two of John's sons, Charles Fairfax and James Reading Fairfax, would work for the company. Sadly,

Charles Fairfax died in 1863 when he was thrown from his horse, leaving James Reading Fairfax to continue the family business.

During these years, not only was there a strong vision with good leadership at the top and a clear division of labor between the partners, it was clear John Fairfax had created an environment where the employees truly felt respected and cared for. Times of crisis often reveal how strong the culture of an organization is. In a sense, the deposits you make in caring for your employees are tested at this time.

In 1841, not long after John Fairfax and Charles Kemp purchased the *Herald*, Australia suffered a severe depression. As we've seen, John was able to save the paper and all his employees' jobs by inspiring their trust in him to accept lower wages for a period of time.

Toward the end of 1842, when the worst of the economic downturn was over, John made this speech to his employees:

"In the relations between employer and employed there should always exist a true feeling of reciprocity. The one expects, and is entitled to receive, fair wages for his work; the other expects, and is entitled to receive, fair work for fair wages. These are the principles on which our firm intends to proceed."

John laid out clear principles of a good working relationship between him and the employees. As times were now better economically, his employees were entitled to be paid fair wages for the work they performed, and he, as the employer, was entitled to expect them to perform fair work for the wages they were paid. On his death in 1877, his employees referred to the "agreeable relations which always subsisted between ourselves and the late Mr. Fairfax," and described him, as noted earlier, as a "kind employer and a valued friend." John Fairfax was indeed a great organizational leader. He had assembled a great team and created an environment in which they flourished.

This positive environment at the *Herald* continued through the next generations. When James Reading Fairfax was about to depart Australia for an overseas trip in 1881, the employees gave him a beautiful, colored, illuminated commemorative scroll that spoke of the cordial relations that existed between him and everyone in the office—a demonstration of their respect for and goodwill toward him and of their earnest desire to welcome him back again. This sense of goodwill would continue to the next generation. On the occasion of the marriages of two of James Reading Fairfax's sons, James Oswald Fairfax and Geoffrey Fairfax, in 1892 and 1891 respectively, the employees gave James a beautiful silver coffee set and Geoffrey a splendid silver tea set.

Organizational Leadership Lessons from My Father

My father, as has been discussed, had a long tenure with the company, first as managing director and later, once it became a public company, as chairman. He tended to leave day-to-day management to Rupert Henderson, the general manager and later, managing director. During this time, the company grew to be a large, diversified media conglomerate. Over the years, my father had assembled a solid team of managers and editors that enabled the company to grow and stay true to its traditions.

What most strikes me about my father in the area of organizational leadership is his open-mindedness. He loved engaging in conversation with a range of people about politics, history, and religion, and he did not mind at all if people disagreed with him. This included the journalists at John Fairfax Ltd. If a journalist had a different point of view than my father, again, that was fine. Obviously, when it came to the editorial position of the *Sydney Morning Herald*, though, that was different. Disagreement was fine, but my father took a keen interest in the editorial position of the *Herald* and always ensured the paper's institutional stands aligned with his values, which he thought best for the issues facing the nation.

I believe this intellectual openness to engaging in discussions about politics and religion was one of my father's best qualities. He was not threatened by people of differing views or those who were different in general. I cannot ever recall him making a disparaging remark about anyone based on their background or point of view. Given the time when he grew up, in the early 1900s, when prejudice occurred in many areas (race, religion, and social class to name but a few), it is all the more remarkable. That is perhaps partly why he was so well respected by all who knew him and worked with him. To actively debate with someone is a strong indication that you respect them, as opposed to shunning debate because you think they are beneath you or you are so much smarter than they are. My father might not always agree with you, but he would be willing to listen and then give you the courtesy of an active debate.

The Great Team-Builder—Abraham Lincoln

We often think of Abraham Lincoln as the leader who abolished slavery and preserved the Union. We focus on his character and his refusal to back down from pursuing noble objectives. All this is true, but Lincoln was also a great organizational leader, a quality we do not always consider.

Doris Kearns Goodwin has written a great biography on Lincoln called *Team of Rivals*. In the book, Goodwin recounts how, once he became president, Lincoln assembled a team of people to help him govern, including some of those he had beaten in 1860 for the Republican Party's nomination for president. Lincoln's cabinet was made up of men very different in personality and skillset from himself and each other but also very able. He created an environment in which his cabinet members not only succeeded individually but also as a team. Over time, Lincoln's former rivals came to greatly admire the man who had defeated them at the Republican Convention.

There is a great contrast between how Lincoln was perceived when he won the Republican nomination for president in 1860 and how he was perceived at the end of his presidency (and by posterity). One newspaper at the time of the convention said the Republican Party had passed over "statesmen and able men" for a "fourth-rate lecturer, who cannot speak good grammar." But history has been kinder to Lincoln. Leo Tolstoy, the great Russian writer, said, ". . . the greatness of Napoleon, Caesar, or Washington is only moonlight by the sun of Lincoln." Tolstoy observed that, compared to other great leaders in history, Lincoln's supremacy was due to "his peculiar moral power and . . . the greatness of his character."

One of the keys to Lincoln's greatness was profound self-confidence. He was not one to boast; he simply knew who he was and what he wanted. He was his own man. This self-confidence was shown, in particular, in his decision to incorporate his main rivals for the Republican presidential nomination into his cabinet. These men included William Seward, a former governor of New York and U.S. senator. Lincoln named Seward, his main opponent, as secretary of state, the preeminent position in the cabinet. He also chose Salmon Chase, the former senator from Ohio and former governor of Ohio, as secretary of the treasury. Edward Bates of Missouri was named attorney general.

Bringing together such a diverse cabinet was not easy. Lincoln had to assuage the egos of confident and strong-willed men who, in the words of John Nicolay, Lincoln's secretary, were "sure to feel that the wrong man had been nominated." But Lincoln wanted the best cabinet possible, composed of men of different skills and personalities. He stated that "we needed the strongest men of the party in the Cabinet," and that he "had no right to deprive the country of their services."

This also meant he had to ignore slights he had suffered. One such slight involved Edwin Stanton, who became secretary of war (the equivalent to today's secretary of defense). Years earlier, Stanton had been hired as a lawyer on a case that originally was to be tried in Chicago, so Lincoln had been asked to be part of the legal team. But when the case was transferred to Cincinnati, no one told Lincoln his services were no longer needed. When Lincoln turned up in Cincinnati, Stanton completely ignored him and would not ask him to join the team for a meal, even though they were staying in the same hotel. But Lincoln was not a man to hold a grudge. He knew he needed someone with Stanton's drive, energy, and passion as his secretary of war.

Lincoln refused to be provoked by petty grievances or slights. He also had a deep self-awareness and was the most even-tempered of the men in his cabinet. He would defuse his own and others' stress by telling humorous stories. At six feet, four inches—which was very tall for the time—he was a big man in stature as well as in his nature.

He also had significant capacity for growth and a great ability to empathize. His ability to understand others' motives gave him political acumen that many did not always recognize at first. This served him well in navigating the political waters during the Civil War. He was not a military man and originally felt he should defer to the generals in the army. But over time, he educated himself in military affairs and strategy. After a succession of mostly unsuccessful appointments, he finally got it right when he named Ulysses S. Grant as the commanding general of the Army in 1864.

Lincoln won the trust of others by putting the cause above his own interests. For instance, in 1854, he was close to winning the votes to become a senator from Illinois. At the time, senators were elected by the state legislature. When it was clear that he was a few votes short, he transferred his votes to Congressman Lyman Trumbull. This ensured that someone who had similar views to Lincoln would be a senator representing Illinois. Trumbull and his allies never forgot Lincoln's support and magnanimity and were to play a key role in his obtaining the Republican presidential nomination in 1860.

He also won trust through his speaking, which, as one reporter noted, "went to the heart because it came from the heart." Lincoln understood that to win people over to your position, you have to appeal to their emotion. He said that to "win a man to your cause," you have to first reach his heart, "the great high road to his reason." His own conviction created conviction in others.

Lincoln also sought and took advice. Early in his presidency, he decided to make one officer a brigadier general. The officer replied that he had voted for Lincoln's opponent in the election but that he would loyally support Lincoln. If there were some act he could not support, the officer said he would resign his commission. Lincoln said that was fair but then added, "When you see me doing anything that for the good of the country ought not to be done, come and tell me so, and why you think so, and then perhaps you won't have any chance to resign your commission."

In particular, Lincoln's relationship with Stanton, his secretary of war, shows how two very different people can form a great team and how good Lincoln was at taking tough feedback. While Lincoln was open, Stanton was secretive. Lincoln was calm amid the storm, while Stanton would work himself up into a frenzy over events. But as Stanton's private secretary, A.E. Johnson, observed, ". . . yet no two men ever did or could work better in harness." They supplemented each other's nature—critical to navigating through and beyond crucible experiences.

Lincoln's stature grew during his presidency, and many who served with him grew to have a profound devotion and even love for the man. In March 1865, a little over a month before he was assassinated, Lincoln gave his second inaugural address upon being re-elected. This speech is commonly regarded as one of the greatest in American presidential history. The London *Spectator* referred to Lincoln's speech as "the noblest which any American President has yet uttered . . ."

It is remarkable to contrast what the members of Lincoln's cabinet and his key leaders thought of him when he won the Republican nomination for president with how they viewed him toward the end of his presidency and certainly after his death. Seward, Lincoln's key rival for the Republican nomination, said Lincoln was "the best and wisest man he [had] ever known." Attorney General Bates said Lincoln "comes very near being a perfect man." Union General Grant said of Lincoln, "He was incontestably the greatest man I ever knew." When Lincoln was assassinated in April 1865, these men of Lincoln's cabinet, who had once had such disdain for him, wept openly. On hearing the news of Lincoln' death, Seward reportedly had tears coursing down his cheeks. One observer said, "Stanton's grief was uncontrollable."

Abraham Lincoln is an excellent case study of a great organizational leader. He truly did find the right people and create an environment in which they could succeed. His cabinet shows the advantages of picking people with diverse skills, whose abilities are different from your own but that complement yours.

Appointing people to your team who are just like you and with whom you are comfortable is so overrated. If you are prepared to tolerate a little discomfort by working with a team comprised of people quite different from you, you can accomplish a lot. Such diversity in perspectives and temperaments is a key factor in being able to weather the storms that accompany crucibles—and emerging on the other side stronger and more able to continue bringing your vision to reality,

Lincoln's self-awareness and self-confidence enabled him to assemble a truly great cabinet, a cabinet of men who may have had large egos, but who were also very talented. A profoundly humble man, he was not threatened by greatness. All that mattered was the cause, saving the Union.

Personally, Lincoln truly lived his values. He represented what his team all hoped they themselves could be. He trusted his team and gave them a chance to succeed or fail. Even when some of his team did fail, he let them go with such dignity that their love and devotion only increased. As Tolstoy so insightfully pointed out, Lincoln's greatness as a leader was due to the greatness of his character—and this was the key to his success as an organizational leader.

Reflection Questions

1. Do you have the right people on your team? If not, what next steps should you take?

2. How have you created an environment for your team to succeed? If this is an area of weakness for you and your organization, what should you do about it?

3. How diverse is your team, in terms of background (race, gender, nationality, upbringing, life experience) as well as skills and personalities?

Chapter 15

MAKING IT ALL HAPPEN

A huge part of successful implementation as a leader is setting a compelling vision, hiring the right people, giving those people defined areas of responsibility, and then getting out of the way.

Ultimately, leadership comes down to implementation. It's great to have vision. It's important to inspire your team with a shared vision. And, you have to get the right people on board and create an environment for them to succeed. But you do have to get things done. Your vision has to become reality.

What are the key ingredients for implementation? They are the summation and culmination of the leadership principles we have been talking about. In essence, each area of leadership builds on itself.

But implementation is not easy. A huge part of successful implementation as a leader is setting a compelling vision, hiring the right people, giving those people defined areas of responsibility, and then getting out of the way. It also means coaching your team, giving them input (though more effectively in the form of questions, not commands), and holding them accountable to results to which you have agreed with them in advance.

Getting out of the Way

For many leaders, holding their team accountable for results is easier than getting out of the way. The desire to micromanage a team can be intoxicating. Hiring the right people and actually trusting them to do their jobs is one of the hardest areas of leadership. It is also one of the biggest reasons for poor implementation.

If your team thinks you do not have confidence in them and are continually second-guessing them, their motivation will decrease. They will take fewer risks and ask your opinion on decisions they know they should make but are afraid to. You will be increasingly drawn in to do more and more of your team's job. At that point, team morale decreases. Your productivity falls. People don't have a sense of autonomy or authority, and they don't feel you trust them. And you can be so focused on doing their work, you don't have enough time to do yours! Needless to say, in this scenario, the work ethic—not to mention the creativity—of your team is bound to fall. In short, one of the greatest keys to implementation is simply getting out of the way and letting people do their jobs.

> In short, one of the greatest keys to implementation is simply getting out of the way and letting people do their jobs.

From Good to Great

One of the most encouraging business books I have read is *Good to Great* by Jim Collins, one of the leading authors and thought leaders on the subject of what makes great companies so successful. He has taught at

Stanford Business School and has written other bestselling books such as *Built to Last* and *How the Mighty Fall*.

Good to Great, which has sold millions of copies, is about results. It looks at the key factors that took companies from being good companies to being great companies. Collins and his team started with the companies that appeared on the Fortune 500 in the U.S. between 1965 and 1995. They looked for companies that had fifteen-year cumulative stock returns at or below the general stock market, punctuated by a transition point, then cumulative returns at least three times the market over the next fifteen years.

Which were the companies that made the cut as good-to-great companies, and who were their CEOs? The list includes leaders such as Darwin Smith of Kimberly-Clark and Colman Mockler of Gillette. Oddly, these CEOs are not household names, nor are these companies you might automatically think of as some of the best led.

What accounts for the dramatic results these companies enjoyed? The CEOs who ran them are, in fact, remarkable individuals. But they are very different from the type of leaders who are often on the front covers of business magazines or invited on news shows. They blend extreme personal humility with intense professional will. Their ego is not for themselves but first and foremost for their companies, for the institution. These leaders are modest but have strong wills; they are humble yet fearless. Let's look more closely at these two leaders.

When Darwin Smith became CEO of Kimberly-Clark, a paper products company, its stock price had fallen markedly over the previous twenty years. Smith closed the company's coated paper mills because he felt this particular business was doomed to mediocrity and led Kimberly-Clark into the fire of the consumer paper products industry, taking on world-class competitors like Procter and Gamble. Many thought this was an unwise move. But twenty-five years later, Kimberly-Clark beat Procter and Gamble in most of the product categories in which they competed.

And who was Darwin Smith? He had previously been the company's mild-mannered in-house lawyer. He was not a well-known figure and did not put on airs of importance. He spent vacations rumbling around his farm, digging holes and moving rocks. But while Smith may have been shy and lacked pretense, he had a fierce resolve.

During the more than fifteen years that Colman Mockler was CEO of Gillette, a maker of razors and other personal care products, he faced multiple attacks by corporate raiders. Many executives, when faced with this situation, would have given in, pocketing millions of dollars from selling their own stock and cashing in on other benefits CEOs often receive when their companies are taken over. But not Colman Mockler. Like Smith, he was not one to take the easy path. He chose to fight off these attacks by reaching out to thousands of investors. He believed the company's huge investments in new technology would pay off.

Gillette's subsequent performance proved him right. Also, he may have been driven and worked hard, but he had balance in his life and a strong Christian faith. Even during the darkest days at Gillette, he did not significantly reduce the amount of time he spent with his family, and he maintained his worship practices.

In contrast to the egocentric styles of many other leaders, Smith and Mockler did not talk about themselves. They talked about the company and the contributions of other executives and would deflect any discussion of their own contribution. Impactful leaders, such as these two men, look out the window to apportion credit to factors outside themselves when things go well and look in the mirror to apportion responsibility when things go poorly.

It is interesting that when seeking to hire "the right people," the leaders Jim Collins wrote about in *Good to Great* placed greater weight on character attributes than on specific educational backgrounds, practical skills, specialized knowledge, or work experience. Their view was not that specific knowledge or skills are unimportant but that these traits are more teachable or learnable than character, work ethic, and values.

So what does all this have to do with implementation? The leaders in Jim Collins's book embody so many, if not all, of the qualities we have been discussing as necessary for great leadership. Many of them faced crucible experiences; for example, Darwin Smith had to cope with a cancer diagnosis two months after becoming CEO of Kimberly-Clark. Above all, they were authentic. They were themselves. They did not put on airs. They seemed to be grounded and have an inherent belief system, a core set of values that did not change and which was clearly displayed in their lives and their character.

These leaders did not always start with a vision for their organization before they attained their positions, but, by assembling a good executive team, they had a foundation to form a shared vision. Given the types of people they were and the teams they assembled, it seems clear these leaders listened to others and sought advice. They clearly understood and embodied the requirements for successful organizational leadership—hiring the right key people and creating an environment for them to succeed.

One key ingredient these leaders embodied that is vital to implementation was that they not only knew what the right thing to do was, they *did* it. They may have been modest and humble, but, as Collins puts it, they had fierce resolve, too. They had a history of making tough decisions, of putting their vision into practice. They not only got the right people on board; they also removed the wrong people. They made tough people decisions. They made tough business decisions.

I said that this book, *Good to Great,* was one of the most encouraging I have read. Why? When I think of the qualities a leader following the principles of Jesus would have, they are very much in line with the qualities the leaders in this book demonstrate. That was not Jim Collins's intention, but I found it encouraging. These were humble leaders who focused on their teams as the reason for their companies' success. It was not about ego; it was about the team and doing what was best for the institution. Following the principles of Jesus does not guarantee success in life or as a leader, but, all things being equal, it will make your chances of success greater.

The Family Legacy—Implementation

When I consider John Fairfax's career, he was clearly good at implementation and a strong manager. His crucible experiences made him stronger. He knew who he was. He had great faith and a good character. He had a clear vision, which those around him embraced. He listened and took advice. He hired great people and created an environment where they could succeed. Who wouldn't have wanted to work for John Fairfax? He was a man you could believe in. Just as Sarah Fairfax, in those dark days on the ship off the west coast of Australia, knew her husband would succeed, those who worked with him also knew he would succeed.

The last thing I would have thought my father was good at was implementation. He was *so* not a manager. That might not be entirely accurate but that was my impression growing up. In fact, many of the reasons I found myself in the situation I did in the years leading up to the takeover were ones that, fairly or unfairly, I blamed on my father. If the company had not gone public in the late 1950s, on his watch, the family would have had greater control, so the company would not have been vulnerable to takeover. Beginning in the late 1950s, my father also gave a significant portion of his shares to my older brother to avoid estate taxes. If he had not done this, other members of the family would not have been able to remove him as chairman temporarily in 1961 and then permanently in 1976.

But maybe it's not that simple when it comes to his implementation acumen. Crucible experiences in life did not destroy him. My father was authentic. He had a strong faith and character. He got on with things. My father may not have been a visionary, but he preserved the vision handed down to him and did help to inspire people within the company with that vision.

He probably did not listen that well or always take advice in some key areas of his life. He may not have been a managerial organizational leader, but he did help to preserve a climate where quality journalists were hired and editorial independence was maintained. He installed as the leading management figure a man who helped grow the company into a large, influential, diversified media conglomerate. So, funnily enough, overall, my father does not look that bad in terms of the key principles required for good implementation.

And what about me? Executives are often called on to make hundreds of decisions a day, some critical ones. You cannot fret over and second-guess every decision. You just have to decide, and if things do not work out, you then have to reassess and make new decisions. At one level, implementation is that simple. That is so not me. I make decisions slowly, agonizingly slow at times. I like to reflect, have alternatives, seek advice, and when I do make a decision, inevitably, I second-guess myself. *Was that the right decision? Did I hurt anyone's feelings? Is everyone okay? What were my motives? What are God's thoughts about this?* I cannot imagine having to make hundreds of decisions every day. The amount of fretting and second-guessing involved in leading a large corporation, given my personality, would stress me out to no end. I am not wired to be the manager who has to implement.

So how did I cope when I was the controlling shareholder for a large media company? Didn't I have to make hundreds of decisions every day? Yes and no. I brought in a terrific chief executive who had established a successful career at a large multinational company and had worked in many countries around the world. He was a great manager who had the skills to implement well. He took advice, got the information he needed, made decisions, did not second-guess himself, and if circumstances changed, he reassessed and took appropriate action. So, day-to-day management decisions were made by him, not by me.

I had to make decisions, often critical ones, but they were those of a bigger-picture strategic nature. They initially involved decisions around the takeover, and later, many were around the issue of refinancing. In key management decisions, I would, of course, give the chief executive my opinion. But basically, I was more in the role of strategic shareholder than implementing chief executive. At that stage, I was not as self-aware as I am now of my strengths and weaknesses, so I saw my unwillingness to be chief executive as more a function of my lack of experience rather than a poor fit with gifts and abilities, which is more how I see it now.

The lesson I take from this is, again, be who you are designed to be! I am not a manager. Not all of us are. Put yourself in a position to succeed. I enjoy advising, coaching, and writing. I have come to realize that one way I lead is through the questions I ask and how I facilitate a group of people. I have found that when you know who you are and put yourself in positions that cater to your strengths, success is not only possible but likely. You may not be the manager on the team, but your contribution to the team, ironically, can facilitate successful implementation.

Great Military Implementation—The Duke of Wellington and Lord Horatio Nelson

When you think of "implementation," you might think of great military commanders. They often make life-and-death decisions where the consequences of success and failure are huge. Their decisions can impact so many lives, even the fate of nations. Good implementation is critical.

Two of the greatest British military commanders in history were Lord Horatio Nelson and the Duke of Wellington. In fact, Nelson and Wellington have long been favorite heroes in my family. John Fairfax, his family, and friends used to play a parlor game in which they would list favorite authors, songs, and mottoes. They would also list their favorite heroes. John's was Nelson and his wife Sarah's was Wellington. The Duke of Wellington is considered, along with the Duke of Marlborough (the great British general of the early 1700s), to be one of Britain's greatest generals. It has been said that in the almost fifty battles he fought, he never lost one.

The Duke of Wellington

Arthur Wellesley, who became the first Duke of Wellington, was born in 1769 and grew up in Ireland as part of the Anglo-Irish ruling class of the day. He showed little interest in his military career, preferring to socialize and play the violin, until his proposal to a young woman of a more prosperous family was rejected. This happened to be the same year, 1793, that the French executed King Louis XVI.

Wellington was a curious mixture. He has been called a control freak who did not easily trust other people and who had to do everything himself. He had a tendency to keep battle plans close to the vest and tended not to keep his commanders fully informed. But he also had compassion. He seemed to genuinely hate war, deriving little pleasure from victory, and in general, conserved his troops, not wanting to waste lives unnecessarily. He was confident and had high self-esteem yet seemed to be modest and somewhat shy, embarrassed when his troops cheered him. He was also cool and calm even in the thick of battle. He inspired his troops by leadership and example, not by great speech making. Wellington was highly energetic and could cope with a huge workload. He was also extremely physically fit and an exceptional horseman. He could go for a long time without eating and, by the standards of the time, drank moderately.

Probably one of Wellington's greatest qualities as a leader was that he was a great strategist. He evaded the enemy with rapid maneuvers and avoided battles until certain of decisive victory. He almost always chose the battleground and would study the terrain carefully. He read avidly and widely and carefully studied Napoleon Bonaparte's master campaigns.

Wellington's finest and best-known victory was the Battle of Waterloo in 1815. In 1814, the Allied armies were at the gates of Paris, and

Napoleon was forced to abdicate as the emperor of France and accept exile on the island of Elba in the Mediterranean. Ten months later, in 1815, Napoleon escaped Elba with fewer than a thousand men. He was able to gather his former commanders and troops to him.

When Napoleon heard that the forces of Wellington, who commanded an Anglo-Allied army, and Field Marshal Gebhard Leberecht von Blucher, who commanded the Prussian army, were physically divided, he was on the march. He headed for Belgium, where Wellington and Blucher were. First, he went after Blucher, defeating him, and then he went after Wellington. He met the British forces at Waterloo.

Napoleon's commanders had reason to fear Wellington. Some of them had faced him in Spain and lost, even when their forces had outnumbered his. However, Napoleon underestimated Wellington. When one of his commanders warned him about Wellington, Napoleon snapped at him, "Because you have been beaten by Wellington you consider him a great general. And now I will tell you that he is a bad general, that the English are bad troops, and that this affair is nothing more serious than eating one's breakfast."

Wellington, on the other hand, did not underestimate Napoleon. He had little regard for the French emperor as a man but immense respect for his military ability. In 1814, a year before the Battle of Waterloo, when someone pointed out that Wellington had never been in combat on the same battlefield as Napoleon, he replied, "No, and I am very glad I never was. I would at any time rather have heard that a reinforcement of forty thousand men had joined the French army than he, Napoleon, had arrived to take command."

Wellington made a sober-minded appraisal of the task ahead of him. Unbeknown to Napoleon, he had carefully chosen the ground at Waterloo for its strategic advantages. He also knew the victory depended on the Prussians, whom Napoleon had earlier defeated, regrouping and joining him on the day of the battle.

There was one moment in the Battle of Waterloo that shows Wellington's leadership ability, his courage and his cool and calm demeanor under fire. The French attacked his position with their cavalry, and Wellington's infantry formed themselves into squares for protection. The French cavalry swirled around the British infantry. Wellington knew that so long as the British soldiers maintained their formations and fired as they had been told, they would be able to withstand the French charge.

Amid the frenzy of the battle, Wellington rode from square to square. He showed his troops that he was with them, and by his presence, he inspired them to hold firm. He projected an air of calm and showed his troops that, even at the height of battle, he was in control of the situation. The British infantry squares held against the French cavalry charge. Late in the day, Blucher's Prussians arrived on the battlefield, turning the tide against the French, leading to the decisive and final defeat of Napoleon.

But despite Wellington's calmness under fire and his brilliance as a strategist, he was not one who relished war. Afterward, he was not sorry to have fought his last battle. He made no secret of the fact that Waterloo was a "close-run thing," won by the narrowest of margins. Weighed down by the terrible loss of life and the loss of companions and his "poor soldiers," he said, "Believe me, nothing except a battle lost can be half so melancholy as a battle won."

What qualities of leadership did Wellington demonstrate? And, how did these qualities enable him to successfully implement his strategies? First of all, he was himself. He was authentic. He had high self-esteem and was self-confident, yet he had an accurate sense of his ability and did not overrate himself compared to others. He sought to learn as much as he could about his enemies, as he did with Napoleon.

Wellington's focus was never on the magnificence of his uniform or appearance. He inspired his troops with who he was and what he had achieved. He was able to admit mistakes and did not pass blame. He was calm under fire and not one to panic in a crisis.

Like all of us, Wellington was not a perfect leader. But while he may not have always confided his plans to his key commanders or sought their input, he did surround himself with people who became like family to him. When any were injured, he would become distraught. Wellington did prefer "ability with a title to ability without"—that is, able men with noble titles—in selecting his personal staff officers. However, he would send home those who did not perform. He respected people no matter their station or status and believed that with privilege comes responsibility.

He was also able to inspire great loyalty from his troops. Wellington's troops had the sense that their commander was a great one, who knew how to win with his great tactical sense, and who would not waste their lives unnecessarily. This kind of assurance breeds a sense of confidence between an army's troops and their leader. Wellington inspired his troops by his leadership—and by his example.

Lord Horatio Nelson

When I was six years old and living in England, my father took me to see HMS *Victory*, which is docked in Portsmouth. HMS *Victory* was Nelson's flagship during his last and most famous battle, the Battle of Trafalgar. My father also took me to see a recreation of the Battle of Trafalgar from the vantage point of the gun deck of HMS *Victory* at Madame Tussaud's Wax Museum in London. You could hear the guns fire and smell their smoke. It felt very realistic. Unfortunately, this exhibit is no longer on display.

Horatio Nelson, who had become Viscount Nelson by the time of his death in 1805, was born in Norfolk, in England, in 1758. The son of a village rector, he was born into a middle-class family. His mother died when he was nine years old, and Nelson joined the British navy when he was twelve. He rose rapidly in rank, becoming captain at the age of nineteen. He was not yet forty when he became a rear admiral.

It is hard to capture the full essence of Nelson's leadership, which has been called "effortless leadership." He did so well in many areas, bold almost to the point of recklessness. He was decisive. Once the plans were set, he exuded an air of calm confidence mixed with resoluteness. He consulted with his key officers, his captains, before battle to such an extent that his captains had no doubt as to what they had to do. He cared for his men—not just the captains but also the junior officers and the crew in general—and was kind and accessible. Nelson achieved success and promotion at a young age, but unlike some in the eighteenth century, he rose up through the ranks because of his ability, not because he was the son of nobility. He made it on merit, and his officers and crew knew that.

Nelson has been called a natural leader. He listened to those who served with him, and he was open and at ease with them, known for a sense of tolerance and an air of informality with junior officers. He instinctively understood that his ability to lead rested not on instilling fear but on winning the goodwill of his officers and crew. One key means that Nelson used to communicate with his officers, including the junior officers, was the dinner table. He also made sure his officers and crew were well fed.

In addition to being bold in his strategy and tactics, Nelson was physically brave. Before his eventual death in battle, he had previously lost an eye and an arm. He was not one to lead from the rear. He was also fearless in other ways, possessing what one admiral called "constitutional courage." He was perceived to have more nerve than any other officer in the British navy.

Nelson cared little for custom in an age when precedent was important. In contrast to the formal hierarchical nature of the British Navy at the time, where control was based on retaining rather than sharing information, his style of leadership was one of high communication with a consensual flavor. He encouraged informality and frankness of discussion, combined with self-confidence, quickness of mind, and a charming manner.

Nelson was admired for having sound judgment and being able to make instant decisions. He had this air of certainty and confidence. People follow and are attracted to leaders who represent certainty, especially in dangerous, fast-moving situations. During those nervous pre-battle hours, he had a surreal calmness about him. All this meant that his officers and crew admired him greatly. If the mark of a leader is how devoted their followers are and how willing they are to follow the leader into battle, then Nelson stands as one of the greatest military leaders in history.

Most of all, those who served with him loved him. One young officer said, "He was perhaps more generally beloved by all ranks of people under him than any Officer in the Service." The English poet Samuel Taylor Coleridge described Nelson's ability to get on with his officers and his crew this way: "Never was a commander so enthusiastically loved by men of all ranks, from the captain of the fleet to the youngest ship-boy."

Nelson was also effective in selecting officers of superior ability. Of the eleven captains of his ships in early 1805, eight were admirals by the end of the war in 1815, when Napoleon was finally defeated. Nelson called his captains his "Band of Brothers." This is a term from Shakespeare's play *Henry V,* which has subsequently been used in a book and mini-series about an American army unit during the Second World War.

There were two defining battles in Nelson's naval career, the Battle of the Nile and the Battle of Trafalgar. The first battle made Nelson a national hero. The second made him an icon for the ages.

During the lead-up to the Battle of the Nile in 1798, Nelson constantly consulted with his senior officers to make sure everyone was on the same page. As his fleet headed toward Alexandria in Egypt, Nelson called together his captains for conferences on his flagship. By the time Nelson's fleet reached Aboukir Bay near Alexandria, where the French fleet was anchored, his captains were so thoroughly acquainted with his battle plans that they almost did not need any further instructions. It was as if the fourteen captains of Nelson's fleet had one mind. One captain said, "Unanimity I believe greater never existed in any squadron."

Indeed, the Battle of the Nile illustrates so many of Nelson's great leadership qualities. His captains knew the man they were working for valued bold decisive action and would support their initiative. When Nelson saw an opportunity for a decisive victory against the French fleet at Aboukir Bay, he did not hesitate. At 5:30 p.m., he sent the fleet straight in. No anchoring to sea and waiting for the next day, giving the enemy time to prepare.

Just as Nelson was decisive in his strategy, sending the fleet straight in, so were his captains decisive and creative in their implementation. One of his captains made a brilliant decision to go on the landward side of the French fleet, which led several other British ships to do the same, catching the French by surprise. This was not Nelson's idea; indeed, he jokingly said that had he had the signal ready, he would have stopped it.

The Battle of Trafalgar in 1805 was the pinnacle of his career and a fine capstone to his life, immortalizing Nelson in the eyes of the British public and making him a hero for the ages. But in the couple of years leading up to his last and most famous battle, Nelson demonstrated abilities that had not always come to light before. During this time, he had to overcome a lack of resources, a lack of shore support, little strategic guidance, and almost no intelligence that did not come from his own efforts.

By this time, Napoleon and France almost completely dominated the western Mediterranean. This separated Nelson from supplies, information, and quick communication with Britain. In spite of these obstacles, he devised a system for obtaining and paying for provisions. He also used a network of British ministers and consuls to get better intelligence and to speed up communication with Britain. Nelson was creative in how he got the job done.

At a meeting of his captains before the Battle of Trafalgar, Nelson explained his tactics. The fleet was to be split into two parallel lines, one led by Nelson, the other led by another admiral under his command. These two lines would sail straight toward the enemy, with no firing until the ships were very close. The line led by Nelson would seem to be heading toward the head of the enemy's line but, at the last minute, would head toward the flagship located in the middle of the enemy's line. The other line of British ships would attack the rear of the enemy's line before the enemy ships could turn back.

Nelson's plan was brilliant and audacious. He aimed to get an overwhelming victory, and his captains all approved of the strategy. Nelson knew his plan would work—in part, because of the greater discipline of the British crews and the superiority of their guns and rate of fire. He knew the weaknesses of the enemy and the strengths of his own captains and ships. He would support his captains. Hence his oft-quoted phrase, "No captain can do very wrong if he places his Ship alongside that of an Enemy." Once the battle plan was laid out, he had the wisdom to delegate the implementation of the plan to his team.

On the morning of October 21, 1805, Nelson had twenty-seven ships, while his French counterpart, Admiral Villeneuve, had a combined French and Spanish fleet of thirty-three. Just before gunfire started, Nelson sent that famous signal to the fleet told to me as a boy by my father: "England expects that every man will do his duty." Originally, his message had read: "England *confides* (in other words, "is confident") that every man will do his duty." That message captured Nelson's heart. He knew and had total confidence that every officer and crewman would do his duty. However, since the signal needed to be sent by flags, it was apparently quicker to use the less evocative word "expects" than "confides."

At the height of the battle, as *Victory* passed through the line of enemy ships, Nelson was hit by a musket ball fired from one of the top masts of a nearby French ship. He knew instantly the wound was fatal. About three hours later, as he was nearing death, one of his captains congratulated him on his brilliant victory. Nelson thanked the captain, saying, "Now I am satisfied. Thank God, I have done my duty."

In January 1806, there was a two-day state funeral for Nelson in London. His coffin was placed on a funeral cart at the Admiralty, and the procession assembled in Hyde Park. One of the most touching things about the funeral procession was that, as Nelson's coffin passed by the crowds, there was complete silence. You could hear a pin drop. Without any instruction, everyone took off their hats. Such was the love, respect, and gratitude the British people felt towards Horatio Nelson. In 1843, a statue of Nelson was placed on a tall column in London's Trafalgar Square, named after his most famous victory, the one that took his life.

There is so much to appreciate and admire about Nelson. He was a self-made man. He had the calm confidence of someone who knew what he was doing. He always led from the front. His crew never doubted his physical bravery, as evidenced by Nelson losing an eye, an arm, and, ultimately, his life in battle. He was also a great seaman. He had sailed around the world, some 45,000 miles, by the time he was a lieutenant.

Not only was Nelson a great military leader, he was also a creative organizational leader. He knew the value of systems, as shown by his creation of a network of consuls in the Mediterranean to give him intelligence, and by his ability to obtain food and supplies under difficult circumstances.

Nelson is a superb example of a leader who was great at implementation. He was clearly authentic. He was likeable. He had character. He believed in bold, decisive action to defend his country against Napoleon, and that was how he lived. His leadership was forged in battles and in his naval service across the globe. Nelson made mistakes, but he learned from them. He grew to be a man who was calm, decisive, and kind—a man who listened, ensuring everyone was on the same page, and who delegated.

By the time of the Battle of Trafalgar, he was at the pinnacle of his leadership ability. If there was ever a leader whose team felt fully heard and listened to, it was Nelson. He was able to clearly impart his vision of how to succeed and defeat Napoleon's navy. He lived his vision of bold decisive action, delegating the implementation of that vision to equally bold and decisive captains, officers, and crew.

Nelson certainly hired the right leaders and created an environment that enabled them to succeed. The loyalty that he inspired in his officers and crew is the equal of or greater than any leader, certainly any military leader. Nelson had the ability to mold his officers and crew into a united force. He gave them clear direction as well as the sense that he had supreme confidence in them. No wonder Nelson is one of the greatest military commanders in history!

Reflection Questions

1. Do you give your team clear direction? If not, how can you ensure you do?
2. Do you empower your team or micromanage them?
3. What next steps will you take to mold your team into a united force committed to making your vision happen?

Chapter 16

STAYING THE COURSE

Great leaders keep going. They never give up. Their
crucible experiences are never the end of their stories.
They learn from and leverage them as opportunities
to write a new chapter of their stories.

Leadership is tough. You continually get knocked down. You have to
get up, again and again and again. And just when you think you cannot take it anymore, you get knocked down one more time.

Yet great leaders keep going. They never give up. They pick themselves
up, dust themselves off, and keep going. That is a huge part of what makes
great leaders great. When faced with obstacle after obstacle, adversity after
adversity, they just don't quit. Their crucible experiences are never the end
of their stories. They learn from and leverage them as opportunities to
write a new chapter of their stories.

When the Going Gets Tough . . .

The importance of perseverance to leadership may be self-evident, but let's look at it specifically in relation to the qualities of leadership we have been discussing—things like authenticity, faith, character, vision, listening to others, finding trustworthy advisers, and organizational leadership.

Consider the crucibles you've been through. Those good intentions you started out with—about being authentic, having faith beyond yourself, and demonstrating character—tend to fade. Tragically, cynicism and defeatism can begin to erode our lofty intentions. Maybe failures and setbacks make men and women in storybooks better people and better leaders, but life, sadly, is not a storybook.

How does the lack of perseverance affect authenticity? When you keep getting beaten up and knocked down, you may get tired of being yourself. Authenticity does not seem to be working. People don't seem to like who you are, the real you. So maybe, you think, you should put on a different persona. Maybe if you seemed more charismatic, more of a take-charge, take-no-prisoners sort of leader, you would look like those other leaders in the magazines or in the movies.

What about your faith? After getting knocked down so many times, it gets difficult, doesn't it, to believe some benevolent, wise force is in control? Your anchor doesn't seem to steady your boat, keep you grounded, as well as it used to.

What about your character? Where have integrity, humility, and doing the right thing gotten you? It seems like everyone else cuts corners. Nobody else you know follows the straight and narrow path. You are tired of getting beaten out by unscrupulous competitors. Why fight it? Why not just give in and start winning for a change?

And then there's vision. Maybe that vision you had feels like a pipe dream—totally impractical. What were you thinking? You had your head in the clouds, thinking the impossible was possible. Well, you have learned your lesson. The impossible is just that. Impossible.

As for shared vision, that's not going to happen. The people in your organization don't get it. They won't get it. They can't get it. They will never get it. Enough said.

As for listening, why bother? Everyone in your organization just gripes and complains anyway. Who wants to listen to that?

Why listen to advisers? All they do is tell you what you don't want to hear. And even if you do listen, what they tell you to do is all too hard and too painful. You wish they would just go away and keep their opinions to themselves.

Oh, and organizational leadership. Getting the right people on the bus and creating the right environment is another impossibility. The right people don't exist. All the people you know whine and complain and are never satisfied. How can you create an environment where such people can succeed?

Clearly it is time to go home, crawl under the covers, and give up.

. . . the Tough Get Going

Many of us have, at times, felt despair and despondency as leaders. We may feel we are inadequate or even hopeless at many (and sometimes all) of the above areas of leadership. The reality is that despair and discouragement are part of leadership. They are part of what leaders go through. That is where perseverance comes in.

There have been few leaders with more perseverance than Abraham Lincoln, whose leadership we've looked at previously. Lincoln suffered from what was at the time called melancholy, or what we might call depression today. He had reason to be depressed. Lincoln lost his mother when he was young, and he lost two sons when they were still children. He twice ran for the U.S. Senate, losing both times. When he did become president, no sooner was he inaugurated than most of the Southern states seceded. Yet he did not give up. He did not crawl under the covers. He doggedly kept on, making decisions and dealing with adversity after adversity. That is what great leaders do. No matter how hard the situation, they keep on going. They take one more step. They make one more decision.

Leadership can be lonely, especially in challenging times. You may have many advisers telling you what to do, but ultimately, they are just that, advisers. At the end of the day, only you can make the decision. Only *you* will have to take responsibility if things go wrong. It will certainly not be the advisers. That is why leadership is often such a lonely, isolated affair.

Leadership that perseveres is about making tough decisions again and again, decisions that may be right or wrong. Whether or not they are right, you can count on them being second-guessed by others and by those who comment on leadership decisions. It is always easier in hindsight, in the clear light of day, when you are not responsible for the consequences of the decision, to comment on whether a given decision someone else made was right or wrong. It is a lot harder in the heat of battle, when you have inadequate information, you may well not have had enough sleep, and you have to make a decision quickly. Great leaders are not immobilized by the thought that the previous decision may have not turned out so well. They move on, trying not to second-guess themselves but rather learning from any mistakes as they make the next gut-wrenching decision.

> Leadership can be lonely, especially in challenging times. You may have many advisers telling you what to do, but ultimately, they are just that, advisers. At the end of the day, only *you* can make the decision.

I think of what my great-great-grandfather, John Fairfax, had to persevere through as a leader—suffering major professional setbacks and personal tragedies. The personal challenges he faced were even more devastating than the business ones.

As I've mentioned, on the voyage out to Australia in 1838, his wife Sarah gave birth to a son, Richard. Soon after they arrived in Sydney, Richard died. John and Sarah had five children: Charles, Emily, James,

Richard, and Edward. Sadly, three of those children would die before John did.

In 1863, John's oldest son, Charles, was out riding when his horse shied and threw him off. Charles died a couple of days later. Then, in 1871, John was coming back from a wedding with his only daughter, Emily. The coachman was drunk and dropped the reins, which made the horses break into a gallop. John leaned out of the carriage to try to grab the reins but fell out. Emily tried to stop her father from falling but fell out, too, hitting her head on a stone. Emily died within the hour.

Sarah nursed her badly injured husband back to health. But as he recovered, Sarah's health declined, in part due to the strain of taking care of her husband. In 1875, she died. Two years later, in 1877, John Fairfax died, too.

While this succession of personal tragedies was devastating, John's faith did not waver. He persevered. On Charles's tombstone is inscribed this quote: "Boast not thyself of tomorrow for thou knowest not what a day may bring forth." John knew that God was in control. We may not understand His plan or why He allows tragedies to happen, like the death of three of John's children and his wife, but God is sovereign. John's faith helped him persevere.

John Fairfax's story reminded me why, in order to develop leadership that perseveres, it is so important to have faith, to believe in something that is eternal and is an anchor for the soul. Without such a touchstone and anchor, it is difficult to see how my great-great-grandfather could have kept going through all the professional challenges and personal tragedies he suffered.

Cultivating Perseverance

Perseverance is actually one of my stronger qualities. It's interesting; I find it much easier to write about my failures, my deficiencies. It may not always be pleasant, but I can write a detailed account of why I failed in a given area of leadership and what great leadership in this area actually looks like. To an extent, this is what I have done in this book. So it is a bit different writing about perseverance when it is actually one of my strengths.

I am not sure if perseverance generally comes from some external motivation or an internal source. For me, I believe it is both. Growing up, as I've noted, I did not want to disappoint my parents. I wanted to live up to their expectations that I would one day be in charge of John Fairfax Ltd. I wanted to live up to the sacred trust that had been passed down through the generations. That sacred trust required a mix of character, ability, and concern for the welfare of others. I desperately wanted to be worthy.

As I was growing up, I worked hard to make sure I was worthy. When I was six, we spent a year in England as my parents waited to adopt my younger brother and sister. During that trip, I spent more time with my father than I had before. That had an impact, as did the school I attended in England, which was more advanced (or so it seemed to me) than my school in Australia. When I returned to Australia, I did much better at school, and for the rest of my school days I was pretty much consistently in the top few, academically. I did not need to be told to apply myself. I knew what was at stake.

When I arrived at Oxford, once again the pressure was on. At Oxford, you can earn first-, second-, or third-class honors. My father, as brilliant as he was, got a second. I wanted to get a second, not what was called a "gentleman's third." (The stereotype of a gentleman's third is of a student who is focused on partying, having a good time, playing sports, and occasionally doing some studying in between.) My biggest fear was that I would not make it, that I would flunk out.

In those days, the way you found out whether you had passed, and what degree you had received, was to go to the Examination Schools building, where the results were posted on a board. Walking to the building, I was nervous. This was it. I looked at the results. When I saw that I had received second-class honors, I was filled with as much joy and pride as I can remember. Later, I was told by my professors that I had achieved a "good second," meaning in the upper end of second-class honors. I had accomplished what I had set out to achieve.

All my life to that point, I had wanted to prove myself to myself. This was a phrase that constantly came to mind. Truth be told, I wanted to prove myself to my parents and my family as well. But when you grow up with all the advantages, in an affluent family that can afford to give you a good private school education, that can afford to send you to Balliol College, Oxford, you have a lot to live up to. You have advantages that few others do. Part of my drive to do well at school, to persevere at Oxford, was to prove myself worthy of what I had been given and what I had been born into. I suppose it was almost a chip on my shoulder. I had a lot to prove, mainly to myself.

The next step in my journey to prepare myself to one day head the family business was to get a job in finance. My parents and I felt there was a lack of understanding of finance within the family involved with the company, and we thought it would be helpful if I had an understanding of corporate finance. If one day I was on the board of the company and another capital-raising scheme was proposed, for instance, this knowledge would enable me to push back against a plan that might dilute family control.

The interesting thing is that I did not have much interest in finance. I still don't. But off I went to seek a job in finance in New York. I was looking for a job, ideally, in investment banking, figuring those were the organizations most closely involved in capital raising and corporate finance. It was not easy to get a job in that area, especially as I was open about the fact that I only wanted to work in New York for three years before going to business school or returning to work for the family company in Australia. Obviously, that was not a good way to get a job, but I felt I should be upfront about it. (Needless to say, that made it difficult for me to get a job in investment banking.)

So, instead, I looked for a job in commercial banking. My parents had some contacts with Chase Manhattan Bank, which helped me get a job there. After nine months of hard work learning about credit analysis, I passed Chase's credit training program and was ready to become a commercial lending officer. At the time, Chase's corporate lending side was broken down by industry. There were divisions focusing on energy, mining, and other areas, such as media. For obvious reasons, I wanted to be part of the media lending division. Fortunately, I was able to get a job in that area. Chase was then a leader in media lending, and it was fun to work in a creative and innovative part of the bank. I ended up in a group whose clients were CBS, advertising agencies, and book publishing companies.

Toward the end of my time at Chase Manhattan Bank, which lasted for three years, I knew I wanted to go to business school. My thought, and my parents' thought, was that while a number of my family had gone to Oxford, none had received an MBA from Harvard Business School. I had actually applied right out of Oxford, but Harvard Business School typically liked you to work for at least two years before you applied. The school looks for diversity in background, including race, ethnicity, gender, international composition, as well as a diversity of business experience. While I did not get into Harvard Business School right out of Oxford, when I applied again, three years later, the fact that I had shown interest and had applied before probably did not hurt.

I remember in the first part of 1985 waiting to find out whether I had been accepted. One evening, when I came home from work and opened my mailbox, there was a letter from Harvard Business School. I walked up to my apartment, sat down, and opened the letter. I had been accepted! I was overjoyed. This would surely help show that I was worth something and deserved a chance to contribute to the family newspaper business and one day, run it. This was another key moment in my life—in proving myself to myself.

But now that I had been accepted, did I want to go there? I knew intellectually that it made sense. Having knowledge of business and finance would help my self-image and also help me seize the opportunity back at John Fairfax Ltd. that my parents wanted for me. But what did *I* want?

I remember telling a friend I wasn't sure I really wanted to go to Harvard Business School. I knew what my duty was, or I felt I did, but I was not sure whether it was something I truly desired to do. Did I *really* enjoy business and finance? I felt conflicted. My friend asked me what I wanted to do. I am not sure I gave him a clear answer. Needless to say, duty won out. Having gotten in, how could I not go? I summoned the perseverance I had mustered while at Oxford; after all, it had served me well then. So on to Harvard Business School, I went.

Taking It to a New Level

I have always loved the Boston area. My parents had friends who lived in a town outside of Boston, and during my time at Oxford, before going to work in New York, I had spent a couple of summers with them. The Boston area seemed to fit my personality. There was this New England sense of hard work, the so-called "Protestant work ethic." Those who were wealthy were understated. Ostentation was frowned on. Being generous with your money and being involved in philanthropy was expected. This fit the type of person I was and wanted to be.

In spite of my uncertainty about going, Harvard Business School was an amazing experience for me. While it was challenging, requiring long hours of work, it wasn't as intimidating as Oxford had been to me at eighteen. By the time I started at Harvard Business School, after graduating from Oxford and working at Chase, my self-confidence was a bit higher. Compared to Oxford, the other people at Harvard Business School seemed more normal. Where the other Philosophy, Politics, and Economics (PPE) students at Balliol all seemed to be Marxists of one variety or another, at Harvard Business School, by definition, the students were in favor of private enterprise and business.

All teaching at Harvard Business School was done using the case study method. (Even accounting, believe it or not, was taught using the case study method.) In this method, you get to study real situations of real companies. You are then asked to analyze the company's situation and make recommendations as to what the company should do. Over the two years of the course, you get to study companies in almost every conceivable situation, from almost every conceivable industry. It gives you an intimate knowledge of business that would normally take a lifetime to accumulate.

At the beginning of each class, the professor asks someone at random to open the case. You have to lay the groundwork for the class discussion by analyzing the situation the designated company is in. Not knowing who is going to be called to open makes the first few minutes pretty frightening, especially for those who may not have studied that case the night before.

In each of my classes, there were about ninety students. We sat in horseshoe-shaped classrooms, in an amphitheater-style setting, with the rear seats higher than the seats at the front. The first day, I walked into class ten to fifteen minutes ahead of time. I figured I wanted to get a good seat. What I did not know is that some had arrived an *hour* ahead of time to get the prime seats! (Since so much of the course grading was based on class participation, you wanted to make sure it was easy for the professor to see you.) The best seats were in the middle, a couple of rows from the front. I ended up sitting a row from the back, on the far right-hand side. The seat you had on your first day was where you sat for the rest of the year. It was not an auspicious beginning.

As soon as class began, and the student who had opened the case had finished speaking, a sea of hands went up. Getting a word in edgewise was a real challenge. Everyone seemed to be forceful, intelligent, and articulate. It was quite intimidating. Invariably, you had a list of three or four points you thought were good. By the time you were picked to say something, someone else had often run through all your good points.

Typically, you had three cases to prepare every evening, which often would take two to three hours each. It was rare to be finished preparing much before eleven or twelve o'clock at night. What helped is that

Harvard Business School encourages its students to form study groups. You spend some time analyzing the cases for the next day, and then compare your analysis with that of the other students in your study group. On any given night, there were some cases where my study group partners could help me, as they might have background in that industry or the type of discipline that was needed to analyze the case. With other cases, I might be able to help them.

After two years, I graduated. It was a grueling and stimulating experience that required a lot of perseverance. And, for better or for worse, after coming out of Harvard Business School you do tend to have some degree of self-confidence!

Putting My Perseverance to Work

During my time back in Australia over Christmas in 1986, I had started thinking that something might need to be done at John Fairfax Ltd. My father was dying, and it was clear to me that the mantle of defending the family company and restoring it to the ideals of its founder now fell to me, at least as far as my parents were concerned. After Christmas, I was back in Boston, finishing up my studies and looking forward to graduation, which would happen in June.

The first few months of 1987 were tough. My father died, and I went back for the funeral. I had studies to finish, and the weight of responsibility of what I would come back to in the family business was upon me. During those months, I talked in the evening to advisers in Australia about what I should do. This included making a takeover bid for the company.

By the time I arrived back in Australia, it seemed the die was cast. I decided to make the takeover bid. There were plans to make, but it seemed the decision had been made. I was determined to press on and restore the company to the ideals of its founder, and see that it was well managed. This was almost a crusade for me. It had been building as I grew up, having been influenced by my father's being thrown out as chairman of the company in 1976, by the abortive capital-raising schemes, and now by my father's recent death. I felt it was my duty to do something.

And so it went. The takeover was launched in late August 1987 and was completed by the end of the year. The other members of my family who were involved in the family business sold their shares to the takeover, and new management was brought in.

I had faced some grueling times before, but this was different. I was fighting to preserve a family legacy, a family ideal. The reality of being responsible for a large media company was quite different from the pressures of studying at Oxford or Harvard or working for a large bank. There were long days of discussion over refinancing, and management challenges. I made numerous trips to the U.S. for refinancing discussions and some business trips to Europe. I was doing what I could to preserve the company. But it was always going to be tough going.

This is where perseverance was somewhat of a challenge for me. The flipside of perseverance is stubbornness, and I do have both. Once I had decided that something needed to be done, there was no turning back. Failure was not an option, in the sense that I had to try. I might die trying, but I could not live with myself if I did not try. Such was my sense of duty.

So persevere I did, through years of refinancing and management difficulties and through a court case in which I was on the witness stand for a month. After the takeover had been completed, we felt we had not received good advice from the financial advisers who had been advising us. This led to a large and very public court case. It was one more challenge to deal with.

In hindsight, as I've acknowledged, I may not have been the right person for the job, given my personality, but I was going to give it my all. But by late 1990, the debt was too much and the company went into receivership. This phase of my life was over. I would have to begin a new chapter to move beyond what was a searing crucible experience.

Reflection Questions

1. Why is perseverance so important to your leadership?
2. What in your experience has helped you persevere? To what thoughts, people, or activities do you turn to help you stay the course?
3. What do you need to do to take your ability to persevere to the next level?

Chapter 17

MOVING BEYOND YOUR CRUCIBLE

Growing up, one of my dearest wishes was that I would never become world-weary. Somehow, through all the trials leading up to the takeover of the family media company, and all the trials since then, I have not become cynical, or lost hope.

The years after the company went into receivership in late 1990 were very difficult for me. Our first year in the United States, Gale and I lived in Chicago, where she had some family and had previously lived for a number of years. The winters in Chicago are very cold, and it is a big city.

I had some friends who were living in Annapolis, Maryland. We moved to Annapolis intending to stay for six months to a year, and we have never moved away. We have now lived in Annapolis for almost thirty years. Annapolis is a great, historic town on the Chesapeake Bay, with great restaurants and shops. It is the state capital of Maryland and the home of the U.S. Naval Academy. It has a mild climate (compared to Chicago, anyway).

While we may be settled now and enjoy our life in Annapolis, those first ten years or so after the company went bankrupt would test every ounce of perseverance I had. My whole life had been built around John Fairfax Ltd. and being prepared to one day run the company. Suddenly, that was over. My purpose in life had been to go into the family business and restore it to the ideals of the founder. That plan was gone. So, in a sense, my purpose in life was gone.

I suffered a tremendous sense of loss—my life's most devastating crucible. As I've mentioned before, I felt like a complete failure. I felt I had let my family down, particularly my father. I felt I had let God down. My perception was that I had helped end one hundred and fifty years of family history. I was devastated and depressed. Some have said that the company might have slipped from family control without the takeover I launched, since, as the generations go by, that tends to happen. That may be true. Again, we will never know. All I knew was that I had tried to save the family company, and I had failed.

Over the years, through the self-doubt and feeling pretty worthless, I tried to figure out what I should do. While I had skills and experience in finance, I was more interested in marketing and strategic planning. But I found it very difficult to get a job. There was not much need for a former media mogul who wanted an entry-level job in marketing somewhere. My résumé and experience were just too different—and not very linear. This inability to get a job did not help my self-esteem. The years went by. My wife was very supportive and understanding. We had a young family. By 1998, we had welcomed two sons and a daughter into our family.

Gradually, my self-esteem began to improve through a series of events. It was like clawing my way up a ladder after being deep down in a cold, dank mineshaft where it was tough to see any light. In 1996, I found a temporary job doing budget analysis for a firm in our area. When I went to the temp agency that placed people with financial and accounting expertise, I tested well on Microsoft Excel. While at Chase Manhattan Bank and at Harvard Business School, I had gained plenty of experience doing financial analysis on Excel. So that experience helped me get this temporary job, which led to a permanent job with an aviation services company in the area.

I spent six years working for this company. I started off doing financial analysis and ending up doing business and marketing analysis, as well as some strategic analysis. When I started at the company, I remember thinking that I must be the lowest-paid graduate in the history of Harvard Business School. This did not help my ego. Still, given how long it had taken me to get a job, I was happy for the work.

Coming out the Other Side

I worked hard and made sure I gave my all to whatever assignment was given me. I never thought the work was beneath me. Colossians 3:23 says, "Whatever you do, work at it with all your heart, as working for the Lord, not for human masters." The next verse says, ". . . it is the Lord Christ you are serving." Ephesians 6:7 says, "Serve wholeheartedly, as if you were serving the Lord, not people," while Colossians 3:17 says, "And whatever you do, whether in word or deed, do it all in the name of the Lord Jesus." These verses mean a lot to me. In some sense, they are the cornerstones of who I am.

It did not matter how I had come to be a financial analyst at an aviation services company. That was my position, and I was going to be faithful "as unto the Lord," as I performed the duties entrusted to me. My sense of duty in my new job was in some strange way similar to my sense of duty when I was in charge of John Fairfax Ltd. Of course, my scope of responsibilities at the aviation services company was a bit smaller.

Over the years, I got on well with my coworkers, receiving good performance reviews. I worked hard and did my best to help those I worked for accomplish and achieve their goals. Over time, I became proficient in the financial and business analysis that was needed. I was a key member of the teams I worked on. Of course, I was not very high up in the hierarchy of the company, but nonetheless, I felt I was doing a good job.

During much of that time, I am not sure whether the people around me knew about my days with the family newspaper company. I did not bring it up, and neither did they. I assumed Australia is a long way from the United States, and that, frankly, the people I worked with did not care that much. As long as I was getting the job done, that was all that mattered.

The years went by, and I seemed to be doing well at the aviation services company, in terms of the work I was doing and how I was regarded. Eventually, my self-esteem recovered to the point that I felt I was not using all the skills and abilities God had given me. It was not about thinking that working at the aviation services company, doing financial and business analysis, was beneath me. It was that God had given me certain gifts and abilities, and I was not fully utilizing them. I was ready for another step in moving past my crucible.

So in 2003, I went to see an executive coach who conducted assessments for people in the mid-stage of their careers. The results that came back, and the coaching sessions we had to help me understand those results, were extremely enlightening. She highlighted my qualities of being reflective, analytical, and a good listener and pointed out that it was a good profile for becoming an executive coach myself. I did not know much about executive coaching, so I began to research it.

I left the aviation services company to learn more, and eventually, did become an executive coach. The woman who introduced me to the practice of executive coaching recommended I attend the upcoming annual conference of the International Coaching Federation (ICF). This was in Denver in November 2003. There were thousands of coaches there from all over the United States, as well as some from different parts of the world. I felt I was among like-minded people. They were good listeners. I listened to them. They listened to me. Everyone seemed to be curious and inquisitive. I found out about some coach training programs. I completed my coach training and became a certified ICF coach.

Becoming an executive coach was another key step on the journey to having a greater sense of self-worth and to being more who I was designed to be. Over time, I came to coach leaders who wanted to ensure their visions became reality. I was drawn to executive coaching around organizational leadership.

My coaching and ability to listen well and ask good questions led to invitations to be on the elder board of my church and the board of my children's school. I spent considerable time in both institutions on strategic planning and governance. Being an adviser on boards was a good fit for my skills and experience and for my personality as a reflective adviser.

But one of the key breakthroughs in my journey to move beyond losing the family media company came from a message I gave in my church in 2008. As I mentioned in the introduction, my pastor asked me if I would give a seven-minute talk during his message about the life of David. He was looking for an illustration of a righteous person falsely persecuted. I told him that I didn't see myself that way, as I had brought a lot of my challenges on myself. But while I did not consider myself a compelling public speaker, if it could help people, I was willing to share my story.

Somehow, despite the fact that there were not any other failed media moguls in the congregation, my story and the lessons learned that I shared seemed to strike a chord. Weeks, even months, after, people came up to me and explained how my story had helped them. Apparently, my authenticity and vulnerability in that message helped others see hope and the potential for healing from their own failures and setbacks. They may not have lost a 150-year-old family empire at a cost of $2.25 billion, but they had lost something. It was as painful to them as my loss was to me. The details of our tragedies might have been different, but the basic emotions of feeling lost, defeated, and even worthless turned out to be more universal than I imagined.

That was where my desire to write this book was born. Writing about my story has not been easy and in fact, has been painful, recounting the mistakes and poor assumptions I have made. But I felt that if sharing my story in a lessons-learned format could help people, then it was worth it. It was by starting to write this book that my journey with Crucible Leadership began.

Today, I am blessed to have an amazing team that has helped me expand Crucible Leadership beyond a book to include a podcast (*Beyond the Crucible*), media appearances, blogs, social media posts, and an assessment—all focused on helping leaders of all levels get beyond their crucible experiences and lead lives of significance.

It has been a tough road. But, as much as I ever have in my life, I now feel I am using my skills and abilities for God's glory, which is a huge part of my purpose in life. Also, as much as I ever have, I feel I am being authentically who I am. I am not fighting my divine design. I am living in light of it. I am doing things that are in keeping with who I am. I am putting myself in situations where my reflective philosophical ability, my advisory ability, and my writing ability are strengths. And, perhaps most importantly, the work I am engaged in is focused on helping others, pointing them toward a life of true significance. I'm using my skills not just to make money but to live in the intentional service of others. (Not to sound too Pollyanna-ish about it but to make the world a better place!)

Not coincidentally, I feel I am receiving more respect than I used to. That is not because I am more or less worthy of respect than I used to be; it is because when we are using more of our skills and abilities, others see a side of us they respect. They see us doing something and doing it well. That engenders respect—and self-respect, as well.

A Voyage of Self-Discovery

It has taken years to get to the point where I am now. It has been a voyage of discovery to find out who I am and to live in light of it. It has taken years to throw off the weight of others' expectations and to only live in light of who God made me to be, to cast a vision all my own and make that vision a reality.

Growing up, one of my dearest wishes was that I would never become world-weary. Somehow, through all the trials leading up to the takeover of the family media company, and all the trials since then, I have not become cynical or lost hope. I have been a bit battered and bruised, but I have persevered. How has this been possible, with all that has happened? It has only been through God's strength.

There are some great Scriptures on perseverance that have encouraged me along the way. These are two of my favorites:

> It has taken years to get to the point where I am now. It has been a voyage of discovery to find out who I am and to live in light of it.

Consider it pure joy, my brothers and sisters, whenever you face trials of many kinds, because you know that the testing of your faith develops perseverance. Let perseverance finish its work so that you may be mature and complete, not lacking anything.

—James 1:2–4

Blessed is the one who perseveres under trial because, having stood the test, that person will receive the crown of life that the Lord has promised to those who love him.

—James 1:12

These Scriptures talk of how trials test our faith and give us the opportunity to persevere, which helps us become more mature. There is a refining fire—the crucible—that trials offer.

I may not consider it "pure joy," when I consider all the trials I have been through, but I absolutely believe that God has a plan for my life, and I try to allow the trials I have been through make me a better person and try, in my own way, to help others. This thought that God did not mean me to be in charge of the family media company but has another purpose for my life has been a source of immense comfort.

The belief that God does not make mistakes has been a huge and helpful thought for me. Without my faith, and the thought that God is in control, there is no way I would have persevered through the trails I have been through. So long as I put my faith in God, and realize that my significance is not in what I can do for God but in what He did for me by sending His Son to die on the cross for my sins, I can put the things of the past behind me, persevere, and move on to live the rest of my story as God intended.

A Man Who Persevered—David

David is one of the great figures of the Bible, and a great biblical example of a man of perseverance. I also discussed his life when sharing lessons about authenticity. The Scriptures call him a man after God's own heart.

David was the youngest son in his family and a shepherd boy when he was anointed as the future king by the prophet Samuel. From an early age, he showed his bravery. He killed wild beasts, such as a lion and a bear, when they attacked the flock of sheep he was protecting.

When the Philistines were gathered for war against the Israelites, one of the Philistines, Goliath—who was, as the Bible records, nine feet tall—challenged the Israelites to send out their champion for a duel. Whichever of the two champions won, his side would win the day. On hearing Goliath's challenge, King Saul and the Israelites were terrified. David, still a shepherd boy, went to Saul and said he would challenge Goliath. As is now a famous story, David felled the mighty Goliath with his slingshot.

From that time on, David was a hero of the people. However, with each success he achieved, Saul's jealousy toward him grew. It did not help when the people sang songs: "Saul has slain his thousands, and David his tens of thousands." (1 Samuel 18:7) So great was Saul's jealousy that he tried to kill David more than once. David had to flee.

Twice while Saul pursued him, David spared the king's life. Once, David was hiding in a cave, which Saul happened to enter. Though he could have killed him then and there, David merely (and secretly) cut off a corner of Saul's robe. The second time, while Saul and his army were sleeping, David and one of his men crept into Saul's camp and took the spear and the water jug near Saul's head, sparing the king's life once again. Each time, Saul was conscience-stricken about how he had treated David. But each time, his contrition was short-lived. Certainly, David did not trust Saul to stop pursuing him.

Eventually, Saul died in a battle with the Philistines, and David became king of Israel. Over time, through a series of conquests, David's kingdom expanded. But, when you are at the height of success, it can be dangerous. David was tempted when he saw a beautiful woman bathing. He found out that the woman was Bathsheba, who was married to one of David's own commanders, Uriah. David wanted Bathsheba for himself, so he knowingly arranged for Uriah to die in battle, telling another commander, "Put Uriah out in front where the fighting is fiercest. Then withdraw from him so he will be struck down and die." (2 Samuel 11:15)

David then took Bathsheba as his wife, and they had a son together. The prophet Nathan confronted David with his sin. David was contrite, confessing, "I have sinned against the Lord." (2 Samuel 12:13) Nathan said that while the Lord would forgive David's sin, David and Bathsheba's son would die. (While God may forgive us our sins, there are consequences.) David and Bathsheba later had another son, Solomon, who would become king after David.

After this, there were some difficult years ahead. David's son, Absalom, plotted against him, and David was forced to flee. Absalom died when his army met David's army. David was then back in control of his kingdom.

David achieved many things in his forty-year reign. When he became king, Israel was not a strong power, and its territory was under threat from the Philistines. By the time he left power, Israel was a mighty nation. David was a courageous man and a great warrior. He had a core of loyal and devoted fighters, called David's Mighty Men, numbering around thirty.

But not only was he a brave and courageous warrior, and a very successful one at that, David was a man of conscience. Yes, he was flawed. Having Uriah killed to marry Bathsheba was no small transgression. Yet each time he sinned, he was contrite. He realized that when we sin, we actually sin against the Lord, not just against other people.

Learning from David's Example

What does David's story have to do with moving beyond a crucible moment? A large part of continuing to press ahead beyond crucibles and persevering lies in not becoming world-weary and not being bitter or vindictive. It is staying true to your values and trying to do the right thing, even when you have blown it or suffered loss.

Just because others may lie and cheat and betray, it does not mean you have to do it. Just because you might have betrayed someone once, as David did in having Uriah killed and then marrying his widow, Bathsheba, does not mean that you can't repent and try to stay true to your values from then on.

David showed remarkable perseverance over the course of his life. He was brave and courageous and a successful warrior. He was a man of integrity and conscience who tried to do the right thing. When confronted with his sin, he confessed it. He tried to live a life the Lord would be proud of. When others betrayed him, including Saul or his own son, Absalom, he did not rejoice in their deaths, he deeply mourned.

Listen to the words of David after his forces defeated Absalom's forces and Absalom was killed: "The king [David] was shaken. He went up to the room over the gateway and wept. As he went, he said: 'O my son Absalom! My son, my son Absalom! If only I had died instead of you—O Absalom, my son, my son!' " (2 Samuel 18:33) On killing a rival and solidifying power, many a leader would rejoice. Even if the rival were a son, they might say, "He betrayed me and rebelled against me. I did nothing to him. Why should I mourn his death?" But not David. He was a man of integrity and forgiveness, who did not hold a grudge.

Despite making a number of mistakes, some of them large ones, David held onto his faith and his character. Despite his flaws, he is considered a great and good leader.

Leading well and not giving up and becoming a cynical, hollow shell amid the crucibles of life and leadership—whether inflicted by others or yourself—requires great focus on leading and living with significance in mind. Such a man was David.

Never Giving Up—Winston Churchill

Winston Churchill was one of the great leaders of the twentieth century. Indeed, Churchill is one of the great leaders in history. His life is also an outstanding example of not allowing mistakes and setbacks to be the end of our stories. He endured many challenges, yet these trials never held him back. He truly did pick himself up, dust himself off, and start all over again. What accounts for Churchill's remarkable ability to press on in pursuit of a life of significance?

Winston Churchill was the son of Lord Randolph Churchill, a prominent Conservative politician in Britain in the late 1800s, and Lady Randolph Churchill (formerly Jenny Jerome), an American heiress. His grandfather was the Duke of Marlborough.

Churchill did not have a close relationship with his parents growing up, and his father was remote. Young Winston did not do well in school and had a poor academic record. But his love of words began while he was at the prestigious English private school Harrow.

Before his political career, he made a name for himself as a war correspondent in Cuba, India, and Sudan, and during the Boer War in South Africa. While Churchill had had his adventures in colonial wars, he was not blind to the horrors of war. He was alarmed by the "composure" or "glibness" with which some members of parliament talked of a possible European war in the years leading up to the First World War.

Churchill won the parliamentary seat of Oldham in 1900 as a member of the Conservative Party. The next turning point in his political career occurred in 1904, when he crossed over and later won Oldham as a member of the Liberal Party in the 1906 election. His crossing over caused a furor. But Churchill was not a party man. The years before the First World War were a happy and productive time for him as he pushed through legislation to help the poor, the unemployed, and the lower-paid working class. In 1911, the Liberal prime minister, H.H. Asquith, appointed Churchill First Lord of the Admiralty. Churchill devoted his energies to building up the Royal Navy.

The first significant political low point in Churchill's life occurred in 1915 when he was removed from the Admiralty over the disastrous Battle of Gallipoli in Turkey. Ironically, while the Gallipoli campaign was a terrible defeat, it features prominently in Australian history. The Australian and New Zealand Army Corps (ANZAC), who were part of the Allied forces, fought valiantly in defeat. The heroism of the Anzacs, as they came to be called, is long remembered in Australia and New Zealand.

In 1922, Churchill was at another low point when he lost his seat in parliament. During the campaign, he was rushed to the hospital for an appendix operation. Churchill later said, "In the twinkling of an eye, I found myself without an office, without a seat, without a party, and without an appendix." The Liberal Party was on the decline in the 1920s as left-of-center voters turned to the British Labour Party as the main opposition to the Conservative Party. It was clear that Churchill's only political future was with the Conservative Party, which he had left in 1904. In 1925, he formally rejoined.

The Conservative Prime Minister, Stanley Baldwin, made Churchill the chancellor of the exchequer, commenting, "I would rather have him making private trouble in the Cabinet than public trouble outside of it." Churchill was overjoyed, commenting that he still had his father's robes. (Lord Randolph Churchill was briefly chancellor of the exchequer in the 1880s.)

The 1920s were a splendid time in Churchill's life. Baldwin called him "the star of the government." However, in 1929, the toughest period of his political life began. These were the ten years in which he was out of political office and out of favor with the leadership of the Conservative Party. This period in Churchill's life has come to be called his "Wilderness Years." During the 1929 stock market crash, Churchill lost a considerable amount of money. Perhaps his confidence was shaken. He began to make political mistakes. He was mired in a crucible experience.

At the time, the new Labour Government of Ramsay MacDonald, together with Stanley Baldwin and his Conservatives, were united in backing gradual progression to self-rule for India. While Churchill played a key role in the creation of the state of Israel and in the independence of Ireland from Britain, here, for some reason, he was on the wrong side of history. He fought a campaign across Britain against self-rule for India. His activities were seen as part of an effort to replace Baldwin as the Conservatives' leader.

Then, in 1931, while in New York City, Churchill looked the wrong way before crossing the road and was knocked down by a fast car. He was quite badly injured. He had lost a lot of money in the stock market crash, he had lost his position in the Conservative Party, and he had been badly hurt—three considerable blows. And the toughest period of his life was still ahead of him. Adolf Hitler was on the rise, capturing power in Germany in 1933, while Churchill was out of power. He could only rail from the sidelines against the pacifism that took hold of Britain.

Churchill's reputation began to rise again over the British government's handling of the German invasion of Czechoslovakia. In 1938, Austria was annexed by Germany. Later, in 1938, Neville Chamberlain, the then British Conservative prime minister, signed the Munich Agreement, allowing Germany to take over the Sudetenland, which was the German-speaking part of Czechoslovakia. However, the Sudetenland included all the elaborate border defenses of Czechoslovakia, meaning that Hitler would be able to walk in and take over the rest of the country.

In 1938, Churchill denounced the Munich Agreement and prophesied that, within months, "the Czechs will be engulfed by the Nazi regime." Churchill said that after dealing with the countries of Central and Eastern Europe, Hitler would then "begin to look westward." Churchill warned that the Munich Agreement was "only the beginning of the reckoning. This is only the first sip, the first foretaste of a bitter cup which will be proffered to us year by year unless by a supreme recovery of moral health and martial vigor, we arise and take our stand for freedom as in the olden time." He was, of course, right about this. With gathering speed, opinion swung against the Munich Agreement and Chamberlain's appeasement policy. In March 1939, Germany invaded the rest of Czechoslovakia and annexed it. In September 1939, Hitler invaded Poland. Due to the fact that Britain and France had guaranteed Poland against invasion, they declared war.

Churchill was now invited to accept his old post of First Lord of the Admiralty, along with a seat in the war cabinet. He was once again back in the thick of things. In May 1940, Chamberlain resigned and Churchill was asked to become prime minister. As he was forming a cabinet, the Germans had begun their decisive campaign against France.

With the backing of the political parties, Churchill held a fair amount of power in his hands. Yet, he believed strongly in parliament and observing appropriate procedural rules. He also had a great deal of respect among the military leaders. He was seen as having been right about Hitler and the dangers of pacifism in the face of aggression. He was overwhelmingly admired and even loved, and perhaps a little feared, within the military. Unlike Hitler, Churchill did not interfere with his military commanders. He respected them. While Churchill and the cabinet made overall strategic decisions, he left the execution of those decisions up to the commanders.

Churchill took power during a desperate time, when Britain yearned for courageous and inspired leadership. Just after he became prime minister in May 1940, he said, "I would say to the House [of Parliament], as I said to those who have joined the government, 'I have nothing to offer but blood, toil, tears and sweat.'" In the same speech, he said his aim was simple and clear: "Victory at all costs, victory in spite of all terror, victory, however long and hard the road may be; for without victory there is no survival."

Churchill set a personal example of ferocious and productive activity. He worked a sixteen-hour day and expected everyone else to do likewise. He had teams of what he called his "dictation secretaries." He worked them very long hours and could be sometimes short-tempered. But they all loved him and were proud to work with him.

Another key factor in his wartime leadership was his oratory. After 330,000 Allied troops were evacuated from the French coastal town of Dunkirk in late May and early June 1940, as German forces were sweeping through France, Churchill gave this famous speech: "We shall not flag or fail. We shall fight in France, we shall fight on the seas and oceans, we shall fight with growing confidence and growing strength in the air, we shall defend our island, whatever the cost may be, we shall fight on the beaches, we shall fight on the landing grounds, we shall fight in the fields and in the streets, we shall fight in the hills. We shall never surrender." After France surrendered in June 1940, Churchill gave another memorable speech: "Let us therefore brace ourselves to our duty and so bear ourselves that if the British Empire and its Commonwealth last for a thousand years men will still say, 'This was their finest hour.'" In late August 1940, when Churchill sensed victory in the Battle of Britain, when the might of the German air force, the Luftwaffe, took on the Royal Air Force, Churchill uttered these now famous words referring to the heroism of the Royal Air Force: "Never in the field of human conflict was so much owed by so many to so few."

However, in July 1945, a few months after Germany surrendered, Churchill suffered what could have been a huge blow. Labour won the election in a landslide, promising a time of peace, including full employment and national health care. It would have been easy for Churchill to feel bitter at a seemingly ungrateful electorate for throwing him out of office. But that is not the way he thought. He got on with life. He sought to alert the world and particularly the United States to the dangers of the Soviet Union, warning, "an iron curtain has descended across the Continent."

Churchill died in 1965. As you might expect, his last words were memorable: "The journey has been enjoyable and well worth making—once!"

Churchill's ability to survive politically, to bounce back, is awe-inspiring. He had moments when he was down, yet this never seemed to hold him back for long. He would always go back into the fray. His attitude reminds me of the line from Shakespeare's *Henry V,* when King Henry is urging his troops to once again attack the gap in the wall of the city of Harfleur in France: "Once more unto the breach, dear friends, once more." That is pure Churchill. He would always have another go.

There are several keys to his ability to persevere and bounce back from crucible after crucible. One was his ability to relax and rejuvenate. While Churchill could work very hard over long periods, he also took time to relax and pursue outside interests. One distraction from the cares of work and duty was painting. Over the course of his life, he painted more than five hundred canvases.

One place that really helped him rejuvenate and recover was Chartwell, which he purchased in 1922 in the county of Kent, about twenty-five miles from Parliament, to function as his country house. He spent many happy times there and would often hold parties there. He tinkered in the garden and even built garden walls.

Another key to his ability to bounce back and carry on was a happy marriage and family life. At a time when marriages among the ruling classes were not always happy, Churchill dearly loved his wife, Clementine, whom he called Clemmie. (Having a life partner who believes in you gives you a much greater ability to carry on.)

One great outlet for his energies was writing. During those times when he was out of power, writing provided a much-needed outlet and a source of income. In fact, writing was his main source of income during his life. He wrote thousands of articles and more than forty books. His books included a record of the First World War called *The World Crisis*, which did very well. In 1945, after his electoral defeat, Churchill began writing his *War Memoirs* about the Second World War. These were incredibly successful. In 1953, he was awarded the Nobel Prize for Literature. At the time, it was calculated that the volumes of Churchill's *War Memoirs* had already sold six million copies in English and had been serialized in fifty newspapers in forty countries.

Another key to his ability to bounce back from setbacks was his magnanimous and forgiving nature. As we've seen, Churchill had not been that close to his father, but in 1906, he wrote a generous book about him. A cousin of Churchill's summed up the book this way: "Few fathers have done less for their sons. Few sons have done more for their fathers."

Churchill was always kind to people, including political opponents. Late in 1940, when former prime minister Neville Chamberlain was ill with terminal cancer, Churchill kept him in the government and would call him to tell him of Allied victories. During the Second World War, Churchill would also take Stanley Baldwin, another former prime minister and rival, to lunch. These were two men whose policies Churchill had, at times, railed against and who had caused him much angst.

Winston Churchill was ambitious. He aimed high. He worked hard, but he also allowed time to relax and pursue creative and restorative outlets. He never allowed mistakes—and he made a number of them—to keep him down. He always moved forward after facing a crucible experience. He never spent much energy on recrimination, shifting the blame, or revenge. As one writer has said, "the absence of hatred left plenty of room for joy in Churchill's life." Hatred, bitterness, and holding onto grudges can be very draining. Like Abraham Lincoln, Churchill forgave and made up.

Churchill's success in life, in the broadest sense, is the stuff of legend. He was not afraid to dare greatly. He was a doer of deeds. He devoted himself fully to the political fray and the causes he championed. He was always in the arena, and he was often knocked down and bloodied. But he always got up and would indeed spend himself for a worthy cause. Churchill is the very epitome of perseverance.

Reflection Questions

1. What's one thing you can do today to keep persevering as you bounce back from your crucible?
2. What negative emotions do you need to confront to help you heal and get beyond your crucible?
3. What does a life of significance look like for you?

CONCLUSION

FROM CRUCIBLE TO SIGNIFICANCE

While this book is about leadership principles, it is also a collection of parables, reflections, and lessons—an assortment of stories that illustrate the leadership principles I hope to highlight. A significant part of this book is about my family and its involvement in John Fairfax Ltd. In particular, it discusses my own life and my role in the family media company, as well as John Fairfax and my father.

When discussing myself in this book there is an irony. I have never been one to talk about myself much. Over the years, I have given few interviews. I would rather listen to someone else talk about his or her life than go on incessantly about myself. Yet, I felt that if I were to talk about leadership, I had to talk about my experiences in John Fairfax Ltd. and my life in general. That is not because I feel that I am such a great leader. In fact—at least in my John Fairfax Ltd. days—I feel that my leadership left much to be desired. But these experiences have all taught me a lot about leadership and life itself. They, together with lessons from my family and from leaders that have come before us, have formed the core of my thoughts about Crucible Leadership.

It is my hope that this book inspires leaders and those who feel called to lead and be better leaders. My hope is that leaders will read this book and stop trying to be who they are not and instead, try to be who they are and who they were designed to be. It is my hope that leaders will have the courage to be people of faith, be it faith in Christ or in some other transcendent way of thought. My hope is that leaders will be people of character and that the crucible experiences they have gone through and will go through will make them better leaders.

It is my hope that leaders will have huge visions that inspire people and nations to be better than they ever thought possible. It is also my hope that large groups of people will be inspired to share that vision. My hope is that leaders will hire the right people and create an environment where these people will succeed and thrive. I would like to see these visions become implemented, to see these visions become reality. Because life is not easy and leaders do get knocked down, I would like to see these leaders persevere and pick themselves up, dust themselves off and start all over again—and, in their new endeavors, aim their lives at a life of significance, a life on purpose that is focused on serving others.

This is a book of lessons on leadership and life. That's because the lessons I have learned, through my own experiences and the experiences of others, are more than just lessons for leadership. I believe they are lessons for life itself. You don't have to see yourself as a leader of an organization to feel that these lessons could be valuable to you.

I believe all those who take a stand and want to make a difference in the world are leaders. Those who inspire others to make a difference are leaders. They may or may not have a formal leadership title. They may or may not be well known. Being a leader is largely a matter of the will. It is a choice. To lead is to take charge of your life and your decisions.

My heart's desire is that every person in every nation be led by a great leader: a leader who is authentic, a person who believes there is a higher purpose, a person of good character, who has integrity and humility, a person who has a huge vision and wants to change the world, a person who will inspire all those around them with a shared vision, a person who will know how to hire the right people and create an environment for them to succeed, a person who can implement a vision, and finally, a person who can persevere and emerge wiser, stronger, and more focused on living a life on purpose, a life of significance, through the inevitable crucible experiences that come along for all of us.

Leaders such as this can have a huge impact in making the world a better place. I hope this book inspires you to become such a leader . . . and sets you on a path to living a life of significance.

RESOURCES TO HELP YOU MOVE BEYOND YOUR CRUCIBLE

Throughout the book, you may have noticed I emphasized the great value of asking questions in your life and leadership. It occurs to me, now that you've finished the book, that you may have an important question on your mind: *Where am I on the road to moving beyond my crucible and toward a life of significance?*

Crucible Leadership can help you answer that question. Right now.

Research we've conducted has found that 49 percent of business leaders have experienced a crucible moment, something so traumatic or painful that it has fundamentally changed their life. And an even greater number of our survey's respondents—nearly two-thirds—said their past failures have held them back.

If you're among that group, we want to help you move beyond your setback. To dive even deeper into to your own crucible experience, and chart a path beyond it, I invite you to scan the QR code on this page. You'll be taken right to our *Life of Significance Assessment*. You'll answer a handful of questions about your values and passions—and any crucible experiences you may have had—and we'll deliver results tailor-made for you that spotlight where you are now—and how you can get to where you want to be.

You'll discover your personality type—are you a World Changer? A Star Performer? An Imagineer?—and action steps you can take to leverage the assessment's insights to launch you toward the personal and professional fulfillment you've always wanted. (You can also take the assessment by typing www.crucibleleadership.com/assessment into your web browser.).

I encourage you to also listen to our *Beyond the Crucible* podcast. I interview men and women from all professions and experiences who share their inspiring and instructive stories of how they've moved past their setbacks and failures to a richer life than they ever imagined. You can find all our podcast episodes at our website, www.crucibleleadership.com.

Always remember, your crucible experiences are not the end of your story. They are, in fact, once you're learned and leveraged the lessons of them, the beginning of a new chapter in your story that can be the most rewarding of your life.

We look forward to helping you navigate your way to a life on purpose—a life of significance.

Warwick

ABOUT THE AUTHOR

Warwick Fairfax is the founder of Crucible Leadership, a philosophical and practical breakthrough in turning business and personal failures into the fuel for igniting a life of significance. He has been hailed by *Forbes* as offering "compelling insights for anyone who would like to wake up feeling inspired by their work, but doesn't." Those insights are rooted not in a checklist of glib to-dos but in his own experience at the epicenter of one of the most spectacular business failures in the history of his home nation of Australia.

Fairfax was only twenty-six when, as the fifth-generation heir to a media empire bearing his family name, he led—and lost—a multibillion-dollar public takeover bid. The result? The company founded by his great-great-grandfather slipped from family control after 150 years, leaving him to examine not only his own shortcomings and losses but also his life's principles and the lessons he learned from family members who came before him and some of history's greatest leaders. It has been by shaping these insights as a leadership adviser that Fairfax has enabled others to learn from their own crucible experiences and emerge to lead a life rooted in who they are. His journey has opened a door for men and women from all walks of life to not only bounce back from failure but to become the leaders they were born to be.

He shares insights from his experience and interviews other leaders who have leveraged their crucible moments to live and lead with significance on the podcast *Beyond the Crucible,* available through all major podcasting channels.

Fairfax holds an undergraduate degree in Philosophy, Politics, and Economics from Oxford University and earned his MBA from Harvard Business School. He is an International Coach Federation (ICF) certified executive coach. He is an Elder at Bay Area Community Church.

He lives in Annapolis, Md., with his wife, Gale. They have three adult children who are in the process of developing their own unique paths to lives of significance.

NOTES AND REFERENCES

Chapter 2

Quotes from John Fairfax family biography
Fairfax, John Fitzgerald. *The Story of John Fairfax*. Sydney: John Fairfax & Sons Pty. Ltd, 1941.

I knew, John, that despair . . .
Fairfax, John Fitzgerald. *The Story of John Fairfax*.

It would be a free . . .
Fairfax, John Fitzgerald. *The Story of John Fairfax*.

In moderation placing all my glory . . .
Fairfax, John Fitzgerald. *The Story of John Fairfax*.

Franklin D. Roosevelt quotes
Smith, Jean Edward. *FDR*. New York: Random House, 2008.

Chapter 3

Quote from Shakespeare's *Hamlet*
Quotes.net, STANDS4 LLC, 2021. "William Shakespeare, Hamlet Quotes." Accessed January 14, 2021. https://www.quotes.net/quote/42920.

Quote from *A Few Good Men*
> Reiner, Rob, dir. *A Few Good Men*. Los Angeles, CA: Castlerock Entertainment, 1992.

Chapter 4

Presidential statistics
> "Presidential Historians Survey 2017." C-SPAN.org, accessed 26 January 2021, https://www.c-span.org/presidentsurvey2017/?page=overall.

Chapter 5

John Fairfax 1856 address to YMCA
> Johnson, Stuart. Macquarie Christian Studies Institute Think Piece, No.4, March 2003.

Quotes from John Fairfax biography
> Fairfax, John F. *The Story of John Fairfax*.

Chapter 6

Strictly speaking, the Greatest Commandment refers to the passage in Matthew 22, and the parallel passage in Mark 12, discussed below. I have called this section the Great Commandments (plural), because there is a relationship between the Ten Commandments found in Exodus 20 and Deuteronomy 5 and the Greatest Commandment.

Chapter 7

England expects that every man will do his duty
> Knight, Roger. *The Pursuit of Victory: The Life and Achievement of Horatio Nelson*. New York: Basic Books, 2005.

Letters from John Fairfax's children
Fairfax, John F. *The Story of John Fairfax.*

Chapter 8

More than his words, his life was his message.
"Mahatma Gandhi." *Time Magazine,* 14 August 2007, accessed 23 January 2021, http://content.time.com/time/world/article/0,8599 ,1653029,00.html.

King George III of England's quote
Rees, James C. *George Washington's Leadership Lessons: What the Father of Our Country Can Teach Us About Effective Leadership and Character.* New York: Wiley, 2007.

Napoleon's quote
Rees, James C. *George Washington's Leadership Lessons: What the Father of Our Country Can Teach Us About Effective Leadership and Character.*

Washington's farewell to the soldiers
Rees, James C. *George Washington's Leadership Lessons: What the Father of Our Country Can Teach Us About Effective Leadership and Character.*

George Washington's Mount Vernon
Hillman, Joseph. "Resignation of Military Commission." mount vernon.org, accessed 26 January 2021, https://www.mountvernon .org/library/digitalhistory/digital-encyclopedia/article/resignation-of -military-commission/.

Chapter 9

Mention of Arthur C. Clarke's article
The Arthur C. Clarke Foundation. Accessed 24 January 2021, https:// www.clarkefoundation.org/arthur-c-clarke-biography/.

The only way of discovering the limits
  "Clarke's Three Laws." *New Scientist Ltd.* Accessed 26 January 2021, https://www.newscientist.com/term/clarkes-three-laws/.

Mention of Johann Strauss's song, "Blue Danube," from *2001: A Space Odyssey*
  Kubrick, Stanly, dir. *2001: A Space Odyssey*. Los Angeles, CA: Metro-Goldwyn-Mayer, 1968.

Regarding the adventures of Perseus, Jason, and Theseus
  Kingsley, Charles. *The Heroes*, (original publisher unknown), 1856.

Without fear to express opinion . . .
  Fairfax, John F. *The Story of John Fairfax.*

Quotes regarding *Sydney Morning Herald*
  Fairfax, John F. *The Story of John Fairfax.*

Chapter 10

Quotes from Walt Disney and the Walt Disney's story
  Greene, Katherine and Richard. *The Man Behind the Magic: The Story of Walt Disney*. New York: Viking Press, 1991.

Disney had only one rule . . .
  Greene, Katherine and Richard. *The Man Behind the Magic: The Story of Walt Disney.*

Mention of song, "Pick Yourself Up" from *Swing Time*
  Stevens, George, dir. *Swing Time*. Hollywood, CA: RKO Radio Pictures, 1936.

Chapter 11

A free, hard-fighting, vigorous newspaper . . .
  Fairfax, John F. *The Biography of John Fairfax.*

Mention of *The Australian* newspaper article
>Lyons, John. "Warwick Fairfax: The Man Behind the Mask." *The Australian*, 12 Nov. 1988 (Saturday edition).

Chapter 12

Mention of story from biography
>Fairfax, John F. *The Biography of John Fairfax.*

His conscientious desire to aim at the realization of a high ideal . . .
>Fairfax, John F. *The Biography of John Fairfax.*

Quotes from George Washington regarding his army
>McCullough, David. *1776.* New York: Simon & Schuster, 2005.

January 16, 1776 and February 16, 1776 Councils of War, George Washington's quotes
>McCullough, David. *1776.*

My God, these fellows have done more work . . .
>McCullough, David. *1776.*

Never were troops in so disgraceful a situation . . .
>McCullough, David. *1776.*

Chapter 13

Quotes from poem by Alfred Lord Tennyson
>Tennyson, Alfred Lord, "The Charge of the Light Brigade," Poetry Foundation, accessed January 14, 2021. https://www.poetry foundation.org/poems/45319/the-charge-of-the-light-brigade.

The tribute to Louis Howe was given by Roosevelt's son Elliott
>Fenster, Julie M. *FDR's Shadow: Louis Howe, the Force That Shaped Franklin and Eleanor Roosevelt.* London: Palgrave Macmillan, 2009.

Admirers he (Roosevelt) had by the millions . . .
"The Presidency: Death of Howe." *Time Magazine*, 27 April 1936, article accessed via web 26 January 2021, http://content.time.com /time/subscriber/article/0,33009,770131-1,00.html.

Chapter 14

1842 speech from John Fairfax to his employees
Fairfax, John F. *The Biography of John Fairfax.*

. . . agreeable relations which always subsisted . . .
Fairfax, John F. *The Biography of John Fairfax.*

Newspaper references
Goodwin, Doris Kearns. *Team of Rivals: The Political Genius of Abraham Lincoln.* New York: Simon & Schuster, 2006.

Quotes in subsequent paragraphs by Abraham Lincoln, A.E. Johnson, London's publication, *Spectator*, and William Seward
Goodwin, Doris Kearns. *Team of Rivals: The Political Genius of Abraham Lincoln.*

He was incontestably the greatest man I ever knew.
Goodwin, Doris Kearns. *Team of Rivals: The Political Genius of Abraham Lincoln.*

Stanton's grief was uncontrollable.
Goodwin, Doris Kearns. *Team of Rivals: The Political Genius of Abraham Lincoln.*

Newspaper quotes regarding Republican Party
Goodwin, Doris Kearns. *Team of Rivals: The Political Genius of Abraham Lincoln.*

Quote about Lincoln by Tolstoy
Rayomand Neville Anklesaria. "The Greatness of Napoleon Caesar History Essay," UniAssignment Centre, submitted 2013, accessed

January 14, 2021. https://www.uniassignment.com/essay-samples/history/the-greatness-of-napoleon-caesar-or-washington-history-essay.php.

Quotes by Lincoln and John Nicolay
Goodwin, Doris Kearns. *Team of Rivals: The Political Genius of Abraham Lincoln.*

Chapter 15

Collins, Jim. *Good to Great: Why Some Companies Make the Leap and Others Don't.* New York: HarperBusiness, 2001.

Quotes by Napoleon and Wellington
Holmes, Richard. *Wellington: The Iron Duke.* New York: HarperCollins, 2003.

Wellington's quotes regarding Waterloo
Creasy, Edward Shepherd. Letter from the field of Waterloo (June 1815), as quoted in *Decisive Battles of the World* (1899).

Nelson's leadership, which has been called "effortless leadership."
Knight, Roger. *The Pursuit of Victory: The Life and Achievement of Horatio Nelson.*

He was also fearless in other ways, possessing what one admiral called "constitutional courage."
Knight, Roger. *The Pursuit of Victory: The Life and Achievement of Horatio Nelson.*

He was perhaps more generally beloved . . .
Knight, Roger. *The Pursuit of Victory: The Life and Achievement of Horatio Nelson.*

Never was a commander so enthusiastically loved . . .
Knight, Roger. *The Pursuit of Victory: The Life and Achievement of Horatio Nelson.*

Unanimity I believe greater never existed . . .
  Knight, Roger. *The Pursuit of Victory: The Life and Achievement of Horatio Nelson.*

No captain can do very wrong . . .
  Knight, Roger. *The Pursuit of Victory: The Life and Achievement of Horatio Nelson.*

England expects that every man will . . . (and other quotes within paragraph)
  Knight, Roger. *The Pursuit of Victory: The Life and Achievement of Horatio Nelson.*

Now I am satisfied . . .
  Knight, Roger. *The Pursuit of Victory: The Life and Achievement of Horatio Nelson.*

Chapter 17

All quoted material from information related to Winston Churchill
  Johnson, Paul. *Churchill.* London: Penguin Publishing Group, 2010.

A free ebook edition is available with the purchase of this book.

To claim your free ebook edition:

1. Visit MorganJamesBOGO.com
2. Sign your name CLEARLY in the space
3. Complete the form and submit a photo of the entire copyright page
4. You or your friend can download the ebook to your preferred device

Print & Digital Together Forever.

Snap a photo   Free ebook   Read anywhere

CPSIA information can be obtained
at www.ICGtesting.com
Printed in the USA
LVHW020025240921
698560LV00002B/10